UNEQUAL PARTNERS

AUSTRIAN INSTITUTE FOR
INTERNATIONAL AFFAIRS SERIES

The Austrian Institute for International Affairs (AIIA) is an independent research institution for the scientific study of current issues of Austrian foreign policy and international relations.

The Vienna Meeting of the Conference on Security and Cooperation in Europe, 1986–1989: A Turning Point in East-West Relations, Stefan Lehne

The European Neutrals in the 1990s: New Challenges and Opportunities, edited by Hanspeter Neuhold

Unequal Partners: A Comparative Analysis of Relations Between Austria and the Federal Republic of Germany and Between Canada and the United States, edited by Harald von Riekhoff and Hanspeter Neuhold

UNEQUAL PARTNERS

A Comparative Analysis of Relations
Between Austria and the Federal Republic
of Germany and Between Canada and
the United States

edited by HARALD VON RIEKHOFF
and HANSPETER NEUHOLD

Westview Press

Boulder • San Francisco • Oxford

Austrian Institute for International Affairs Series

Copyright © 1993 by Westview Press, Inc.

Published in 1993 in the United States of America by Westview Press, Inc., 5500 Central Avenue, Boulder, Colorado 80301-2877, and in the United Kingdom by Westview Press, 36 Lonsdale Road, Summertown, Oxford OX2 7EW

A CIP catalog record for this book is available from the Library of Congress.
ISBN 0-8133-8314-5

This book was typeset by Susanna Mai, AIIA.

Printed and bound in the United States of America

The paper used in this publication meets the requirements of the American National Standard for Permanence of Paper for Printed Library Materials Z39.48-1984.

10   9   8   7   6   5   4   3   2   1

Contents

Figures and Tables

xi

Preface

The theoretical core of this book has been the focus of a Carleton University research project on the foreign policy in asymmetrical dyads. The theory had been tested with reference to Canadian-U.S. relations, but the chapters presented in this book broaden the empirical basis by focusing on two such unequal partnerships, Austria and the Federal Republic of Germany, on the one hand, and Canada and the United States, on the other, and by distinguishing between different dimensions, notably the historical, political, economic, cultural, and media aspects of the relationships. The combination of a comparative approach with a multidimensional treatment transcends the standard literature on inequality in international relations, which is generally confined to a single dyad and rarely encompasses more than the political or economic aspects of that relationship.

This study has deliberately created its own, albeit reversed, asymmetry, as it is written from the perspective of the subordinate rather than the dominant actors. It thereby tries to redress, even if only in a small way, the customary neglect of the smaller states at the expense of a natural preoccupation with the policies of the major international actors like the United States and the Federal Republic of Germany.

We are greatly indebted to Dr. Elisabeth Mach, Cultural and Press Affairs Counselor at the Austrian Embassy in Ottawa, Dr. Elke Schmitz, Cultural Counsellor at the Embassy of the Federal Republic of Germany in Ottawa, and to Professor Frederick Engelmann of the University of Alberta, who provided valuable assistance and encouragement throughout the long planning process for the symposium in Ottawa where the chapters appearing in this volume were originally presented as conference papers. Brenda Sutherland typed the manuscript with customary vigor and exemplary cheerfulness, and Susanna Mai completed the volume at the Austrian Institute for International Affairs. We are also indebted to Westview Press for including the book in the Austrian Institute for International Affairs Series and for their editing assistance. We are grateful for the financial assistance that was provided by the Austrian Foreign Ministry, the Canadian Department of External Affairs, and the Social Sciences and Humanities Research Council of Canada.

Harald von Riekhoff
Hanspeter Neuhold

PART ONE

Overview

1

Introduction:
Toward a Comparison of Relations
Between Austria/FRG and
Canada/United States

Harald von Riekhoff

Bilateral relations between Austria and the Federal Republic of Germany (FRG) and between Canada and the United States can be examined from the more general perspective of relations between unequal partners. An unequal partnership denotes relations between countries that have a common or closely related language, relatively homogeneous cultures, geographic proximity, a high level of transactions, and a significant inequality of power. Charles Doran views partnerships of this type as "an alternative to either integration or autarky,"[1] under conditions in which autarky is impossible because of the high degree of interdependence and integration is unacceptable, at least for the smaller partner, for one reason or another. It should be noted that the term "smaller" is used in the sense of "less powerful" throughout this volume; it is applied to Canada, for example, in relation to the United States, although in terms of geographic size Canada is bigger than the United States.

A number of other countries would fit this definition of unequal partnership in addition to the four selected for this study, as for example Ireland and Great Britain, New Zealand and Australia (although proximity here is relative in the absence of other immediate neighbors), Norway and Sweden, and

---

1. Charles F. Doran, *Forgotten Partnership: U.S.-Canadian Relations Today,* Toronto (1984), p. 260.

Portugal and Spain. Perhaps one might also add Switzerland and the FRG, although the common language, as is also true for Canada, does not encompass the entire population of the smaller partner.

The chapters in this study single out, in the following order, four distinct dimensions that affect relations between unequal partners: historical, political, economic, and cultural. For organizational purposes media relations have been treated as part of the section devoted to culture, although they are equally relevant to the political economy of the two partnerships. From the perspective of the subordinate country, which is the one taken here, the relationship with the superordinate partner is characterized by an underlying tension between socioeconomic forces (which normally work toward increased integration with the major partner) and political — and in the Austrian case legal — considerations (which work toward preservation of the autonomy and distinctiveness of the smaller actor). The historical dimension allows observation of the unfolding of this dialectical process through time. The impact of the cultural dimension appears to be essentially ambivalent. On the one hand, cultural homogeneity would tend to facilitate integration, while on the other hand culture shapes a distinct national identity and thereby helps the subordinate actor in maintaining its commitment to political autonomy in the face of economic counterpressures.

Similarities and Differences

Political scientists comparing the two unequal partnerships selected here are likely to discover greater similarities between them than would historians. The latter are methodologically more predisposed to emphasize the uniqueness of situations or cases, but political scientists search for patterns and attempt generalizations. The distinction is more than methodological, however, because the history of the two partnerships reveals far more distinctive than common features. The history of Canadian-U.S. relations has been quite stable for more than a century and the underlying power ratio has not changed dramatically during that period. In contrast, Austrian-German relations have been far more varied, moving between equal and unequal partnership (at one time favoring Austria and at another Germany, or rather the numerous German states), and even occupation by Nazi Germany, when the relationship ceased to have the characteristic of an international dyad altogether.

Both dyads are similar insofar as they meet the criteria of an unequal partnership specified above. The respective power ratio, using gross national product (GNP) and population, is roughly comparable between the two partnerships and has remained relatively stable since 1955. One can also note a certain similarity in the underlying problem of subordinate actors in unequal partnerships: their great vulnerability to actions and decisions taken by the superordinate power over which they have little or no influence and the pervasive influence of the latter in the media and cultural spheres of the smaller actor. Austrians and Canadians alike seem to be afflicted with a type of neurosis in which they perceive themselves as neglected, their existence being ignored or taken for granted. Such perception is not always accurate, nor is it necessarily a liability during negotiations to be sheltered under relative obscurity, but the feeling does little to enhance the self-esteem of the smaller partner. Another common feature is the tendency of the smaller partners to dwell more on the problematic aspects of the relationship than to stress the demonstrable benefits that accrue from it, chief among them the easy access to a much larger market, to innovative ideas and trends, and to military protection. The contribution of the FRG to permanently neutral Austria's security is much more limited and indirect than the corresponding U.S. guardian role of Canadian security. Although the recognition of these benefits tends to be implicit rather than publicly expressed, it is nevertheless reflected in the generally favorable attitudes that Austrians and Canadians have toward their principal partner. As Hanspeter Neuhold notes in his chapter, opinion polls show that Austrians rank the FRG first among the countries with which Austria should have a particularly close relationship. In Peyton Lyon's study of Canadian elite images, 63 percent of his elite respondents identify the United States as Canada's best friend.[2]

The identification of common features in the selected dyads can improve our understanding of the nature of relations between closely linked but unequal powers. The search for concordance should not, however, blind us to the existence of very considerable differences between the two cases. The two partnerships operate at different levels of the international power hierarchy. Austrian-FRG relations involve a small country and a major international actor and have essentially a bilateral, or at most a regional, orientation. In contrast, Canadian-U.S. relations are between a middle power and a superpower. The purely bilateral aspects of that relationship cannot be effectively insulated from the global concerns of the superpower, and they thereby impose special problems and costs for the conduct of bilateral relations. The superpower agenda is permanently overcrowded. It is therefore difficult even for a special partner like Canada to get an adequate hearing. All too often the particular national interests of the smaller partner will have to be sacrificed or deferred for the common good of the Atlantic Alliance or

2. Cited in Peyton V. Lyon and Brian W. Tomlin (eds.), *Canada as an International Actor,* Toronto (1979), p. 85.

the broader Western community as defined by the superpower. As David Leyton-Brown's chapter notes, Canada frequently suffers from the sideswipe phenomenon, the negative fallout stemming from the wars of the Titans, in other words, international confrontations on trade and monetary issues among the U.S., the European Community (EC), Japan, and other emerging trading blocs.

The fact that, as member of the North Atlantic Treaty Organization (NATO), Canada is a U.S. military ally and with the U.S. manages an integrated North American air defense command, has multiple ramifications for bilateral relations that do not apply to Austria because of its neutral status. NATO membership imposes certain constraints on Canadian foreign policy and makes Canada more susceptible to U.S. pressure on issues such as paying a fair share of NATO's defense costs and testing cruise missiles on Canadian territory. As a result, Canadian strategic doctrine and the structure of its defense establishment, with the exception of its international peacekeeping contingent, is much more closely patterned on the U.S. model than is true for Austria's military structure vis-à-vis the Federal Republic.

Canada's economic dependence on the United States for trade and investment exceeds the corresponding Austrian dependence by more than a factor of two. Austria's external trade with the entire EC affects a smaller proportion of its total foreign trade than does Canada's bilateral trade with the United States alone. The 1972 free trade deal with the EC left Austria with more maneuverability than Canada enjoyed vis-à-vis the United States prior to their signing of a free trade agreement (FTA) with it in 1987. When Austria beds down with Germany on economic matters, it is normally in conjunction with other EC and European Free Trade Association (EFTA) countries, whereas Canada faces the United States in a much more isolated context, which has been intensified following the conclusion of the FTA. Thus the costs to Canada of joining the United States in a bilateral free trade regime are potentially much greater than they would be for Austria. The 1972 agreement corresponded to the model of a classical free trade treaty, whereas the Canadian-U.S. accord, despite its name, has the features of a "common market plus" agreement.

Theoretical Approaches

There exist several theoretical approaches that seek to explain the phenomenon we have labeled unequal partners. The work of Peter Katzenstein on disjoined partners, the Carleton Project on Foreign Policy in Asymmetrical Dyads, and Henry Jacek's opening chapter for this volume are particularly relevant and will be discussed here briefly.

In his highly original analysis of Austro-German relations since 1815, Peter Katzenstein rejects the popular thesis that there exists a natural trend toward political unification between culturally homogeneous states.[3] As Katzenstein demonstrates, smaller states like Austria have manifested a surprising measure of political resilience that appears to defy the logic of gravity, the intensity of transactions, as well as linguistic and cultural similarity. Katzenstein attributes this apparent anomaly to the existence of strong counterpressures and to the effective assertion of political autonomy that neutralize copressures and integrative trends. Prior to 1914, the German elites of the Austro-Hungarian Empire periodically revived the option of political unification with Germany. This served as a political crisis strategy when they faced the threat of social revolution or unacceptable demands by non-German ethnic groups. In the long run, however, the economic benefits of maintaining and administering the Habsburg Empire far outweighed the political attraction of integration with Germany. True enough, after the disaster of the World War I, all major political forces in Austria saw salvation for their suddenly small country in a union with Germany. Yet, after World War II, the counterpressures against integration were even stronger, with the logic of political attractions and economic benefits now being reversed. After 1955, Austria experienced greater economic interdependence with Germany than during earlier phases but showed less political interest and concern in German affairs because the FRG no longer enjoyed the status of a Great Power and suffered from the trauma of an externally imposed political division.

Katzenstein's core concept of disjoined partners corresponds closely to that of unequal partners as developed in this volume. We have refrained from using the same terminology, partly in order to avoid infringement of academic "patent rights" but more importantly because disjoined partners implies the existence of a prior union. Such an assumption would be appropriate for some phases in Austro-German relations, but it would greatly reduce the scope for a comparative analysis because dyads such as Canada-United States and New Zealand-Australia, which otherwise meet our definitional criteria, would be excluded. Another major distinction is the emphasis on the inequality of power between unequal partners. In contrast, inequality is not a condition for disjoined partners, and, for most of the period to 1918, the relationship between Austria and Germany (or Prussia) proceeded on the basis of equality.

---

3. Peter J. Katzenstein, *Disjoined Partners: Austria and Germany Since 1815*, Berkeley (1976).

Another theoretical formulation of relations between unequal partners was developed by the Carleton Project on Foreign Policy in Asymmetrical Dyads.[4] The two principal characteristics defining asymmetrical dyads are: first, a significant inequality in the capacity of the two partners to influence the relationship, and second, intense involvement on the part of the subordinate actor in concentrating the weight of its foreign policy and its international transactions on the superordinate member. Like Katzenstein's disjoined partners, the theory of asymmetrical dyads recognizes the interplay between diverse copressures and counterpressures and their joint effect on integration. In particular, the theory stresses the fundamental tension between the subordinate partner's goal of economic well-being and the goal of preserving its political autonomy. An intensification of cooperation and international transactions with the more powerful partner will be perceived as benefiting economic well-being but undermining political autonomy. This inherent dilemma might in part explain the frequent shifts and starts in the foreign policy of the subordinate country as it fluctuates between cooperative behavior and strategies designed to regulate the relationship, strategies that frequently generate a conflictual response from the target.

After testing the theory for Canadian-U.S. relations for 1963–1972, Dolan and Tomlin reformulated the original theory to incorporate the impact of the current state of the superordinate nation's economy on the foreign policy of the subordinate actor. Under the reformulated theory, economic well-being and political autonomy will be perceived as competing goals not at all times, as the theory originally formulated, but only during periods of economic boom when the economy of the superordinate partner is performing well and a reinforcement of relations will be expected to spread the economic benefits to the subordinate nation. When the economy of the superordinate country is performing in an unsatisfactory manner, then regulatory behavior designed to diminish vulnerability to the superordinate country and to reduce ties would not only serve political autonomy concerns but might also appear to be the appropriate strategy for economic damage control. Such regulatory thinking was reflected in Canada's national energy policy of 1980, which sought to increase national control and autonomy in the energy sector. The

---

4. For a statement of the core theory, see Brian W. Tomlin, Michael B. Dolan, Harald von Riekhoff, and Maureen A. Molot, "Foreign Policies of Subordinate States in Asymmetrical Dyads," *Jerusalem Journal of International Relations* 5 (September 1981), pp. 14–40. For the subsequent modification of the theory, see Michael B. Dolan and Brian W. Tomlin (eds.), "Foreign Policy in Asymmetrical Dyads: Theoretical Reformulation and Empirical Analysis, Canada-United States Relations, 1963–1972," *International Studies Quarterly* 28 (September 1984), pp. 349–368.

policy was fashioned in reaction to the world energy crisis, which appeared to leave the United States more vulnerable to the vagaries of the international energy market than Canada.

The third theoretical explanation of the behavior of unequal partners is found in Henry Jacek's chapter of this volume in which he sets out to compare the two dyads so that "we can begin filtering out relationships that are unique to each dyad versus highlighting propositions common to unequal partnerships." The most important common features of the two dyads are stated in three propositions. The first proposition notes that the smaller partners have developed a stronger collective organizational structure for their societies, in order to deal more effectively with the superordinate actors. Jacek argues that the dense network of interest organizations allows the political economy of the smaller partner "to mobilize more quickly and decisively in pursuit of national policy objectives."[5] The system of organized interest groups in the FRG, although strong by North American standards, is weaker than the Austrian analogue. In comparison with the United States, Canada has a more group-conscious, stronger interest group society. The authority and governmental characteristics of Canadian interest groups resemble those of West European nations, and its unions have outperformed their U.S. counterparts in growth and union density. Jacek's first proposition naturally prompts the question: To what extent is the more densely organized social network of the smaller partners in direct response to the challenges posed by the unequal partnership, or is it merely a function of size because social bonding is more easily achieved in smaller societies? Another question concerns the capacity of social elites to utilize the dense organizational network in order to respond to the demands of public policy.[6] Even if one accepts that this capacity exists, it does not by its existence guarantee a corresponding willingness to use it. One is reminded of the examples of Canada's "third option" strategy of 1972, which sought to diversify international transactions in order to reduce vulnerability to the United States, and of the 1980 national energy policy. In both instances, the unwillingness of Canadian economic elites to support these public policy initiatives contributed substantially to their eventual demise.

Jacek's second proposition is strongly influenced by Alexander Gershenkron's thesis of delayed industrial development. According to Jacek, smaller countries in unequal partnerships place greater reliance on state intervention using mixed public/private enterprises and economic and social

---

5. Henry J. Jacek, "Large State/Small State Relations in the North American Political Economy: Are There Lessons from Europe?" *The American Review of Canadian Studies* 17 (Winter 1987–1988), p. 428.

6. Ibidem.

regulation. In both Austria and Canada, the public sector plays a major role in their respective national economies — one that is significantly stronger than in the economies of their corresponding big partners. The extended authority of the states of smaller countries over their national economies in part compensates them for their natural disadvantages vis-à-vis the Great Powers, which benefit from larger internal markets and from their ability to influence developments in the global economy. Smaller partners such as Austria and Canada often appear to overcome the size handicap, and it is not uncommon for them to outperform their big partners when indicators such as per capita GNP growth and the rate of unemployment are used. One may ask, however, whether all the instruments of state regulation and the multiplicity of public enterprises, which Jacek cites as evidence of a more centralized direction of the Canadian economy, even approximate the corresponding impact on the U.S. economy that is provided by the annual U.S. defense budget. Despite U.S. distaste for regulation, this may be seen as regulation by other means. Moreover, in Austria, the "grand coalition" government formed in 1987 has embarked on a policy of privatization and deregulation.

Jacek's third proposition focuses on the cultural and psychological attributes of smaller partners in dyadic relations. Generally, smaller nations in unequal partnerships tend to be more conservative, more committed to a traditional life style, more cautious, and less risk acceptant in their behavior. The risks facing them are higher, including the risk of absorption by their superordinate partners. Despite this general proposition, we may encounter historical phases in which the prevailing climate of opinion in the subordinate partners is more optimistic and bullish than is the corresponding mood of the superordinate actors. One may note the Canadian mood of confidence during the early years of the Trudeau government and contrast it with the malaise and introspectiveness that befell the United States in the wake of the Vietnam War. Similarly, Hans Heinz Fabris' chapter on Austrian media depicts the 1970s — the so-called Kreisky era — as a period of considerable Austrian optimism, self-confidence, and innovation. This differed sharply from the continued preoccupation of the FRG with the problem of German division, the introspective mood of German artists, and the sober, if not morose, climate of German public opinion.

Historical Dimension of Relations
Between Unequal Partners

In his overview, Frederick Engelmann describes the Austro-German relationship as possessing one common language, one and one-half histories, and two states. He observes that the two countries are gradually moving toward two histories because the shared component is being crowded out by quite distinct recent experiences. The historical relationship between Austria and Germany has not only been characterized by different forms of inequality and equality but also by considerable ambiguity as Austria has asserted varying degrees of sovereignty and autonomy vis-à-vis its German neighbor(s).

In his comprehensive chapter on Austro-German relations since 1815, Günter Bischof traces the different stages of that relationship, which at times manifested attributes of an equal partnership, of an unequal partnership, and even of complete absorption. It is Bischof's principal thesis that Austria, with its cosmopolitan European foreign policy, exercised a restraining influence on Germany to the ultimate benefit of the latter and of Europe as a whole. True to its heraldic symbol of a double eagle, Austria traditionally exercised the dual function of maintaining an internal balance within the system of German states while upholding the broader European balance-of-power system. Austria's exclusion from the German states system after 1866 and its decline as a Great Power opened the way for Prussian hegemony within Germany and for German nationalism and thus created the "German problem" in European politics. Perhaps one should add to Bischof's thesis that as Austria's capacity to restrain Germany declined, the respective roles were somewhat reversed. Prior to World War I, it was German influence that frequently had a moderating effect on Austria's Balkan policy, although, with tragic consequences for both, such restraint was not exercised by Germany on its Austrian ally during the 1914 crisis.

As Bischof observes, Austrians naturally identify with the grandeur of the imperial history but have had more difficulty in coming to terms with the more recent history as a small state. The failure to identify with the new status is best captured by the title of Ernst Hoor's history of Austria during the interwar period, *Staat ohne Nation, Republik ohne Republikaner* (State without Nation, Republic without Republicans). In view of the interwar trauma, what is quite remarkable is the relative speed with which Austrians after 1955 have come to accept the rationale of an independent Austrian state, which itself is not a novelty in Austro-German relations, and, moreover, the fact that they have also come to identify themselves as a nation distinct from the German one. The rapid formation of a distinct national identity was facilitated by the disastrous experience of World War II and the welcome opportunity to recover full sovereignty and to escape political division.

When we consider the historical component of national identity, it is interesting to note that both Austrians and Germans continue to refer to each other in order to complete the historical picture. In this respect, the two countries resemble equal rather than unequal partners. No such reciprocity exists in Canadian-U.S. relations. Neither now nor historically has Canada figured in shaping a U.S. national identity. Conversely, the United States figures dominantly, albeit somewhat paradoxically, in Canadian national identity. On the one hand, the affinity and pervasive presence of U.S. culture leave little fertile ground on which a distinct Canadian identity can flourish. On the other hand, much of what constitutes a Canadian identity has developed in reaction to the United States. This is a residual nationalism that is sustained by the awareness of not being American, a benign form of "un-American" activity.

In his chapter dealing with the defense of Canadian nationalism among English-speaking intellectuals, Joseph Levitt singles out three key attributes that he believes have sustained a Canadian national identity distinct from that of the United States: commitment to the British connection; preference for a British-style parliamentary political system; and the belief in the success of a separate Canadian transcontinental economy.

These three factors have been diluted over time, if they have not become altogether irrelevant. The British connection ceased to be a major factor in Canadian political life and national identity with the demise of Britain as a world power after World War II and with the relative decline of immigration from the British Isles. While preserving a British-style parliamentary democracy, Canada has adopted many features of the U.S. political system, among them the extensive use of media, the style of party conventions, the enhanced role of legislative committees, and the introduction of a formal bill of rights. Finally, the nineteenth-century dream of a separate Canadian transcontinental economy has given way to the postwar reality of an integrated North American continental economy that was expanded and formalized by the 1987 Canadian-U.S. FTA.

If Canadian national identity thus rests on these three pillars, it would be difficult to escape the conclusion that we are inspecting a picturesque ruin. One may, however, use a different interpretation and argue that the three factors that Levitt identifies were not so much the effective causes of Canadian national identity as merely a convenient rationale offered by English-Canadian nationalists to explain and defend their nationalist convictions. The origins of the latter were probably more intangible and complex. They may be more readily explained by reference to a different historical experience and by socialization into a political culture that, in several principal aspects, is as distinct from that of the United States as, in other aspects, Quebec society is distinct from the rest of English-speaking Canada.

Political Dimension

The chapters by Hanspeter Neuhold and David Leyton-Brown address the political dimension of relations between Austria and Canada and their respective big partners. In both cases, political relations are extensive in scope and intimate in form — the very image of good neighbors — but they are not unproblematic. Neuhold draws attention to several irritants in relations between Vienna and Bonn, notably Austrian objections to the construction of a nuclear power plant at Wackersdorf close to the Austrian border and, most recently, the dispute over the transit of heavy German trucks through Austria.

Despite occasional complications, the political relations between Austria and the FRG have been considerably more stable and less volatile than the corresponding relations between Canada and the United States. Although the prevailing mode of Canadian-U.S. relations has been cooperative, there have been periods of sharp conflict, if not crisis. Moreover, at the time, the conflicts were not seen as merely temporary aberrations but as evidence of a more fundamental breakpoint. Seen in retrospect, these instances of serious disturbance, however, did not serve as the breakpoint that changed the essential nature of the relationship.[7]

This poses the obvious question why Canadian-U.S. relations have been more problematic than their Austro-German counterparts. Even if we exclude the possibility of inferior diplomatic conflict management skills by the former two — Kal Holsti speaks of a highly developed diplomatic culture of conflict accommodation in Canadian-U.S. relations[8] — there are two other principal reasons that may explain this apparent anomaly between the two unequal partnerships. First, the sheer magnitude of mutual transactions, both in absolute and in relative terms, is substantially higher in the Canadian-U.S. dyad, thereby creating greater scope for the emergence of conflictual issues. Second, as Neuhold points out, Austria's degree of political dependence on the FRG is less than Canadian dependence on the United States. Katzen-

---

7. The theme of continuity and dramatic change in Canadian-U.S. relations is addressed by Stephen Clarkson, *Canada and the Reagan Challenge,* Toronto (1982); David Leyton-Brown, *Weathering the Storm: Canadian-U.S. Relations, 1980–1983,* Toronto (1985); and Harald von Riekhoff and Brian W. Tomlin, "The Politics of Interdependence: Canada-United States Intergovernmental Relations," in Jon H. Pammett and Brian W. Tomlin (eds.), *The Integration Question: Political Economy and Public Policy in Canada and North America,* Toronto (1984), pp. 144–162.

8. Kal Holsti, "Canada and the United States," in S. Spiegel and K. Waltz (eds.), *Conflict in World Politics,* Cambridge, Mass. (1971), p. 390.

stein speaks of a pluralistic pattern of Austro-FRG relations after 1955, with
Austria having intimate cultural and social links with the FRG but not sharing the same political concerns.[9] As a neutral country, Austria does not pursue a joint security policy with the Federal Republic and does not operate
within the same international institutional framework.

Despite the importance and scope of relations with their respective principal partners, both Austria and Canada have shown a preference for con-
ducting relations on an ad hoc basis and for avoiding formal institutional
mechanisms to ensure cooperation. It is not that the smaller partners object
to cooperation; but they have an instinctive fear that institutionalized forms
of cooperation would reduce their capacities to maneuver and would formally entrench the dominance of the superordinate partners. The present
Canadian government under Prime Minister Mulroney appears to have shed
some of these reservations. It has moved from the customary ad hoc management of issues to what Joseph Jockel styled semi-institutionalized consultation, which relies on regular annual summits of the U.S. president and
the Canadian prime minister and quarterly minisummits at the foreign minister level. More significant, the FTA establishes a formal bilateral dispute
settlement mechanism. David Leyton-Brown regards it as a turning point
that creates a different context for the conduct of bilateral relations even in
areas that are not covered by the FTA.

Economic Dimension

Canadian dependence on the United States for trade and investment is
more than twice as great as Austrian dependence on the FRG. This may explain why Canadians tend to view their economic dependence with greater
concern than do Austrians. As Neuhold indicates, only 9 percent of Austrians
regarded economic relations with Germany as too close. In contrast, 61 percent of Canadians thought the amount of U.S. investment in Canada was
sufficient and did not want to see an increase in it.[10] Yet, as the chapter by
Georg Winckler shows, using a number of significant economic indicators of

---

9. Peter Katzenstein, *Disjoined Partners,* p. 30.

10. Canadian Institute of Public Opinion, "The Gallup Report," (2 July 1987 and 16
    June 1988), cited in Glen Williams, "Regions within Region: Canada in the Con-
    tinent," in Michael S. Whittington and Glen Williams, *Canadian Politics in the
    1990s,* 3d. ed., Scarborough, Ontario (1990). Concern over U.S. investment in
    Canada reached a peak in 1975, with 71 percent viewing the amount of U.S. in-
    vestment as sufficient, and concern has declined somewhat thereafter.

economic behavior, the Austrian economy correlates more closely with the German one than does the Canadian economy vis-à-vis that of the United States. Winckler addresses this apparent paradox by arguing that "direct economic linkages between the FRG and Austria play a less significant role in moving the Austrian macroeconomy along the West German path than do the policy decisions of the government or of the social partners." The deliberate actions of the Austrian Central Bank with respect to exchange rates and the actions of the social partners with respect to price and wage policies tend to "transmit the impact of the German economy to the Austrian one" in an effort to protect Austria's competitive position vis-à-vis its principal partner.

Mark Schultz's contribution to this volume — as that by Frederick Engelmann — deviates from the general approach of dyadic relations research in which Austrian and Canadian experts usually deal with their country's relations with the respective dominant actors or — as in the case of the two "synthetic" chapters by Henry J. Jacek and this writer — with a "synthetic," comparative analysis of the two dyads. However, an analysis of the fundamental change in Austrian policy that culminated in the application for membership in the EC in 1989 may also be of interest to Austrian readers, although or because it was written from the viewpoint of a Canadian.

Previously Austria had been satisfied with free trade accords with the Communities but had avoided full membership because it was afraid this might jeopardize its neutral status. But with the EC's move toward a single market in 1992, there were growing concerns that nonmembership might lead to increased discrimination and to economic costs as well as to Austria's gradual marginalization in European affairs. Supporters of EC membership, interestingly, reversed the previous neutrality argument. They now claim that full-fledged membership would place Austria in a better position to influence EC decisions from within and thus to prevent any Community action that might undermine Austria's independence, and as a result, its neutrality.

Austria's decision to apply for membership in the EC raises an important question that has interesting political and theoretical implications. Do free trade treaties or similar economic arrangements between unequal partners lead to political integration? In his study of several relevant historical precedents, Peyton Lyon found no evidence of such linkage, at least when political unification did not figure as a principal goal at the very outset.[11] The Austrian example invites a reexamination of the linkage hypothesis. In this particular instance, however, it is not a political union in the traditional sense but an integration into an international political community. It should be

11. Peyton Lyon, *Canada-United States Free Trade and Canadian Independence,* Ottawa (1975).

borne in mind that Austria insists on preserving its neutrality, which, at least according to the traditional definition, rules out full participation in a common foreign and eventual common security policy of the EC.

If Austria's decision to seek membership in the EC reversed a thirty-year-old convention, the conclusion of a FTA with the United States in 1987 broke with a century-old taboo that considered full-fledged free trade with the United States an unacceptable risk for Canadian political independence. Bruce Wilkinson's chapter obliquely touches on the FTA without entering into a comprehensive debate on the possible gains and losses resulting from it for Canada. In his analysis of the 1987 antidumping action brought by the U.S. government against the Saskatchewan potash industry, he raises the broader question of whether the bilateral FTA will provide protection against periodic attempts by the United States to use antidumping and countervailing laws "not just to create a 'level playing field' but to protect declining industries." Wilkinson finds little in the FTA that might help reduce Canadian vulnerability to similar U.S. actions in the future. Existing U.S. antidumping and countervailing laws and regulations remain unaffected by the FTA. In addition, the dispute settlement procedure provided under the agreement can merely be used to decide whether determinations have been made in strict accordance with existing national laws, not whether they are inherently justified.

Culture and Media Relations

The closing section of this volume addresses cultural and media relations between unequal partners. The conditions of asymmetry can be seen to affect the cultural and information sphere in at least two important areas: the attention ratio and the overall political economy of culture. In both cases examined here, the subordinate partners have a disproportionately greater knowledge of public affairs, media content, and cultural developments in the superordinate countries than applies conversely. The superordinate partners can operate, albeit at some cost (particularly in negotiation situations), by practicing benign neglect toward their smaller partners. For the latter such neglect would be a recipe for disaster.

The political economy of culture affects mobility and competitiveness in that particular sphere. Writers, artists, and performers from the smaller country in an asymmetrical pair tend to gravitate toward the superordinate country, attracted by the cultural dynamism and career opportunities that the latter provides. There is no equivalent flow of cultural talents in a reverse direction. It is interesting to note that high career mobility in the cultural field is not fully duplicated in other spheres of activity. Mobility is more constrained in the economic sector and is virtually nonexistent in political life. Adolf Haslinger's chapter draws attention to the fact that a book by an Austrian writer must be sold in Germany in order to guarantee its literary and commercial success. The same rule generally applies to Canadian authors, although their dependence on the big partner is somewhat mitigated by a larger domestic market. Thus Austrian and Canadian cultural and media products generally operate under the disadvantage of a smaller domestic market; moreover, one in which they must face stiff competition from their big partner. The data presented in the chapters by Hans Heinz Fabris and Frederick and Martha Fletcher clearly attest to this double predicament.

Although the respective statistics may vary somewhat between sectors, the underlying problem facing both Austria and Canada is strikingly similar. The dominance of the superordinate country in the sphere of culture and media is extensive. Fabris draws attention to the obvious commercial and technological benefits provided by the Big Brother connection. He contrasts these benefits with the related problems of maintaining a distinct identity and of debating issues of particular national concern under conditions of strong cultural penetration by the big partner. Fabris credits the growth of indigenous Austrian magazines and journals during the 1970s for having opened the delayed national debate of Austria's role during the years of Nazi occupation.

The Fletchers argue along the same line when they state that cultural dominance makes it difficult to recognize and consequently to pursue one's national interest. Depending on where one places the accent, Canada finds itself in either an easier or a more difficult situation than Austria. The situation is better for Canada insofar as it offers a larger domestic market for its cultural products than does Austria. However, Austria is in a better position to cope with foreign penetration because of a well-established tradition of government ownership, regulation, and subsidies. Instead of the Austrian state monopoly over electronic media, Canada has a mixed system of private and public ownership of television and broadcasting. This reflects a fundamental ambivalence regarding the appropriate role of the state. Moreover, Canadian attempts to regulate cultural and media activities for the purpose of strengthening their national content have led to confrontations with the United States which tends to interpret such assertions of cultural nationalism as challenges to such basic principles as the free market and free flow of information.

There are at least two aspects in which the cultural relations of the two dyads differ quite fundamentally. Unlike Canada, Austria is the heir of an ancient and great cultural tradition that helps explain the natural confidence of Austrians in their culture and their highly developed sense of cultural identity. Nothing comparable exists in Canada. In his chapter on Canadian literature, Stanley Fogel criticizes the efforts of the Canadian literary establishment to promote a Canadian national identity in their literary works and literary criticism. In Fogel's opinion, national identities are inflated constructs, the products of commercial advertising and politics rather than artistic creations. Instead of constructing a literary landscape that would serve to shape a national identity, he urges the literary establishment to follow a deconstructionist paradigm. Fogel's prescription is not likely to go unchallenged, for it may be argued that something will first have to be constructed before there can be any meaningful deconstructionist effort.

The other significant cultural difference between Austria and Canada is the high degree of reciprocity of cultural influence between Austria and Germany that has no counterpart in Canadian-U.S. cultural relations. In fact, the cultural cross-influences are so strong between Austria and Germany that, in this particular sphere at least, the conditions of asymmetry are largely erased. (West)German literary reviews and anthologies include Austrian writers without observing any distinctions, even though, as Haslinger reminds us, there are differences in style, thematic preoccupation, and historical interpretation that set postwar Austrian writers apart from their (West) German counterparts. There exists no comparable reciprocity in U.S.-Canadian cultural relations, and the pattern of influence here is almost exclusively unidirectional. The United States requires no contribution from Canada to define its cultural role and self-image. Although some Canadian writers and artists are known to a few U.S. cognoscenti, they are not exactly household words. No U.S. literary critic is likely to identify Margaret Atwood or Robertson Davies among the most significant American writers of our time in the same manner in which Austrian writers Thomas Bernhard and Peter Handke have been ranked, together with Heinrich Böll and Günter Grass, as the four greatest contemporary German writers.

Conclusion

Recently we have witnessed major changes that are likely to have important consequences for Austrian and Canadian relations with their respective big partners. Austria's bid for membership in the EC, if successful, will entail a restructuring of its relations with its German neighbor, although at this stage one can construct diverging scenarios about the precise impact of such a development. One might plausibly argue that EC membership would reinforce Austria's dependence on the FRG by simply grafting a multilateral dimension onto the existing bilateral relations. The argument gains credibility because a united Germany would be the undisputed leader of the Community. Conversely, membership in the EC would reduce Austrian reliance on the intermediary role of the Federal Republic; moreover, as Fabris suggests, it might accelerate the globalization of Austria's economy and media and thereby reduce the strong dependence on a single partner.

The other critical development for Austrian-FRG relations has been the entirely unpredicted and rapid movement toward German unification following the disintegration of Soviet imperial dominance over Eastern Europe. As a minimum consequence, a unified Germany will accentuate the power discrepancy of this particular unequal partnership. With the decline of interbloc confrontation in Europe, Austria's status as a neutral state will become less conspicuous because former parties to the Warsaw Pact will, at least temporarily, acquire a similar status either on a de facto or de jure basis. Moreover, neutrality will probably provide less leverage for Austrian foreign policy because the need for third-party mediation in East-West conflicts will diminish. The gradual devaluation of Austrian neutrality does not foreclose other avenues for Austrian foreign policy engagement. Neuhold draws attention to Austrian efforts to revive in some form the historical *Mitteleuropa* concept by forging a network of cooperative ties involving cultural, economic, ecological, and, eventually perhaps, political issues among former entities of the Habsburg monarchy. The disintegration of communism in Eastern Europe and the consequent loosening of bloc affiliation broadens the scope of such cooperative regional ventures and promises to increase the potential membership of such a group.

The Canadian-U.S. FTA has the potential for substantially restructuring the traditional continental relationship between the two countries. Because the agreement did not enter into force until 1989, there is insufficient evidence to draw any definitive conclusions of its ultimate economic (let alone political) consequences for Canada. No recent issues, save the abortive attempt to amend the Canadian constitution in order to accommodate Quebec's particular needs, has divided Canadian opinion more sharply than the FTA.

Its critics interpret the FTA as a clear breakpoint in bilateral relations that will lead to a fundamental transformation of the Canadian economy, the erosion of its cultural distinctiveness, and the effective surrender of Canadian sovereignty. Defenders of the agreement are more inclined to view it as a logical progression toward increased trade liberalization following the Kennedy and Tokyo rounds. To support their case they cite trade statistics that indicate that, prior to the agreement, 90 percent of Canadian exports entered the United States duty-free and the average duty on the remaining portion varied from 4 to 6 percent. In the face of these figures, the cataclysmic image of the FTA by critics may appear unrealistic and over-dramatized. Leyton-Brown's position is of particular interest for this debate insofar as he manages to integrate the two bipolarized positions. In purely economic terms, he finds the FTA to be consistent with Canada's long-term bilateral and multilateral strategy to secure favorable access to world markets. The agreement merely placed the bilateral approach on a fast track. In political terms, however, he finds the opposite argument to be more credible:

> The FTA is a departure, marking not an attempt to escape from the American
> orbit but an embracing of the bilateral relationship. It is a turning point which
> creates new bilateral mechanisms and from which all aspects of the relationship,
> whether directly and explicitly covered by the agreement or not, will be conducted
> in a different context.[12]

In a similar vein, Doern and Tomlin conclude that the institutionalization of relations as provided by the agreement will have a profound impact on decision making by making way for a "greater U.S. presence in all areas of Canadian decision making, required by the notification and consultation provisions."[13] The authors evaluate the probable consequences of the FTA on Canadian policy capability, i.e., the ability of governments to spend, tax, and regulate, in various policy areas. Their multidimensional treatment avoids the simplistic all-out acceptance or rejection which has characterized much of the FTA debate in Canada. They anticipate a mixed outcome of gains and losses in Canada's capacity to make trade policy. The capacity to shape industrial policy has clearly been weakened by removing restrictions on U.S. direct investment and by concessions on trade in services. In turn, the capacity to make energy policy may have been marginally weakened, with benefits from assured access to the U.S. energy market compensating for concessions with respect to export taxes, export control, and differential prices. Finally, the capacity to conduct social policy has not been harmed by the FTA and may actually have been strengthened.[14]

Doern's and Tomlin's generally favorable interpretation will, without doubt, be challenged by other analysts, in particular as it relates to the social policy sphere. Thus Donald Smiley, one of Canada's most eminent political scientists, warns that the ultimate thrust of any free trade treaty between Canada and the United States is toward greater harmonization of public policy. Canada will experience most of this pressure, in part, because the United States as the superordinate actor will establish the norms and, in part, because the level of economic and social intervention is higher in Canada,

---

12. David Leyton-Brown, below, p. 150.

13. Bruce Doern and Brian Tomlin, *Faith and Fear: The Free Trade Story*, Toronto (1991), p. 96.

14. Ibidem, p. 96.

thus making the latter the primary target of any leveling efforts. According to Smiley, policy harmonization "challenges Canadian distinctiveness in a very direct way" because Canadian nationalism is defined essentially in political rather than in cultural, ethnic, or religious terms.[15]

In a balanced argument which avoids the polemics which the issue has generated in Canada, Denis Stairs emphasizes that the FTA will reduce the maneuverability of the Canadian state in areas of public policy.[16] The FTA explicitly restricts the Canadian government's capacity to regulate important economic sectors such as energy and foreign investment. It will also expose the Canadian government to greater pressure from U.S. corporations objecting to subsidies and from Canadian producers demanding deregulation in order to provide them with an equal chance to compete in the U.S. market. It is not merely the capacity for independent action that will be impaired by the FTA but the willingness to take such action. Exposing Canadians more directly to the philosophy and reality of U.S. competition may reduce their willingness to use their sovereignty in ways different from the United States.

For Canada the choice of endorsing free trade highlighted the central dilemma of the weaker partner in an asymmetrical dyad, i.e., opting for greater integration because of the expected economic benefits despite the risks to political autonomy and national identity. The choice involved a leap of faith, as former Finance Minister Donald Macdonald called it, or perhaps a leap in the dark, as a more critical analyst has styled it.[17] Such a leap marks a notable departure from the preference for risk avoidance that has normally characterized Canadian policy.

From the Canadian perspective, the FTA broke with two well-established principles in Canadian-U.S. relations: the principle that a comprehensive free trade treaty must be avoided and that formal institutional arrangements for the management of bilateral conflicts should be minimized. It was feared that free trade might irreparably weaken the decision making latitude of the Canadian state and that an institutional mechanism for bilateral conflict management would be overly intrusive and would, moreover, give statutory form to the unequal power relationship.

---

15. Donald Smiley, "A Note on Canadian-American Free Trade and Canadian Policy Autonomy," in Marc Gold and David Leyton-Brown (eds.), *Trade-Offs on Free Trade: The Canada-U.S. Free Trade Agreement,* Toronto (1988), pp. 441–445.

16. Denis Stairs, "Non-Economic Implications of a Comprehensive Canada-U.S. Free Trade Agreement," in Allan Maslove and Stanley Winer (eds.), *Knocking on the Back Door: Canadian Perspectives on the Political Economy of Free Trade with the United States,* Halifax (1987), pp. 79–100.

17. Denis Stairs, "The Impact on Public Policy: A Leap of Faith," in Marc Gold and David Leyton-Brown (eds.), *Trade-Offs on Free Trade,* p. 454.

In recent years the first principle suffered gradual erosion from Canada's declining international economic competitiveness and the consequent need for structural adjustment. For the Mulroney government and for business interests, the FTA represented the most, and perhaps the only, effective shock treatment to launch structural adjustment and eventual economic recovery. Reservations about an institutionalized mechanism for the management of bilateral conflicts were gradually supplanted by growing concerns with U.S. neoprotectionism as witnessed by a sharp increase in the application of trade remedy laws in response to demands by U.S. special interests. Given the "atomized, highly adversarial, litigation-prone system of U.S. government," in which special interests drive the system, administrations in Washington have been hard-pressed to find an acceptable solution to bilateral disputes with Canada, even when they were committed to do so.[18] Allan Gotlieb, Canada's former ambassador in Washington and a key player in the FTA negotiations, has been the most articulate proponent of a new framework for Canadian-U.S. relations which would depart from the traditional approach of ad hoc improvisation and would rely increasingly on the rule of law and on bilateral institutions in order to "abridge the new power of public pressure and special interests through objective intermediation."[19] Adherence to a set of rules regularizing bilateral relations might go some way to level the disparity of power even though they are likely to reflect disproportionately the preferences of the stronger party; moreover, the latter will be in a better position to alter or bypass these rules.

For Canadian negotiators the inclusion of an institutionalized mechanism for dispute settlement was a *sine qua non* for the completion of the FTA, and negotiations almost broke down over the failure to achieve an acceptable formula. The dispute settlement provisions contained in the final treaty fall far short of Canada's original demands. Two serious flaws, in particular, weaken the efficacy of the agreed method. First, decisions of the binational review panels are nonbinding except for disputes involving countervail and antidumping duties. Second, the panels' scope for decision making is severely curtailed by the fact that, prior to the creation of a harmonized system of trade remedy laws, they can merely rule on the correct application of existing national laws rather than of treaty law.[20]

18. Allan Gotlieb, "Keeping the U.S. trade gate open," *Globe and Mail,* Toronto, 9 March 1992.

19. Allan Gotlieb, "The United States in Canadian Foreign Policy," O. D. Skelton Memorial Lecture, Toronto, 10 December 1991.

20. A critical assessment of the dispute settlement provisions is given by Bruce Fisher, "Politics of FTA Trade Disputes," *International Perspectives* (September/October 1990), pp. 17–20. For a more favorable evaluation, see Joseph

In their seminal work, *Power and Interdependence,* Keohane and Nye have argued that under conditions of complex interdependence, such as exist in Canadian-U.S. relations, power disparities will be mitigated by close elite networks, transgovernmental and transnational coalitions, and the existence of international regimes.[21] Doran has questioned the adequacy of the complex interdependence model for explaining Canadian-U.S. relations because it fails to make adequate allowance for the obvious asymmetry of size and disparity in bargaining strength in this particular dyad.[22]

In closing, we will use the three-year record of dispute settlements under the FTA to address two related questions, namely whether the codification of dispute settlement procedures as part of the bilateral Canadian-U.S. trade regime will reduce the politicization of conflicts and whether it will mitigate the power disparity between the two partners.

Kidd notes that "it could be that FTA institutions will serve to limit the degree to which politicization will be a determinant of Canadian success," but cautions this may not prove true in the long run.[23] If by politicization we mean the tendency to seek maximum publicity for a conflict and to drive it to the top of the decision making ladder, then the FTA has at least partially succeeded during the 1989–1991 short-run period to contain the politicization of bilateral conflicts. The mere fact that recourse can be taken to review panels provides for a breathing space and allows governments to react in a more low-key manner. In this context, it is interesting to compare the measured response of the Canadian government to the current dispute over duties on softwood-lumber imports. When the identical issue occurred in 1986, it immediately produced a mini-crisis in Canadian-U.S. relations and almost derailed further FTA negotiations. The binational, quasi-judicial review panels also appear to have preserved an arm's length relationship from political pressures. In the nineteen decisions which the review panels have made during the first three years, there was only one instance, involving a U.S. import prohibition on Pacific lobster, in which the verdict was divided along national lines.[24]

McKinney, "Dispute Settlement under the U.S.-Canada Free Trade Agreement," *Journal of World Trade* 25 (December 1991), pp. 117–130.

21. Robert Keohane and Joseph Nye, Jr., *Power and Interdependence: World Politics in Transition,* Boston (1977), pp. 23–27; 165–218.

22. Charles Doran, *Forgotten Partnership,* pp. 53–64.

23. Michael Kidd, "Complex Interdependence, Canada-U.S. Relations and the Free Trade Agreement," unpublished paper, Carleton University, Department of Political Science (1992), p. 13.

24. Anthony Chapman, "Canada-U.S. Trade Disputes," *Current Issue Review* 91–1E, Library of Parliament, Ottawa, 22 January 1991, p. 17.

As Kidd has cautioned, the existence of a formalized mechanism for trade dispute settlement does not guarantee the nonpoliticization of issues. The issues decided by the review panels so far have not been items of the highest significance. The response to an unfavorable panel decision on a significant issue, such as softwood-lumber or steel imports, or a streak of decisions which are consistently unfavorable to one party, may prompt a highly politicized reaction by the loser.

Depoliticization of disputes may be a sound prescription for effective conflict management, but does it actually work for the benefit of the weaker party? Doran observes that "politicization as a hypothetical tool in Canada-U.S. relations has generally held more appeal in Canada than in the United States."[25] A highly politicized dispute with the United States is more likely to produce a unified Canadian national front, and thereby enhance bargaining leverage, than a comparable situation in the United States. But as was indicated above, the chances of improving the outcome of a dispute by driving it to the top of the U.S. decision making ladder are much diminished in the current U.S. domestic political environment.

Finally, one can examine the actual record of FTA dispute settlements to ascertain whether the codification of rules of conflict management as part of the free trade regime does mitigate the underlying power disparity between the two countries by moving from a power-driven to a rule-dominant relationship. During the first three years after the treaty took effect, i.e., between 1988 and 1991, a total of twenty-four trade-related disputes were submitted to binational review panels. In all but two of these cases, the panels were authorized to make binding rulings involving countervail and anti-dumping duties. Canada initiated nineteen reviews, the U.S. the remaining five. Canada's disproportionate reliance on the dispute settlement provisions reflects a much stronger interest in their function; moreover, Canada almost automatically becomes the challenger because of the much greater frequency with which the U.S. applies trade remedy laws.

It is much more difficult to go beyond these elementary statistics and to make a qualitative judgement about the outcome of decisions made by the review panels. Of the nineteen decisions taken in three years — five were still pending at the end of 1991 — five appear to have upheld the Canadian position, seven supported the U.S. position, and seven represented ties or compromise verdicts.[26] In the case of compromise decisions, it is particularly difficult to determine with precision whether the outcome was closer to a

25. Charles Doran, *Forgotten Partnership*, p. 69.

26. A list of cases and a synopsis of completed cases were provided by the Canadian Secretariat of the Canadian-United States Trade Commission, Ottawa (1992).

win/win or a win/loss solution. As the record indicates, the bilateral review panels managed to reverse a number of U.S. decisions that had been unfavorable to Canadian interests, and they did so with considerably greater speed, lower expense, and a higher success rate than might have been achieved by relying on the vagaries of an unregulated political process.

2

Unequal Partners: The Historical, Political, Economic, and Cultural Dimensions of the Austrian-FRG/Canadian-U.S. Dyads

Henry J. Jacek

Students of comparative country studies pick their comparisons for many practical reasons relating to both their language skills and their cultural interests. Thus, the choice of comparisons often forecloses addressing interesting theoretical questions. There are many excellent individual country studies of Austria, the FRG, Canada, and the United States. There are even a few analyses of relations between Austria and the FRG and between Canada and the United States.[1] What has been lacking to date and is now

---

1. For studies of the European countries see Peter J. Katzenstein, *Disjoined Partners: Austria and Germany Since 1815*, Berkeley (1976). For North America see Charles F. Doran and John H. Sigler (eds.), *Canada and the United States: Enduring Friendship, Persistent Stress*, Englewood Cliffs, N.J. (1985); and the five published reports of the Asymmetrical Dyads and Foreign Policy Project: Brian W. Tomlin, Michael B. Dolan, Harald von Riekhoff, and Maureen Appel Molot, "Foreign Policies of Subordinate States in Asymmetrical Dyads," *Jerusalem Journal of International Relations* (September 1981), pp. 14–40; Michael B. Dolan, Brian W. Tomlin, and Harald von Riekhoff, "Integration and Autonomy in Canada-United States Relations, 1963–1972," *Canadian Journal of Political Science* 15 (June 1982), pp. 331–363; Michael B. Dolan, Brian W. Tomlin, Harald von Riekhoff, and Maureen Appel Molot, "Asymmetrical Dyads and Foreign Policy: Canada-U.S. Relations, 1963–1972," *Journal of Conflict Resolution* 26 (September 1982), pp. 387–422; Harald von Riekhoff and Brian W. Tomlin, "The

clearly the next step is a comparison of the two partnerships themselves. In this way we can begin filtering out relationships that are unique to each dyad versus highlighting propositions common to unequal partnerships.

What is especially interesting about these two dyads is their *relative* cultural and linguistic homogeneity. Thus, the question is put best by Peter Katzenstein. "What needs to be explained ... is the resilience of the politically autonomous nation-state. With growing interdependence why does integration not succeed autonomy? Why do partners remain disjoined?"[2] To this line of analysis on disjoined partners is added the concept of asymmetry that was a key part of the Carleton project.

How do we approach the analysis of the dyads of unequal partners? Overall there would seem to be a number of broad dimensions to consider such as the historical, political, economic, and cultural dimensions. The latter one could include the diffusion of cultural content by the media. The key questions of history of partners revolve around the development of unique nationalities, especially on the part of the subordinate partner, and the reconciliation of each to their separate and unequal existences. The contemporary political dimension is concerned with the relationship between state actors in each dyad. Influencing the previous two dimensions is the economic development of each country as influenced by the other and as set in the context of regional and the international economies. Finally, the cultural dimension includes a diverse set of phenomena from arts and literature to the popular transmission of information, perceptions, and values, and their impact on the relations between the unequal partners.

The Methodology of Studying Unequal Partners

In selecting cases of unequal partnerships it seems important for theoretical development that we select dyads that have large asymmetries in population size and economic weight, as well as dyads that share a relatively homogeneous cultural and linguistic unit and are in close physical proximity to

---

Politics of Interdependence: Canada-United States Intergovernmental Relations," in John Pammett and Brian W. Tomlin (eds.), *The Integration Question: Political Economy and Public Policy in Canada and North America*, Toronto (1984), pp. 144–162; and Michael B. Dolan and Brian W. Tomlin, "Foreign Policy in Asymmetrical Dyads: Theoretical Reformulation and Empirical Analysis, Canada-United States Relations, 1963–1972," *International Studies Quarterly* 28 (September 1984), pp. 349–368.

2.   Katzenstein, *Disjoined Partners*, p. 4.

one another. By controlling for language, culture, and geographical closeness we make an important start toward eliminating factors extraneous to the size relationship. Some might recognize this as the "Most Similar Systems' Design" described by Adam Przeworski and Henry Teune.[3] The purpose of this type of design is to minimize the number of variables so we can isolate the exact relationship between the independent variable, superordinate or subordinate status in a dyad, and the dependent variables, that is, their historical, political, economic, and cultural relationships. Such a design combines the assumptions of the traditional "area studies" approach in the humanities and social sciences with social science research designs that have as their ideal the experiment in the physical sciences.

The notion of close geographical proximity in comparative research has been neglected over the last generation. Studies that seek to compare "neighboring, closely related communities" are called *concomitant variation studies.*[4] Such a consideration goes beyond the most similar systems design because it takes into account communications between countries that diffuse information, perceptions, and values and harmonizes them. Thus, the dyad has a tendency to be immunized continually and to reject cultural influences from outside the dyad. This harmonization of culture is greatly aided by a dominant commonly shared language in comparison to the rest of the world. The sharing of the dominant language, German for the European dyad and English for the North American one, is vitally important because it facilitates continual close cultural relationships and ensures their continuation. In addition, this cultural affinity transmitted through a common language should be reflected by a high level of intersociety social and economic communications, once again in comparison with the rest of the world.

The Historical Web of Social, Political, and Economic Organization

Besides the relatively homogeneous cultural affinity within each dyad, the vagaries of historical experience have led to an almost identical size differential within each dyad today. In both partnerships, the smaller of the two is

---

3. Adam Przeworski and Henry Teune, *The Logic of Comparative Social Inquiry,* New York (1970), pp. 32–34.

4. Raoul Naroll, "Some Thoughts on Comparative Method in Cultural Anthropology," in Hubert Blalock, Jr., and Ann Blalock (eds.), *Methodology in Social Research,* New York (1968), p. 240.

approximately 11 to 12 percent of the larger partner's population size (see Table 2.1). Austria's population is now 9.5 percent of its major partner after German unification.

TABLE 2.1

Population of the Countries in the Austrian-FRG/Canadian-U.S. Dyads

Country	Austria	FRG	Canada	United States
Population	7,550,000	61,015,300 (79,200,000)*	25,359,800	236,681,000
Percentage of the population size of the larger partner	(12) (9.5)*	(100)	(11)	(100)

* Represents adjusted population figures after German unification.

Source: The Europa Year Book 1987: A World Survey, London (1987), vol. I, Austria, pp. 402–424, Canada, pp. 651–683, FRG, pp. 1164–1208; vol. II, United States, pp. 2839–2929.

Thus, whatever the impact of relative size in each dyad, that impact will not be affected by variations in the current relative size of the smaller country.

Historically how has each smaller country responded to its large neighbor? Our first working hypothesis is that in order to deal with the international scene and a large neighbor it cannot control but must respond to, the subordinate country has developed a stronger collective organizational structure for its society. A dense, powerful net of interest organizations, especially economic ones, allows a smaller country to mobilize more quickly and decisively in pursuit of national public policies. Such a net indicates associations that are capable of performing a public policy role in addition to the interest representation functions commonly ascribed to such groups. Thus, these organizations function as agents of public policy and should be seen not only as the pleaders of special interests.[5]

---

5. For a theoretical analysis along these lines see Wolfgang Streeck and Philippe C. Schmitter, "Community, market, state, and associations? The prospective

Austria and Canada are more densely organized per capita compared to their large neighbors. More importantly, the authority of association leaders over their members is relatively greater. Thus, the organizational elites are more capable of responding positively to the demands of public policy.[6] This is most clearly seen when one examines the organization of interests among business, labor, the professions, and agriculture.

In Austria, the diversified capital base — private domestic, private foreign, and public domestic — is more than matched in a complex organization of business interests, centralized associations, both compulsory and voluntary, interest associations for state enterprises, and sectoral and subsectoral organizations.[7] A fairly well-known characteristic of Austrian interest politics is the phenomenon of the chamber system, whereby all persons gainfully employed and all enterprises are compelled by state statute to be represented by an appropriate chamber association.[8] At the same time, there is a panoply of parallel voluntary associations that provide expert technical advice to the corresponding chamber organization. There is an association for public enterprises exclusively from which private firms are excluded, namely the *Arbeitsgemeinschaft der Österreichischen Gemeinwirtschaft* (AdÖG). At the same time, there exists the voluntary League of Austrian Industrialists, the *Vereinigung Österreichischer Industrieller* (VÖI), as well as sectoral and sub-

contribution of interest governance to social order," in Wolfgang Streeck and Philippe C. Schmitter, *Private Interest Government: Beyond Market and State,* Beverly Hills (1985), pp. 1–29.

6. As regards Canada, some details on the use of business interest associations to implement public policies in the area of energy conservation, conversion of imperial weights and measures to the metric system, and wage and price controls can be found in Henry J. Jacek, "Pluralist and Corporatist Intermediation, Activities of Business Interest Associations, and Corporate Profits: Some Evidence from Canada," *Comparative Politics* 18 (July 1986), pp. 419–437. For a similar and recent analysis of Austria from the same perspective see Bernd Marin, "Austria: The Paradigm Case of Liberal Corporatism?" in Wyn Grant (ed.), *The Political Economy of Corporatism,* London (1985), pp. 89–125.

7. My knowledge of the organization of business interests in Austria, Canada, the United States, and West Germany is based primarily on my participation in the Organization of Business Interests Project headed by Philippe Schmitter and Wolfgang Streeck. The countries included in this project are Austria, Canada, Denmark, the FRG, Italy, the Netherlands, Sweden, Switzerland, Spain, the United Kingdom, and the United States. I am a Canadian coordinator on this project.

8. Bernd Marin, "Organizing Interests by Interest Organizations: Associational Prerequisites of Cooperation in Austria," *International Political Science Review* 4, no. 9 (1983), p. 210.

sectoral business interest associations. These voluntary business associations complement the compulsory chambers in another way by giving special representation to large firms or to sectoral and subsectoral interests with distinctive properties or problems.

Similarly, Austrian workers are just as well-organized. The organization of Austrian labor, both in its centralization and high density, has been given a predominant position in explaining the successful management of Austria's economy.[9] Labor's integration into consensual decision making, under the watchful eye of the government, along with the similarly well-organized professions and farmers, allows the various interests to make important concessions in economic decision making. This system, usually called the Social Partnership, leads to a no-surprise, relatively predictable, dependable system in which all major economic interests achieve their primary goals by mutually sacrificing secondary goals. The strong interest organizations ensure that the agreements are implemented. The West German interest group system, although impressive by North American standards, is weaker than its Austrian analogue.

When an examination is made of the two North American countries, one can see a more group-conscious, stronger interest group society in Canada.[10] In many ways, the system of business interest associations in Canada appears to be a smaller replica of the system in the United States, but there are differences. First, with a much smaller population, Canada does, nevertheless, tend to reproduce associations with similar-sounding names and functions. In addition, many Canadian corporations, indeed, probably most large- and medium-sized firms, also belong to associations based in the United States. Thus, Canadian business belongs to a very dense web of business interest associations and thereby increases the likelihood of concerted collective action. Second, there are present in Canada subnational multisectoral peak associations of business such as the Employers' Council of British Columbia and the *Conseil du patronat du Québec* (CPQ). In terms of their organizational strength, ability to represent business in their respective territories, authority over their member firms, and practice of striking deals with organized labor in the same territory, there are no counterparts to them in the United States.

---

9. Franz Traxler, *Evolution gewerkschaftlicher Interessenvertretung*, Frankfurt and Vienna (1982); Fritz W. Scharpf, *The Political Calculus of Inflation and Unemployment in Western Europe*, Cambridge, Mass. (1987), p. 52.

10. For a summary of evidence that economic interest associations have greater legitimacy in Canada compared to the United States, see Robert Presthus, *Elites in the Policy Process*, London (1974).

At times, the authority or governmental characteristics of business interest associations seem more like what we would expect on the European continent rather than in North America. This is especially so in Quebec. In addition to the powerful role of the CPQ noted above, some sectors have associations that can make policies generally binding, that is, the guidelines and rules apply to members and nonmembers alike. In at least one case, membership is compulsory. "Every person in the construction industry in Quebec who employs at least one worker must by law belong to the Association des entrepreneurs en construction du Québec (AECQ)."[11]

The robustness in the organization of business interest associations in Canada is matched by the dynamism of Canadian trade unions. Over the past generation "the Canadian labour movement has outperformed its American counterpart in terms of union growth, union density, and certification outcomes."[12] By 1985, union density (that is the percentage of potential or eligible union members who actually belong to a trade union) fell to 18 percent of nonfarm employment "in the United States, while in Canada the union density in 1985 remained at 39 percent."[13] As Rose and Chaison show, the energy of the Canadian labor movement is seen among all three major types: private sector international unions, private sector Canadian unions, and public sector Canadian unions.[14] Clearly, there is something about the characteristics of Canada itself in contrast to characteristics of the United States that affects these sharp discontinuities on the North American continent.

To an important degree what makes this dynamism so interesting to analysts of national industrial and economic strategies is that the health of Canadian unions and the industries within which they are located often seems to vary together. Contrary to arguments that old-style militant unions weaken economic efficiency by restraining market forces, many Canadian sectors with strong unions, such as steel,[15] automobiles, electrical products,

---

11. William D. Coleman, "State corporatism as a sectoral phenomenon: the case of the Quebec construction industry," in Alan Cawson (ed.), *Organized Interests and the State: Studies in Neo-Corporatism,* London (1985), p. 114.

12. Joseph B. Rose and Gary N. Chaison, "The State of the Unions: United States and Canada," *Journal of Labour Research* 6 (Winter 1985), p. 108.

13. Joseph B. Rose and Gary N. Chaison, "The State of the Unions Revisited: The United States and Canada," a paper presented to the annual meeting of the Canadian Industrial Relations Association, McMaster University, Hamilton (June 1987), p. 3. This excellent paper not only documents the detailed nature but also the circumstances surrounding these divergent national trends.

14. Ibidem, pp. 3 f.

15. One can catch the flavor of this counterintuitive finding by examining the Steel Company of Canada (Stelco). This company is one of the two dominant

fish processing, and meat packing, also appear healthier and more internationally competitive than their U.S. counterparts. Canadian unions reject concessionary bargaining and the introduction of harsher work conditions modeled on U.S. factories in the 1980s.[16] Since 1971 the volume of strikes has been twice as high in Canada, the frequency has been substantially higher and the number of workers involved in any given strike has been over 25 percent more.[17] Despite their militancy, however, Canadian workers are willing to accept substantially lower wage rates.[18] Part of this is because Canadians have more extensive welfare state provisions, such as universal medical care coverage, as well as "legally mandated holidays and vacations with pay."[19]

In the third broad division of the North American economic structure, that of the professions, the same divergence in attachment to collective action is observed. Although the Canadian tendency to strong professional associations was not intended originally to help implement Canadian macroeconomic politics, over the last twenty years these associations have increasingly become agents of macroeconomic policy. Their specific function as macroeconomic policy agents is to contain the professional fee increases that are extracted from the national income, especially those fees paid out from the public purse.

Since the beginning of the professions in Canada, there have been controversies over who should be allowed to engage in each profession, what standards should be followed, and, indeed, whether any regulation at all should take place. The basic conflict resulted from the clash of two value systems. The first tradition is the European one. This tradition contains the core idea that it is the organized profession as a unified whole that possesses professional rights, and thus individual professionals must submit to regula-

---

corporations in the Canadian steel production sector, is highly efficient and competitive in North American and world markets, produces very high quality steel, and is the only steel company in North America to have opened a new greenfield works, in Nanticoke, Ontario, over the past generation. Yet this company is organized and led by very militant local union leaders affiliated with the United Steelworkers of America. For an explanation of the political history of Stelco's largest union local see Bill Freeman, *1005: Political Life in a Union Local,* Toronto (1982).

16. Roy J. Adams, "Industrial-Relations Systems: An International Comparison," *Working Paper No. 274,* Faculty of Business, McMaster University, Hamilton (March 1987), p. 27.

17. Ibidem, p. 32.

18. In 1985 the hourly compensation of Canadian industrial workers was only 84 percent of that of similar workers in the United States; ibidem, p. 38.

19. Ibidem, p. 42.

tion by the professional group.[20] Practitioners who exercise the profession's skills and techniques and who purport to follow its ethical standards must answer to their peers with strong standards of self-regulation — standards that are overseen, however, by government.

The second tradition comes from the United States. Its core idea is completely opposed to the first in that the skills, techniques, and standards of conduct are under the control of the individual. The individual professional is subject to regulation by the market, thus giving freedom to both the professional and client to reach a mutually acceptable contractional arrangement.

Much of the political and economic history of the professions in Canada revolves around the clash of these two traditions. Throughout the nineteenth century, the issue was accelerated by the large influx of immigrants with certified professional qualifications from many different places, the existence of private professional schools in Canada itself, and the recognized shortage of professionals in general. Attempts to upgrade standards, whether by government or by rudimentary professional organizations, were seen as elitist and detrimental to the youth in rural areas where primary and secondary educational facilities were limited.

Often professional groups had two associations, one British and European-oriented and another market-oriented association representing professionals from the United States. During the twentieth century, the first organization tended to win out as a standard-setting body as the proportion of immigrants declined, as solidarity increased among the existing professionals, and most important, as the government supported strong peer self-regulation as a way to raise standards. But at the same time, the elitist character of the European-style organization was modified in order to make the professional association more responsive to the diverse elements within the profession and to make its leadership selection more democratic.

In many cases, two types of associations continue side-by-side, representing the same profession, but performing complementary functions. The first organization, compulsory in character, functions as a standard-setting body. It licenses the professional, collects yearly fees, attempts to provide continuing professional education, hears grievances from the public, and has the power to penalize practitioners financially, including suspension and the denial of the right to practice permanently. The second organization is voluntary and seeks to represent the financial interest of the individual practitioners.

---

20. This idea is explained very well in Carolyn J. Tuohy, "Private Government, Property, and Professionalism," *Canadian Journal of Political Science* 9 (December 1976), pp. 668–681.

As governmental authorities move to use both types of associations for macroeconomic policy implementation purposes, tensions increase both within the profession and between the two types of organizations. First, the licensing powers of the first type are used to restrict individual entry into the profession on the assumption that the fewer the professionals, the lower will be the aggregate professional bill for society and, where applicable, the public purse. Second, the second type of organization is used as a fee-setting body after negotiations with the government as the representative of the consuming public.[21]

Finally, strong associational government is also present in the fourth pillar of the modern economy, that of agriculture. Canadian agriculture is distinctive from that of the United States by the involvement of agricultural associations in marketing boards, in agricultural public enterprises, and in collective marketing arrangements with business interest associations representing the Canadian food-processing industry. In contrast, agriculture in the United States has tended to rely on different mechanisms such as subsidies, price supports, or government purchases of agricultural produce or its processed products.

Canadian agricultural marketing boards are a diverse group of federal and provincial institutions. It is clear, however, that they exist to serve primarily the agricultural community, especially the family farm. Although most boards negotiate or set the prices the processors must pay to farmers for their produce, some boards have strong powers to limit the supply of agricultural production and the entry of new farmers. This is most clearly seen in the case of milk, chicken, turkey, and egg production.[22]

---

21. This Austrian-like pattern of dual associability is most clearly seen in the organization of physicians and surgeons in the Canadian provinces. In nine out of the ten provinces, there is a College of Physicians and Surgeons that is the compulsory standard-setting body, but voluntary organizations exist to represent the financial interests of these practitioners. Where the disagreements over the best way to proceed in defining these material interests are especially severe (as in Ontario), there are competing voluntary organizations, sometimes as many as three. Only in Saskatchewan is there no voluntary organization. The decision to disband the voluntary association there was taken in the Great Depression as a cost-cutting measure.

22. For a detailed explanation of how these marketing boards work and their relationship to farmers' organizations and business interest groups, see William D. Coleman and Henry J. Jacek, "The Roles and Activities of Business Interest Associations in Canada," *Canadian Journal of Political Science* 16 (June 1983), pp. 257–280. Although Canadian farmers are more willing to support marketing boards and government help to farmers, there are important sources of resistance to both agricultural supply management and public enterprise in the

Summing up, within the central European and North American dyads, the relative histories of the smaller political economies are similar. Both are relatively more likely to possess a dense net of producer-based economic interest associations with strong powers of self-regulation that lend themselves to quick mobilization as agents of national macroeconomic policy. Because Canada, although a North American country, must cope with its large neighbor to the south, it has taken on some characteristics associated with European patterns of societal and economic organization and public policy, especially those properties found in the small political economies such as Austria.

The Role of the State

As important as a society-centered concentration of organizations is to the survival of the subordinate country in each dyad, such a pattern is far from sufficient to maintain national autonomy. The character of the state is important as well. What is needed is a strong state. This can be shown in a number of ways. However, our basic overarching hypothesis about the role of the state is that the smaller country places a greater reliance on state intervention in the economy, particularly by the use of public and mixed public/private enterprises and by the use of economic and social regulation.

The specific internal historical reasons within each subordinate country for such a development may differ, but the advantages of a large state role sustain this pattern. In Austria, the chaos after World War II and the resulting weakness of the private sector led to a large-scale nationalization of formerly German assets, a decision even supported by conservative interests.[23] In Canada, it was clear that Canadian control of the economy would be lost without a state-led building of the transportation and communication infrastructure. Just as important was the provision of a steady supply of inexpensive energy to Canadian industry and the occasional development of industry itself.

The importance of the state in the economy in the smaller country in each dyad can be seen in various ways. The size of the public sector, including

agricultural division. See Grace Skogstad, "Interest Groups, Representation, and Conflict Management in the Standing Committees of the House of Commons," *Canadian Journal of Political Science* 18 (December 1985), pp. 739–772.

23. On this point see Leland Stauber, "The Nationalizations and Political Stalemate after World War II," in Leland Stauber, *A New Program for Democratic Socialism: Lessons from the Market-Planning Experience in Austria,* Carbondale (1987), pp. 79–116.

both pure public enterprises and mixed public/private businesses, is an important indicator. The size is measured both by assets held by the state and by employment provided. In both subordinate countries, we see very large, indeed, among the largest, business enterprises owned by the state. These enterprises, as well as other medium-sized businesses, have been used to cushion the work force from strong swings toward unemployment.

What is also impressive about this large public sector role in the small states is the support of political elites for this role irrespective of party, although we recognize that parties of the left have a deep ideological, as well as pragmatic, commitment to a large public sector role. Perhaps this point is made clearer by contrasting the major right and left parties, not only within each country, but also within each dyad. First, looking at the conservative parties, it is clear that the *Österreichische Volkspartei* (ÖVP) has had a more favorable position toward state intervention compared to the *Christlich-Demokratische Union* (CDU). In turn, the Progressive Conservative party of Canada (PC) has been more tolerant of government expenditures and enterprises compared to the Republican party of the United States (Grand Old Party – GOP). Especially at the provincial level, many of the large infra-structure state enterprises in Canada were set up for the benefit of private businesses and for their development.

In Europe, the most left wing of the major socialist parties in recent years is the *Sozialistische Partei Österreichs* (SPÖ – since 1991 *Sozialdemokratische Partei Österreichs*), certainly more so than the *Sozialdemokratische Partei Deutschlands* (SPD). The former has been strongly influenced by its own indigenous Austro-Marxist tradition, as well as by the Swedish socialists' commitment to an extensive welfare state network, although seemingly untouched by the social market economy ideas prevalent in West Germany. In North America, there is an active socialist party in Canada that has had a major public policy impact, especially at the provincial level.[24] In contrast, in the United States there are only isolated socialists and no party of any note.[25]

---

24. For a careful analysis that shows the specific type of impact the New Democratic party has had, see William M. Chandler, "Canadian Socialism and Policy Impact: Contagion from the Left?" *Canadian Journal of Political Science* 10 (December 1977), pp. 755–780.

25. For a passionate plea by the most electorally successful American socialist in the 1980s, see Bernard Sanders, "This Country needs a Third Political Party," *The New York Times*, 3 January 1989, p. A19. Sanders served eight years as mayor of Burlington, Vermont, and received 29 percent of the popular vote for the U.S. House of Representatives from Vermont in the 8 November 1988 U.S. congressional elections.

The Democratic party is a middle-of-the-road liberal party and considerably to the right of its Canadian counterpart, the Liberal party of Canada.

The tendency in each small country for all parties to support a strong public sector is reinforced by the way power and authority is exercised. In the smaller state, decision-making powers tend to be more concentrated in the executive and senior levels of the bureaucracy, whereas in the larger state the legislature has a relatively larger role. The independence of U.S. members of congress is well-known, whereas the form of parliamentary government in Canada emphasizes cabinet domination of the legislature to which it is fused.[26] In Austria, the independence of the legislature is severely constrained by the corporatist policy agreements made elsewhere. These agreements are so limiting of parliamentary discussion and independence that "about 85 percent of all legislative proposals in economic and social policy are unanimous as a result of pre-parliamentary, inter-associational consensus formation."[27]

There are also significant institutional differences in the relationship of the central bank and the political executive. In the smaller country there is a closer connection between the two, once again an indication of a greater concentration of central institutional power. On the one hand, the Federal Reserve in the United States has both the legal authority and the technical expertise to pursue its insulation from pressure by the president, the cabinet, or the congress.[28] In Canada, on the other hand, the minister of finance is able to give directives to the Bank of Canada. If there is a policy disagreement, the governor and the other directors of the Bank of Canada have no choice but to resign.[29] In Europe, the *Deutsche Bundesbank* is charged with

---

26. On this point, see Mark Sproule-Jones, "The Enduring Colony? Political Institutions and Political Science in Canada," *Publius: The Journal of Federalism* 14 (Winter 1984), pp. 93–108; C.E.S. Franks, *The Parliament of Canada*, Toronto (1987); and Michael M. Atkinson, "Parliamentary Government in Canada," in Michael S. Whittington and Glen Williams (eds.), *Canadian Politics in the 1990s*, 3d ed., Scarborough (1990), pp. 336–358.

27. Bernd Marin, *Austria: The Paradigm Case of Liberal Corporatism?*, p. 101.

28. See John T. Woolley, "Monetarists and the Politics of Monetary Policy," *The Annals* 459 (January 1982), pp. 148–160.

29. However, the political costs may be extensive. See, for example, Peter C. Newman, "The Carnage of the Coyne Affair," in Peter C. Newman, *Renegade in Power: The Diefenbaker Years*, Toronto (1963), pp. 295–321. My understanding of the relationship between the Federal Reserve and the U.S. cabinet, on the one hand, and the Bank of Canada and the minister of finance, on the other, has been greatly aided by a discussion with my colleague Bill Coleman. However, I have not described the many nuances in these relationships.

the task of safeguarding the value of the Deutsche Mark and is independent of directives from the government. Indeed, the institutional differences between the FRG and Austria are very great, namely "the German Bundesbank enjoys a much greater degree of statutory and practical independence from the federal government than does the Austrian Nationalbank."[30]

This more coherent organization of state authority in the smaller country is necessary because the economic forces work against small country economic prosperity. The generation of wealth needs political support and action that is less necessary in the larger country. In contrast, the relatively better (in historical development terms) economic performance of the superordinate partner is due to its larger internal market and its ability to influence the larger global economic community.

In each of our two unequal partnerships, the subordinate nation has experienced retarded economic growth over the past century. The size of internal markets seems key to explaining these variations. However, whatever the cause, the retarded development is always in focus in the evolution of Austrian and Canadian macroeconomic policies.

The concept of delayed economic development and its impact on societies is a well-researched area by economic historians; the most well-known is Alexander Gershenkron.[31] His understanding of this phenomenon arises out of his research on nineteenth-century economic history, including that of Central Europe. Nonetheless, his analysis can be extended to North America as well.[32]

The major elements of Gershenkron's analysis revolve around the tension that exists in a delayed political economy between the existing level of economic development and the country's wealth potential. Reinforcing this basic tension is the booming economic development of the neighbor next door. The economic response of the smaller country is similar to the political response. The emphasis is on concentration and coordination among institutions. Domestic economic competition is, in practice, not an important value to be pursued, although in large world markets it is encouraged. Monopolies

30. Fritz W. Scharpf, "Economic and Institutional Constraints of Full-Employment Strategies: Sweden, Austria, and West Germany, 1973–1982," in John H. Goldthorpe (ed.), *Order and Conflict in Contemporary Capitalism: Studies in the Political Economy of Western European Nations,* Oxford (1984), pp. 257–290.

31. Alexander Gershenkron, *Economic Backwardness in Historical Perspective,* New York (1965).

32. For two examples see H.V. Nelles, *The Politics of Development: Forests, Mines, and Hydro-Electric Power in Ontario 1849–1941,* Toronto (1974), p. 305; Michael M. Atkinson and William D. Coleman, *The State, Business, and Industrial Change in Canada,* Toronto (1989), pp. 33–35, 39.

are tolerated, and the economy is directed and guided, in an important degree, by nonmarket institutions such as the associations described earlier, as well as by public enterprises and by the judicious use of state capital.

Yet even these measures are not sufficient. The smaller country recognizes the advantage of trade with the large neighbor next door in terms of its large market, close transportation links, knowledge of the large country's state of affairs through the mass media, and the ease of commercial communication because of a common language and relatively similar culture. Thus, if the disparity of the economic performance of the two partners increases or concerns are publicly raised about the subordinate country's future competitive economic performance, then the smaller partner will seek closer economic ties and guaranteed commercial access to the larger country's domestic market.

In 1972, because of concern about the future of Austrian economic growth, Austria entered into agreements with the European Economic Community (EEC) and the European Coal and Steel Community (ECSC) that greatly liberalized trade rules between these two parties. The evolution of these agreements continues. The main target for Austria was, of course, its large German neighbor. Strong growth of Austrian exports to West Germany has occurred in two central sectors of any modern industrial economy, namely chemicals and machinery. Thus, there are clear indicators of a successful impact of these free trade treaties from the Austrian perspective. Additional evidence shows that Austria's exports, as a percentage of its GNP, have grown steadily since 1973. There has been important new growth since the recession year of 1982 so that over half of Austria's exports to the EEC are with the Federal Republic. Since 1960, manufactured exports, as a percentage of exports to the FRG, have increased and primary resource commodities, including agricultural products, have decreased.

But even these successful developments have not soothed the economic fears of many Austrians. Only full membership in the EC will do. This is true of both major political parties.[33]

In the 1980s, Canada also became apprehensive about its economic future. First, one of the major worries centered on the state of Canadian manufacturing. The size of the Canadian market was seen as an impediment to successful marketing in the three big blocs of consumers of the EC, Japan, and the United States, which were increasingly dominating world trade. Second, the comparative per capita wealth ratios of Canadians versus Americans began to change unfavorably for the Canadians in the 1980s. All through the

---

33. For a discussion of Austrian apprehensions for the future despite the current prosperity, see "Financial Times Survey: Austria," *Financial Times*, 16 May 1989, sec 3, pp. 1–6.

1970s, Canadian GNP per capita grew at a faster rate than that of the United States. By 1980, this had ended. This was even more disastrous to Canada than it might seem because the Canadian base was lower than the U.S. one to begin with. As a result, 1978 saw the beginning of a long sustained slide of the Canadian standard of living vis-à-vis the average U.S. citizen. Thus, it was no wonder that many Canadians began to view greater access to the U.S. economy as worth the risk to the degree of political autonomy actually enjoyed by the Canadian state in the recent past.

Values, Culture, and the Media

Although each set is culturally integrated compared with the other partners, the relative population size and comparative economic power of each country vis-à-vis its neighbor affects its perceptions. This is true even when a subordinate country has in its own eyes an ambivalent size perception, as does Canada. The big nation has a tradition of confident, aggressive nationalism and a more positive view of its future destiny despite occasional and even major setbacks. It has a willingness to consume and invest, and, overall, it is a country at home on the world stage.

In contrast, because of its subordinate position within the same cultural area the smaller partner displays an adherence to the values we would associate with caution and pessimism, such as less faith in the future, less willingness to risk capital and reputation, and greater reserve and restraint. Thus, the populace of these smaller nations seem much more deliberate and careful, more reticent in proclaiming the society's comparative advantages, more frugal as measured by personal saving rates, and more appreciative of a quiet but pleasant social life. Although those most desirous of fame and fortune are drawn by the magnet of affluence in the larger economy, the preferred position of most inhabitants of the smaller country is to stay home and enjoy moderate prosperity.

In personal characteristics, the larger country's population prizes freedom, in both their associative and economic behavior. They see life more as a series of opportunities rather than risks; consequently, voluntary action and aggressive individualism is prized. In the subordinate member of the dyad, group solidarity receives emphasis, obligations are more readily accepted, duty to the society is a more important virtue than individual calculations. In sum, such cautiousness and feelings of insecurity on the part of the subordinate country generate values that emphasize tradition, deference to the law, reliance on public authorities for direction, and elitism in general.

One property of unequal partners is the flow of information through the mass media, especially when there is a common dominant language and culture uniting the two. This flow is asymmetric in that the knowledge of the state of affairs in the superordinate country is well-known to the elites and citizens of the subordinate society, but the reverse is not true. As Mildred A. Schwartz argues, "Characteristically, information about the conduct of politics spreads from the United States to Canada."[34] The latter country, like any small partner, then accepts what is useful, rejects what is not, and adapts still other practices. Similar patterns of information influence exist between Austria and the Federal Republic.[35]

Such an asymmetric relationship is often lamented by the cultural elites in the small country. Yet, this uneven flow of knowledge about each other works to the advantage of the subordinate country and, indeed, may help ensure its survival and autonomy. This unbalanced relationship in news and information allows the smaller society to make adjustments quickly in public policy in order to cope with the changing relationship. This gives the small partner more lead time in dealing with problems.

But despite the advantage the asymmetry of ideas, information, and knowledge of the other partner gives to the smaller society, this imbalance reinforces the feelings of insecurity of the subordinate partner. It is a case of wanting to be recognized, of desiring a more important recognized position in the world order, and of obtaining respect. The collective ego is fed by a psychological need that runs counter to the economic and political self-interest of the subordinate player. When more is known about the smaller country and its coping mechanisms by the leaders and population in the larger country, then there are specific actions to be criticized. The small country cannot have it both ways.

---

34. Mildred A. Schwartz, "American Influence on the Conduct of Canadian Politics," in Richard A. Preston (ed.), *The Influence of the United States on Canadian Development: Eleven Case Studies,* Durham (1972), p. 110. Other contributors in this volume also note the similar spread of information from the United States to Canada in such areas as scholarship, economic behavior, labor organizations and relations, Canadian literature, and Canadian speech patterns.

35. See Hubert Feichtlbauer, "The Media," in Kurt Steiner (ed.), *Modern Austria,* Palo Alto, Cal. (1981), pp. 279–298; and Hans Heinz Fabris, "The Media," in Jim Sweeney and Josef Weidenholzer (eds.), *Austria: A Study in Modern Achievement,* Aldershot (1988), pp. 236–244.

Toward a Conclusion

The problems faced by small countries vis-à-vis their large neighbors have been summarized well by S. N. Eisenstadt.[36] The perennial question is: How can these countries develop both economically and in a social and cultural sense that is not inferior to their large neighbors yet maintain their political autonomy? As he sees it, the major drawback is the small domestic market that does not provide a critical mass for economic and technological development at a competitive rate so that this market can both retain and draw in sufficient amounts of investment capital. The economic solution is to be a specialized trading nation. Yet, at the same time, these countries want to insulate themselves and their domestic cultures from their large neighbors that flood in through the electronic and printed media. The political solutions involve strong executive, political, and organizational leadership while maintaining the form, if not the substance, of open, representative legislatures.

In his work on small countries in general and Austria in particular, Peter Katzenstein has elaborated at great length on these mechanisms in two important volumes.[37] A key part of economic adaptation was the persistent attempt to get foreign automobile manufacturers to locate in Austria through the use of subsidies and thus to reduce the flow of consumer payouts for foreign-produced cars with high markups.[38] In a similar vein, Canada also made a dramatic move to reduce its balance-of-payments problem in automotive products resulting in the Automotive Products Trade Agreement of 1965.[39]

These types of solutions must survive external complaints from political leaders in the large neighbor (when they recognize the advantage gained by the small partner) as well as domestic social forces that believe considerations other than economic development should matter. Yet the institutional mechanisms and distinct policy-making procedures persist. Austria's economic success has survived the green politics stimulated from the Federal

---

36. S. N. Eisenstadt, "Reflections on Centre-Periphery Relations and Small European States," in Risto Alapuro et al. (eds.), *Small States in Comparative Perspective: Essays for Erik Allardt*, Oslo (1985), pp. 41–49.

37. Peter Katzenstein, *Corporatism and Change: Austria, Switzerland, and the Politics of Industry*, Ithaca and New York (1984); and Katzenstein, *Small States in World Markets: Industrial Policy in Europe*, Ithaca and New York (1985).

38. Katzenstein, *Corporatism and Change*, p. 58.

39. Gilbert R. Winham, *Trading with Canada: The Canada-U.S. Free Trade Agreement*, New York (1988), pp. 51 f.

Republic[40], and Canada's national government has coped with increased regional loyalties backed up by more-developed and professional provincial bureaucracies.[41]

The exact ways in which these small states maintain their political and cultural autonomy while creating wealth for their citizens is largely an unmapped area. This chapter proposes hypotheses to guide us initially as we explore this research agenda. Others have proposed complementary research strategies as well,[42] and a beginning has been made. As the research proceeds, we should be better able to articulate an explanation to the question why political and cultural fragmentation exists despite the integrating pressures of language and economy.

40. Peter Gerlich, Edgar Grande, and Wolfgang C. Müller, "Corporatism in Crisis: Stability and Change of Social Partnership in Austria," *Political Studies* 36 (June 1988), pp. 209–223.

41. See the cogent analysis by Gilbert R. Winham on the growing power of the Canadian provinces and how the national government has coped with this trend in one of the most critical public policy areas of Canadian life, namely trade policy, in *International Trade and the Tokyo Round Negotiations*, Princeton (1986), pp. 332–342.

42. See, for example, Mildred A. Schwartz, "Comparing United States and Canadian Public Policy: A Review of Strategies," *Policy Studies Journal* 14 (June 1986), pp. 566–579. Also reprinted in Robert J. Jackson, Doreen Jackson, and Nicolas Baxter-Moore (eds.), *Contemporary Canadian Politics: Readings and Notes,* Scarborough (1987), pp. 323–335. For one example in the use of part of this research strategy that compares large nation/small nation public policies, see Henry Jacek, "Large State/Small State Relations in the North American Political Economy: Are There Lessons from Europe?" *The American Review of Canadian Studies* 17 (Winter 1987–1988), pp. 419–438.

PART TWO

Historical Relations

3

The Austro-German Relationship: One Language, One and One-Half Histories, Two States

Frederick C. Engelmann

Since 1919, the Austro-German relationship has indeed been an unequal one. Between the world wars, Germany had ten times as many people as Austria; between 1945 and 1990 the FRG — the German state we speak about here — had eight times Austria's population. German investment dominated the First Austrian Republic and plays an important part in the Second. Austria spent seven years under occupation by Hitler Germany, after which it was occupied by the victorious Big Four. Today's Austria is, in a formal sense, completely independent of Germany. No comprehensive economic or military treaty binds the two. The dependence is a consequence of the common language and, over the long haul, a half-shared history.

One Language

On paper, it certainly looks like the two countries share one language. The Salzach, a minor part of the frontier but the part that symbolizes it, marks a linguistic division characterized mostly by different words for some fruit and vegetables. Because Austrians would claim that Bavarians speak an ordinary kind of Austrian, the Salzach does not really mark a spoken language barrier. However, Germans living north of the Main do not like to concede that Austrians *speak* the same language. Fortunately, Austrian higher schools (and some of the others) make a real effort to teach their students an enunciation that *can* be understood by the northern neighbor. This may be considered fortunate because Austria's economy would be in rough shape without the large numbers of German tourists who come south in summer and winter.

Because the written language is essentially the same, there is, again essentially, one literature. Goethe and Schiller are appreciated in Austria the way Shakespeare is in California, and only the most rabid Austrian chauvinist would claim that Grillparzer is their equal. Vienna's most prestigious non-musical stage, the Burgtheater, prides itself on being intelligible to all Germans; in fact, it even claims to monitor the German language.

The common language helps trade and literature. It also has important implications for communications. There was a brief time from 1930 to 1933 when Austria was inundated by the Nazi press. Even after that press was outlawed in Austria, most radio receivers were able to receive Hitler's speeches, which were listened to eagerly by hundreds of thousands of Austrian Nazis and apprehensively by tens of thousands of Austrian Jews and other anti-Nazis. Today, German newspapers generally outclass their Austrian cousins in quality, but they are only scarcely read in Vienna. Many Austrians are able to receive German television. Until cable television completely takes over Austria, however, it can hardly be said to be flooded by the German airwaves. To the occasional visitor to Austria, it appears that the greatest German influence comes through the periodical press. For the somewhat sophisticated readers, the German *Der Spiegel* is more interesting than the Austrian *profil*, and the unsophisticated German periodicals have no peers southeast of the Salzach.

When Austria was basking in the warmth of the Moscow Declaration, in the early years of the Second Republic, German was officially perceived more as the language of Hitler than the language of Goethe. For that reason, the basic language course was not called "German" but *"Unterrichtssprache"* (language of instruction). This was soon felt to be a bit ridiculous, and a wag, applying the word to Felix Hurdes, the minister of education, called it *"Hurdestanisch."* The German language was soon officially reinstituted. Julius Raab, chancellor from 1953 to 1961, referred thus to the one-language, two-states theme: "Our mother tongue is German, but our fatherland is Austria."

One and One-Half Histories

Berlin certainly was not the first German capital, but neither was Vienna. The first city worthy of this name was Zlata Praha, the "golden Prague," *Prag* in German. The Czech metropolis, built to some extent as a German city, was the residence of the Holy Roman emperors in the fourteenth century. Their court chancellery did, in fact, standardize the German language. German history, of course, is much older. Some would consider the battle of the Teutoburg Forest (A.D. 9) to have been the originating point, though its beginnings are placed more realistically with the crowning of Charlemagne (A.D. 800) or of Otto I (A.D. 962), whose jeweled crown can still be seen in Vienna. The latter date is close to the beginning of the reign of the Babenbergs in Austria (A.D. 976) and to the first use of the name *Ostarrichi* (A.D. 996). Austrian prominence in German lands began when Rudolf von Habsburg, German king since 1273, became duke of Austria in 1278. His progeny ruled Austria until 1918.

During the four centuries — cumulatively speaking — during which the Habsburgs were dukes (later archdukes) of Austria and German kings and Holy Roman emperors, it makes some sense to say that Germany and Austria had one history. One could extend this period to 1806, the end of the empire, or even to 1866, the end of the German Federation.

This would make for less than one and one-half histories, but more is involved. The Habsburgs were German kings, but from the early sixteenth century on their main interest was in their non-German possessions, especially Hungary, which was not even in the Holy Roman Empire. Also, during much of Austria's "German" centuries, German identity anywhere was, at most, weak. The eventual unifiers of Germany, the Hohenzollerns, did not gain importance until the second half of the seventeenth century.

This historical connection became stormy in 1740 when the male Habsburg line died out and the heiress, Maria Theresa, became reigning archduchess at the same time that her Hohenzollern contemporary, Frederick II (the Great) became king of Prussia. While others coalesced against Maria Theresa, Frederick, in a most unchivalrous way, invaded and grabbed prosperous Silesia. He held it in two subsequent wars, and, by the time of the French Revolution, Prussia and Austria had become equal powers within the empire. The empire finally expired under Napoleon's onslaught. A few years later, Prussia contributed more than Austria to his defeat. Only the superior diplomatic skill of Metternich (not of Austrian origin) enabled Austria to claim the formal leadership of the new German Federation.

All it took to tip the balance of power away from Austria was an able Prussian king, Wilhelm I, and an even more able first minister, Bismarck. In the early 1860s, Bismarck persuaded the Austrians to make common cause against the Danes. After arguments over the spoils of that war, Bismarck allied with the newly united Italy — no friend of the Habsburgs — and Prussia crushed Austria in the brief war of 1866. In his attempt to unify Germany under Prussia, Bismarck decided to ignore the Habsburgs and their largely non-German holdings. Allied with the other German princes Prussia defeated France, and Bismarck twisted the knife by proclaiming Wilhelm a German emperor in the Hall of Mirrors of Versailles in 1871. He soon formed an alliance with Austria to prevent Russian aggression and Austrian expansion in the Balkans. After 1890, both German and Austrian leadership left much to be desired, and the two countries entered World War I. Although Germany survived the war reasonably well in geographic terms, Austria-Hungary was dismembered. The small (German-)Austria was, in Clemenceau's contemptuous words, "what is left" after the other nationalities were allowed to satisfy their territorial aspirations.

Almost everyone in Austria, certainly German Nationalists and Social Democrats, wanted the *Anschluß* — union with the young German republic. The victorious Allies, however, would not permit this. A fairly good relationship developed between the big and the little brothers, and German investments helped the Austrian economy. This relationship changed drastically in 1930, when the Great Depression made a strong party out of Adolf Hitler's *Nationalsozialistische Deutsche Arbeiterpartei* (NSDAP). Although many Austrians would like to see Hitler go down in history as a German and Beethoven as an Austrian, it was the other way around. Born in the Austrian border town of Braunau, Hitler had an irrepressible desire to bring Austria "home into the [German] empire." From Austria, he brought hatred of Jews and Slavs and an essentially revolutionary frame of mind. Once his party became important, he subjected Austria to an incessant propaganda campaign.

By the time Hitler seized power in 1933, the appeal of an *Anschluß* in Austria had weakened considerably. Austria's Christian Social party had come to enjoy governing the country, and the Social Democrats wanted to have nothing to do with Nazis. Unfortunately, Chancellor Dollfuß felt that he could keep Austria independent only by allying with Mussolini, who demanded an Austria without Nazis *and* without Social Democrats. Because this objective could not be reached by democratic means, Dollfuß set up a dictatorship, outlawed the Nazis, and sent the Social Democrats into submission. Because he could not improve the economy, Hitler's now clandestine propaganda line gained more and more supporters. In 1936, he wrested some concessions from the Austrian dictatorship. In early 1938, he felt that Mussolini would tolerate a forcible *Anschluß*, and he was right. On 13 March 1938, Vienna greeted him as a liberator. Four weeks later, more than 99 percent of Austria's Aryan population said "ja" to the already executed *Anschluß*.

About four years later, it had become obvious to many Austrians that Hitler could only bring them blood and tears. By then, it was too late. Not only had Austria lost its 200,000 Jews (of whom, fortunately, two-thirds survived in exile), but also tens of thousands of its Aryan sons. Much of Vienna was destroyed in air raids, including the world-renowned opera house and the roof of the cathedral.

The politicians who gathered in Vienna after the liberation by Soviet troops in April 1945 were certain that they wanted a distinct Austrian history. This realization was facilitated by the will of the Allies and the fact that there was, at that time, no Germany. Unlike the divided Germany, Austria fortunately managed to stay united. In 1943, the Allied foreign ministers meeting in Moscow had declared Austria to have been the first victim of Hitler's aggression. Whether fully correct or not, the Moscow Declaration helped Austria's Second Republic immeasurably. Austria might have done well to remember it during the presidential election of 1986, when Waldheim claimed "only to have done his duty" to Hitler's Germany. When it became clear in 1955 that no part of Austria would be in the Soviet orbit, relations with the German Democratic Republic (GDR) continued to be cool. Relations with the FRG are cordial, but Austria's neutrality and the Federal Republic's Western alliance and EC membership make sure that, despite broad trade relations, Austria and the FRG continue to have distinct histories, at least as long as these differences exist.

Two States

The Holy Roman Empire could hardly be called a state. The emperor was little more than a feudal overlord. After the Peace of Westphalia in 1648, the major components of the empire, not the empire itself, were recognized as states. Certainly once the Habsburgs became emperors, the empire did not have the essential quality of a state, namely, the monopoly of force.[1] Its component territorial states did, however, with literally hundreds of units, which were finally reduced to dozens by Napoleon. In this sense, what is now Austria and what is now Germany and their legal predecessors never were one state.

---

1. See inter alia, Friedrich Glum, *Die staatsrechtliche Struktur der Bundesrepublik Deutschland,* Bonn (1965); Viola Herms Drath, *Germany in World Politics*, New York and London (1979).

Though possibly with some difficulty, one can agree on these legal predecessors. This is easier in the case of Austria, the core of which was formed by
the eastern Habsburg lands since the thirteenth century. Mentioned earlier
were the *Ostarrichi* of the House of Babenberg, which will celebrate its mil-
lennium in 1996, but, like the Holy Roman Empire, *Ostarrichi* went through
an interregnum around 1250. Since then the Habsburgs reigned continuously
until 1918 over Lower Austria, Upper Austria, and Styria, and they soon
acquired Carinthia, Tyrol, and Carniola (the present Slovenia).

Bella gerant alii, tu, felix Austria, nube (Let others wage wars; thou, fortunate Austria, marry) became a most meaningful slogan. Though the Spanish
acquisition of the Austrian Habsburgs lasted only half a century and the
acquisition of the Lowlands only into the eighteenth century, Bohemia and
Hungary stayed with the Habsburgs until 1918. With the Josephinian cen-
tralization (1780–1790) and the creation of the Austrian Empire (1804), the
Habsburg lands truly became one state. After the Habsburg defeat in the
German War of 1866, Hungary (today, Hungary, Croatia, Slovakia, and
Transylvania) became a separate state. The end of World War I brought the
formation of Czechoslovakia and Yugoslavia and the rebirth of Poland. The
First Republic of Austria became the new, sharply reduced incarnation of the
Austrian state.

It is misleading to speak of a German *state* prior to 1871. Its legal predecessor is best represented by in the Kingdom of Prussia. Its rulers, the house
of Hohenzollern, originated but 100 miles northeast of the Habsburgs. Like
the Habsburgs, they moved east, but farther north, and in 1415 they became
the Electors of Brandenburg. In this position, the Hohenzollerns existed quietly for about 250 years until Frederick William, the Great Elector, elevated
Brandenburg to a well-organized, fairly important state. A militarism possibly unequalled since Rome, but organized as well as Sparta, and expansion to
the east symbolized the transmutation of Brandenburg into the Kingdom of
Prussia, creating the state most likely to challenge the Austrian state for
German hegemony. After the Congress of Vienna, Prussia consolidated the
western territories, which gave it a resource-rich area that was ideal for
entering the industrial revolution.

Already discussed were the steady gains of Prussia over Austria from
1740 to 1866. By 1871, the one, though federated, state of Germany and the
now two states of Austria and Hungary gave the Hohenzollerns and Habsburgs similar magnitudes in area and in population. But here the similarity
ended. With the exception of a sizeable Polish minority, the population of
Germany spoke German. It was held together by a common prosperous
economy, a strong army and bureaucracy, and an uncanny ability to trans-
form postfeudal dynastic rivalries (there were still over twenty dynasties) into
a possibly unequalled nationalism. Austria-Hungary, however, was less than

25 percent German, was somewhat less prosperous, and was equipped with traditional but antiquated armies and bureaucracies. Its Austrian state was rent by national strife that led to collapse at the time of the military defeat of 1918.

As has already been mentioned, the events of 1918–1919 brought about a condition of unprecedented asymmetry for the two now separate states — asymmetry that was maintained only by the Allied prohibition of the *Anschluß*. There were now ten times as many people in Germany as in Austria because Germany, no matter how much it had been humiliated in 1919, had only lost one-tenth of its population.

On 13 March 1938 Austria ceased to exist. There was, for the first time, one German state. The state of 1871 had been united (according to Bismarck) by "blood and iron". The Greater Germany of 1938 was united without blood and with a negligible amount of iron. Both blood and iron came into play only a few years later. This time, Austria came out unscathed, though after suffering heavy war losses and ten years of four-power occupation. The Germany in the borders of 1937, however, became a dream. There were to be two states — one of them in the Soviet orbit — and Poland was transported 100 miles to the West.

Although there were, until 1990, really three German-speaking states (not counting Liechtenstein and multilingual Switzerland), this book deals with the FRG as it existed before reunification. The use of the term "two states" for the FRG and Austria, without question, is correct. As already mentioned, the two states are not united economically or allied militarily, but they have cordial relations. Differences in their forms of government are obvious to the political scientist but hardly to the layman. The world hardly cares that the German chancellor is nominated by the president and elected by Parliament, but the Austrian chancellor is nominated by the president only. It hardly cares that Germany has a more important second chamber than Austria. It barely knew, before the Waldheim election and crisis of 1986, that the Austrian president is elected by the people whereas the German president is not.

The political parties in the two states are very similar, with the exception of the third party, which is more liberal in Germany and more nationalist in Austria. Both states have strongly organized interest groups. However, Austria with its compulsory-membership chambers sustains a much stronger neocorporatist system, the social partnership. Whereas Germany's political economy is more flexible, Austria's has produced an amazing socioeconomic peace.

Conclusion

What would the title of this chapter be if it applied to the relationship between Canada and the United States? The last part, "two states," would be the same. What about "one and one-half histories?" By now, I would claim, there are more than 1.9 histories, and inching toward two histories. Until the Official Languages Act of 1969, some people might have claimed that "one language" would fit in the title. Today, all Canadians *know* better, and most also *feel* that Canada is bilingual.

To the political scientist, the two relationships are similar. They are only most vaguely similar to the historian. Austrians tried to come to grips with their new size in 1919. They did not succeed. Not that they tried to reconquer anything, except possibly the Alto Adige, or *Südtirol*. But many wanted the truncated state to become part of Germany. Only the failure of success in this question made Austrians accept their state of 1919 — by now, almost all of them love it. Germans had no such problem in 1919, except with their revisionists. The problem came after the Nazi collapse. Until the dramatic events in Eastern Europe that commenced in the autumn of 1989, it was generally assumed that West Germans had come to grips with division and were satisfied with the undoubted fact that they are a major economic power that is earning the respect of the world. In any case, there are no Germans known to me, personally or by publication, who are seeking another *Anschluß* of Austria.

One can conclude that there is not a question about two states, nor about one language. If one and one-half histories is today's state of affairs, then, in one generation, it will grow to become at least 1.6. The unequal partnership will continue, but it will likely remain politically irrelevant. Despite occasional flaps, the respect these two unequal partners have come to have for each other in recent decades remains undiminished.

4

The Historical Roots of a Special Relationship: Austro-German Relations Between Hegemony and Equality

Günter Bischof

Canada's former Prime Minister Pierre Elliott Trudeau once told an American audience: "Living next to you is in some ways like sleeping with an elephant. No matter how friendly or even-tempered is the beast, if I may call it that, one is affected by every twitch and grunt."[1]

This metaphor might sum up the nature of U.S.-Canadian relations, but it does not characterize Austrian and Prussian cohabitation in the territorial structure that we call "Germany."[2] As a matter of fact, until 1866 there were at least two elephants in the bed of the Holy Roman Empire (which became the German Confederation with the Congress of Vienna in 1815). In the prolonged struggle for supremacy in Germany between Austria and Prussia, the north German beast turned out to be the stronger one. Bismarck's Prussia unified the German nation state with "blood and iron" in the wars of 1866

---

1. Quoted in Andrew H. Malcolm, *The Canadians,* Toronto and New York (1985), p. 165.

2. For two excellent recent collections of essays on the Austro-German relationship see Robert A. Kann and Friedrich E. Prinz (eds.), *Deutschland und Österreich. Ein bilaterales Geschichtsbuch*, Vienna and Munich (1980); Heinrich Lutz and Helmut Rumpler (eds.), "Österreich und die deutsche Frage im 19. und 20. Jahrhundert. Probleme der politisch-staatlichen und soziokulturellen Differenzierung im deutschen Mitteleuropa," in Grete Klingenstein et al. (eds.), *Wiener Beiträge zur Geschichte der Neuzeit*, vol. 9, Vienna (1982); see also Peter Katzenstein's methodologically innovative study, *Disjoined Partners: Austria and Germany since 1815*, Berkeley, Los Angeles, and London (1976).

and 1870–1871. Austria was excluded. Germany acted like an elephant toward Austria during the two world wars. In the 1930s, in the events that led to the *Anschluß* — Austria's annexation to Hitler's Germany — the National Socialists did not treat Austria with kid gloves. During World War II, when Austria was absorbed by the Third *Reich*, Austro-German relations were at their closest. Only their common defeat in World War II humbled both the Austrians and the Germans, and since 1945/1955 they have learned to live next to each other with mutual respect for each other's sovereignty. The Germans discarded their tendency to exercise varied forms of hegemony in the political arena, as had been their inclination between 1870 and 1945. In the post-World War II era, in a central Europe dismembered by the victorious Allies, the two Germanies and Austria became relative equals similar to their pre-Königgrätz (1866) relationship.

Austro-German relations, in short, have been characterized by great mutations over a thousand-year period in history. The ups and downs of this relationship have resulted from the ever-changing territorial changes in the center of Europe; the changing balance of power in the center of Europe has always profoundly affected the European balance. In this sense the study of relations between the principal central European powers constitutes a crucial chapter in European history.

The terms "Austria," "Prussia," and "Germany" have to be used with great caution. Erich Zöllner has shown how Austria experienced dramatic mutations in its territory as well as in its political, dynastic, and constitutional content over a period of 1,000 years (the same can be said of Germany).[3] The little Bavarian "Eastern march" on the Danube of the tenth century was very different from the "Casa d'Austria" that exercised limited hegemony over the many territories of the Holy Roman Empire in the sixteenth century, ruling an empire in which "the sun never set."[4] It was this Austrian hegemony in Germany that Prussia challenged in the nineteenth century with its design to form a German nation state, excluding Austria. On the basis of its continuous territorial growth in the eighteenth and nineteenth centuries then, Prussia entered the path for predominance in Protestant northern Germany. This augmentation of power in Germany also made Prussia a Eu-

---

3. Erich Zöllner, "Formen und Wandlungen des Österreichbegriffes," in Hugo Hantsch, Eric Voegelin, and Franco Valsecchi (eds.), *Historica. Studien zum geschichtlichen Denken und Forschen,* Vienna, Freiburg, and Basle (1965), pp. 63–89; see also Gerald Stourzh, "Vom Reich zur Republik. Notizen zu Brüchen und Wandlungen im Österreichbewußtsein," *Wiener Journal* no. 1 (March 1987), pp. 19–21, and no. 2 (April 1987), pp. 17–19.

4. R.J.W. Evans, *The Making of the Habsburg Monarchy, 1550–1700,* London and New York (1979), Chapter 8.

ropean power. Prussia's rise to power in central Europe is somewhat comparable to the unchecked territorial, political, and economic growth of the United States on the North American continent, making it the hegemon in the Americas.

With the exclusion of the multinational Austria as a stabilizing factor in German affairs, Germany embarked on what many historians consider a *"Sonderweg"* (1870–1945). Was "that dreamy and dangerous nonsense called German nationality,"[5] as the British statesman Disraeli put it, the source of all evil? Germany's late national unification set it on a peculiar path toward aggressive expansionism after 1870. It quickly became clear that a strong and united Germany in the center of Europe was bound to be destabilizing for the European balance of power. If viewed from the vantage point of the international system, the unification of Germany under Prussian leadership has directly led to the "German problem."[6] The exclusion of Austria from Germany, as a balancing factor against Prussian predominance, can be seen as a crucial element in the origins of the German problem. The old Habsburg monarchy with its universalist European foreign policy was never narrowly central European. After all, Metternich's "system" — no matter how repressive and conservative it was domestically — secured the balance of power in Germany and in Europe. Once Austria lost its role in preserving the equilibrium in central Europe, the European powers ("the international system") had to take on that function, with very mixed success. The German problem was solved after World War II through the dismemberment of Nazi Germany. With the breathtaking speed of German unification in 1990, the traditional hard questions emerge again: Will a unified Germany become aggressive once more, or, will it become the key nation to speed up the process of European unification?

The "Elimination" of Austria from Germany

The Congress of Vienna set up a "dualist system" in Germany. For almost 1,000 years, the Holy Roman Empire had represented the overarch-

---

5. Quoted in Thomas Nipperdey, *Deutsche Geschichte 1800–1866. Bürgerwelt und starker Staat,* Munich (1983), p. 623.

6. Wolf D. Gruner has examined the interrelationship of the German question and the international system. See *Die deutsche Frage. Ein Problem der europäischen Geschichte seit 1800,* Munich (1984); for a critique of the *"Sonderweg* thesis," see Helga Grebing, *Der deutsche Sonderweg in Europa 1806–1945. Eine Kritik,* Stuttgart (1986).

ing brace for the multitude of German semisovereign territories (around 300 in 1800), before it unceremoniously met extinction during the upheavals of the Napoleonic Wars in 1806.[7]

The statesmen at the Congress of Vienna reinjected traditional order and legitimacy into the European state system, which the radical ideas of the French Revolution, exported by Napoleon's irresistible armies, had so gravely disturbed. Metternich's and Castlereagh's political philosophy and balance-of-power thinking put the stamp on the Congress. Their principal goals were to recreate the traditional European balance of power and reestablish the legitimate dynastic order. The conservative monarchies and their anticonstitutional rule were on the ascendancy one last time. All national-revolutionary elements had to be thwarted since they posed a mortal threat to dynastic-feudal states like Austria.[8]

For Germany this demanded paring back its national ambitions. The statesmen in Vienna did not allow Germany nor Italy to form nation states. Austria became the dominant power in Italy, but lost its former territorial positions in southern Germany. Prussian demands for aggrandizement with all of Saxony were thwarted as well; instead, it was compensated with rich industrial territories on the Rhine. In 1815, the roots were sown for Prussian hegemony in Germany. Meanwhile, it had to settle for sharing power and influence in Germany with Austria and the "third Germany."

After endless negotiations, a new federal order was established in Germany. The "three Germanies" — Austria, Prussia, and the third Germany, the small- and middle-sized states — maintained a rough balance of power in the German Confederation (a "German *Trias*"[9]). The forty-two German territorial states sent their representatives to the Paulskirche in Frankfurt, where the federal parliament (the *Bundestag*) met. The original Austro-Prussian consensus for a strong executive had given way to the demands of the third Germany. The mid-sized south German kingdoms and principalities had no desire to be crushed by the two giants in the north and south. It was this third Germany that played an important role in helping maintain the German balance between the two hegemonic powers.[10] Moreover, Metter-

---

7.   Walther Hubatsch, "Österreich und Preußen 1740–1848," in Robert A. Kann and Friedrich E. Prinz (eds.), *Deutschland und Österreich*, p. 102; C.A. Macartney, *The Habsburg Empire, 1790–1918*, New York (1969), pp. 147–198.

8.   Edward Vose Gulick, *Europe's Classical Balance of Power: A Case History of the Theory and Practice of One of the Great Concepts of European Statecraft*, New York and London (1955); see also Nipperdey, *Deutsche Geschichte*, pp. 82–101.

9.   Nipperdey, *Deutsche Geschichte*, p. 356.

10. For the role of the third Germany see Michael Derndarsky, "Österreich und der

nich's repressive system ("Carlsbad Decrees," etc.) made sure that the national idea would not triumph in Germany after 1815, even though he could not prevent the establishment of a constitutional government in the south German states. It is indeed as Thomas Nipperdey has written in his brilliant *Deutsche Geschichte*, the "unity of reaction" managed to prevent the "unity of the nation."[11]

Nipperdey has also argued that the loose organization of the German Confederation was a "misfortune" for German history. It represented the victory of the restorative forces. All it achieved was the guarantee of stability in the center of Europe; but it did not secure freedom and national unity for the Germans.[12] Yet, one is tempted to doubt whether a German Confederation with strong executive powers under Prussian leadership might have acted as a more stabilizing factor in the international arena than did the "small-German Reich" dominated by Prussia fifty years later. True, Austria would have been included in a strong and centralized federation and could have exercised a restraining influence on Prussian chauvinism. But in an ardently nationalist Germany one wonders for how long.

Next to its reactionary government, the essence of the Habsburg monarchy lay in its multinational make-up. Austria was "anti-national in an age of nationality."[13] Non-German territories of the Habsburg Empire such as Galicia and Hungary were always a thorn in the flesh of the German nationalists, both in Germany and in Austria. It would never have occurred to Metternich that he ought to make a choice between his Italian, German, or Slav territories. Archduke Albrecht later summarized the philosophy of state of the Habsburgs: "The dynasty may not favor anybody exclusively in a polyglot empire, peopled by many nationalities and races. Like a good mother she must demonstrate equal love toward all her children."[14] It may sound naive, but this is how the multinational Habsburg Empire tried to survive in an age of nationalism.

Deutsche Bund 1815–1866," in Lutz and Rumpler (eds.), *Österreich und die deutsche Frage*, pp. 92–116 (here p. 108); for the role of the smaller states of the third Germany between Prussia and Austria see Theodor Schieder, "Die mittleren Staaten im System der großen Mächte," *Historische Zeitschrift* 232 (June 1981), pp. 590–596; Nipperdey, *Deutsche Geschichte*, pp. 344–357.

11. Nipperdey, *Deutsche Geschichte*, p. 355.

12. Ibidem, p. 97.

13. Waltraud *Heindl*, "Die österreichische Bürokratie," in Lutz and Rumpler (eds.), *Österreich und die deutsche Frage*, pp. 73–91 (here p. 83).

14. Quoted by Brigitte Hamann, "Die Habsburger und die Deutsche Frage im 19. Jahrhundert," in Lutz and Rumpler (eds.), *Österreich und die deutsche Frage*, pp. 212–230 (here p. 222).

Metternich not only denied the existence of the national idea, he also saw the conservative influence of his principle of legitimacy as the guarantor of stability in all the Habsburg lands. In Metternich's view, stability in Austria guaranteed European equipoise. The foreign policy of a multinational empire perforce had to be European and universalist rather than German and parochial. Part of Austria's larger task in Europe also demanded that it preserve the balance of power in central Europe, for the German balance constituted an important prop for the European equilibrium, as Edward Vose Gulick has argued convincingly:

> One of the substantial props of the European balance was, oddly enough, the political disunity of Germany, because the division of sovereignty in that area gave to the state system itself a surprisingly stable center. The German atoms could not easily be pressed into an explosive molecule, so to speak; and Europe could count on the German center to be relatively incapable of offensive warfare. On the other hand, the atoms did tend to coalesce into a resistant molecule whenever outside powers sought to move into or through Germany. A disunited Germany not only did not threaten Europe – a negative virtue – but stood positively as a potential bulwark against the conquest of central Europe by a non-German power. When viewed from the point of view of a European statesman who was deeply motivated by balance-of-power concepts, German disunity was better for the security and duration of the state system than German unity, however sympathetically one may feel toward German patriots in the nineteenth century who struggled for unification. Such unification, although granting fulfillment to those patriots, would at the same time dangerously revolutionize the state system.[15]

From the European perspective of maintaining the balance of power, Metternich's policy of keeping Germany divided was skilled statesmanship; from the German nationalist viewpoint, Metternich represented a major roadblock toward the achievement of nationalist goals — given that the Austrian chancellor was a Rhinelander, it represented outright betrayal.

Roy Austensen has argued that Prince Felix Schwarzenberg's plans in the early 1850s were a continuation of Metternich's German policy rather than a struggle to gain predominance in a *"großdeutsches Reich* of seventy million."[16] Austensen stresses that Austria never showed similar nationalist

---

15. Paul *Schröder* makes the point about Austria's "European" foreign policy in "Austro-German Relations: Divergent Views of the Disjoined Partnership," *Central European History* 11 (September 1978), p. 310; for the quote see Gulick, *Europe's Classical Balance of Power*, pp. 130 f.

16. Roy A. Austensen, "Einheit oder Einigkeit? Another Look at Metternich's View of the German Dilemma," *German Studies Review* 6 (February 1983), pp. 41–57; Paul Schröder has also called Austrian foreign policy throughout the neoabsolutist era "basically defensive ... its aim to retain what Austria possessed." See his

ambitions to be active in Germany as did Prussia; it never tried to absorb Germany into Austria. From the perspective of German nationalists, however, Schwarzenberg's plan to include all of multinational Austria, namely millions of Slavs and Magyars, in Germany was unacceptable and blocked German unification.

Prussia circumvented Austrian political roadblocks by unifying Germany first in the economic sphere. While Metternich tried to preserve the equilibrium in Germany and Europe, Prussia established the *Zollverein* in 1834 and assumed de facto leadership in Germany. With the German Customs Union, Prussia united most of the third Germany under its economic leadership. This economic unification represented a giant step on the road to the political unification of a *"kleindeutsch"* German national state. In spite of the fact that the South German states wanted Austria to join the union, Metternich decided to stay out for economic and domestic political reasons — a fateful step as it turned out.[17] The thinking of Friedrich von Motz, the Prussian finance minister, probably expressed the view of many German nationalists. Motz advocated German unification in a big and strong national state since Austria proved to be unable to solve the German question; it was domestically too brittle and too involved in European matters. Therefore, Austria had to be eliminated from decision making in Germany. Prussia was called on to unify Germany. The Customs Union represented the preliminary step for political unification, argued Motz.[18] The prominent Austrian economic historian Herbert Matis has called the *Zollverein* "the catalyst for unification."[19] Prussia gained a position of hegemony in Germany in the economic field, whereas Austria was isolated from the huge German market by high tariffs.

In the years after the Revolution of 1848, Austria desperately tried to preserve its interests in Germany. With the defeat of the revolutionaries all over the monarchy, the new emperor, Francis Joseph, blocked the constitution drafted by the "National Assembly" meeting at the Paulskirche, even though Austrian representatives had participated in the liberal parliamentary reform

---

"Austro-German Relations," p. 310. For a sharp critique of such pro-Austrian analyses see Alan Sked, *The Decline and Fall of the Habsburg Empire 1815–1918*, London and New York (1989), pp. 154–156, 167 f.

17. Macartney, *The Habsburg Empire*, pp. 260 f.

18. Nipperdey, *Deutsche Geschichte*, p. 359.

19. Herbert Matis, "Deutsch-Österreichische Wirtschaftsbeziehungen 1815–1938 – Aus österreichischer Sicht," in Kann and Prinz (eds.), *Deutschland und Österreich*, pp. 370–397 (here p. 373).

movement in Frankfurt in 1848–1849.[20] The ambivalence of the Austrians in the Paulskirche has been characterized as "wondering how they can unite with Germany without uniting with Germany — like trying to kiss a girl with your back turned on her."[21]

In the 1850s, the Prussians were winning the struggle for supremacy in Germany, both on the economic and political fronts. In the economic sphere, Austrian attempts to join the German Customs Union did not come to fruition. The plan of Austrian minister of commerce Karl Bruck for a "Central European Customs Union" reflected the fact that Austria's failure to join the German Customs Union had set the stage for Austria's exclusion from German affairs. Bruck's plan represented the *pendant* in the economic sphere to Schwarzenberg's efforts to create the *"Reich* of seventy million" in the political arena. Bruck's desperate attempt to establish a German economic *Mitteleuropa* with Austrian participation failed.

In the political sphere, Prussia did not yet succeed in establishing a *"Kleindeutschland"* under its leadership. Schwarzenberg's "Olmütz Punctation" threatened war in case of a *kleindeutsch* solution to the German problem. Francis Joseph's prime minister Schwarzenberg thwarted Prussian plans to have the Austrian Empire "thrown out" of Germany.[22] Austria remained the presiding power in the German Confederation. Olmütz, however, added insult to injury among German nationalists. The deadlock between the two principal powers in the German Confederation continued throughout the 1850s and early 1860s. Meanwhile, Prussia further increased its economic preponderance, while Austria tried to preserve its ill-fated political leadership. All Austrian efforts to be included in the German Customs Union failed. It was indeed a "conflict-ridden" period in Austro-German relations, as Peter Katzenstein has maintained.[23]

In the 1850s, then, Otto von Bismarck, the "Iron Chancellor" who would succeed in unifying Germany in the 1860s, redefined Prussia's role in Ger-

---

20. For the complicated interaction of the German and the Austrian revolutions in 1848 see Nipperdey, *Deutsche Geschichte,* pp. 595–673.

21. Macartney, *The Habsburg Empire,* p. 353.

22. It was Heinrich Friedjung who coined the phrase in his famous book *The Struggle for Supremacy in Germany 1859–1866,* New York (1935); Roy Austensen called it a "struggle for survival in Germany," in "Austria and the 'Struggle for Supremacy in Germany,' 1848–1864," *Journal of Modern History* 52 (June 1980), pp. 195–225 (here p. 222); see also Adam Wandruszka, "Großdeutsche und Kleindeutsche Ideologie 1840–1871," in Kann and Prinz (eds.), *Deutschland und Österreich,* pp. 110–142 (here p. 128).

23. Katzenstein, *Disjoined Partners,* pp. 35–96; for a critique of Katzenstein see Schröder, *Austro-German Relations,* pp. 306–312.

many as Berlin's envoy to the *Bundestag*. Bismarck's ideas eventually became decisive in the Prussian councils of state. He came to the conclusion that the German national question could only be resolved politically with the exclusion of Austria from Germany. Bismarck argued that

a German Prussia will always be too fat ... , if Austria wants to keep the room to maneuver that she desires. Our policy has no other parade ground but Germany, and if only because of our deep geographical roots therein ... We are breathing one another's air (*"wir atmen einer dem anderen die Luft vom Munde weg"*), one of us will have to give way, or be removed by the other (*"einer muß weichen oder vom anderen 'gewichen werden' "*).[24]

Bismarck warned Berlin not to enter "sentimental alliances" with Austria during the Crimean War.[25] Austria's odd anti-Russian policy during this war led to its international isolation and permanent antagonism with Russia. This eventually allowed Prussia to challenge Austria on the battlefield. Russia became Austria's deadly enemy for the next half-century because Francis Joseph had not supported Russian ambitions in the Danube Principalities during the Crimean War. From now on, Prussia could rely on Russian neutrality in case of war with Austria. In the long run, moreover, Austria eventually would need Prussian support against the Czar's aggressive stirring of pan-Slavism in the Balkans.

When Italy challenged Austria in 1859, Prussia remained neutral, in spite of widespread demands in the third Germany to lend military support to the embattled Habsburg monarchy. Austria lost and relinquished most of its Italian possessions. In an age of intensifying nationalism, Austria's universal "European" foreign policy clashed with Prussia's determination to unite Germany in the *kleindeutsch* solution. In the 1860s, Vienna was too late to start concentrating on German affairs. The fledgling economic giant, Prussia, under Bismarck's able leadership, embarked on its policy of political unification of the "German nation." In the fateful battle of Königgrätz/Sadowa the superior Prussian military machine defeated the Austrian forces.[26]

For Austria's position in Germany, Königgrätz proved to be as similarly disastrous a blow as Montcalm's defeat at Quebec in 1759 turned out to be for French interests in North America. Austria and France were no longer in a position to compete for hegemony in Germany and North America. For

---

24. Letter from Bismarck to Leopold von Gerlach (December 1853), quoted in Andreas Hillgruber, *Otto von Bismarck. Gründer der europäischen Großmacht Deutsches Reich*, Göttingen (1978), p. 26.

25. Hillgruber, *Bismarck*, p. 27.

26. On Königgrätz see Wolfgang von Groote and Ursula von Gersdorff (eds.), *Entscheidung 1866. Der Krieg zwischen Österreich und Preußen*, Stuttgart (1966).

both the Austrians and the Canadians these disastrous military defeats constituted the beginning of their unequal partnership with their neighbors, the two budding industrial giants.[27]

After Königgrätz, Bismarck convinced his king to grant the Austrians a mild peace, thus setting the stage for allowing the foes of 1866 to enter into an alliance treaty in 1879. Nevertheless, in 1866 the Austrians were eliminated from Germany. One thousand years of common Austro-German history ended, but the cultural and economic ties were not severed. Austria's demise in the German Confederation came as abruptly as the end of the Holy Roman Empire. The new North German Confederation under Prussian leadership helped pave the way for a *kleindeutsch* solution for Germany. After the military decision of 1866, came the defeat of France in 1870 and the proclamation of the German *Reich* in 1871. The Prussian nationalists finally had a unified German nation to be proud of. In fact, they were so full of hubris that they proclaimed their new empire from the Versailles Hall of Mirrors. This egregious humiliation of France set the tone for the new brand of German relations with the outside world.

From Königgrätz to World War I

A few generations of German historians, starting with Sybel and Treitschke, came to view German unification as the culmination of German history. What these historians failed to see is that the formation of a strong German national state in the center of Europe posed an immediate threat to the European balance of power.[28] Some contemporaries saw the writing on the wall. Carl Jakob Burckhardt recognized Bismarck's founding of the German Empire with "blood and iron" as an assault on European history and as the self-destruction of German history. The perceptive Swiss historian

---

27. For brief accounts of the battle of Quebec see Udo Sautter, *Geschichte Kanadas,* Stuttgart (1972), pp. 80 f.; and Edgar W. McInnis, The *Unguarded Frontier: A History of American-Canadian Relations,* New York (1942), pp. 41–45.

28. For a brief historiographical survey of the *"Reichsgründung"* see Michael Stürmer, *Die Reichsgründung. Deutscher Nationalstaat und europäisches Gleichgewicht im Zeitalter Bismarcks,* Munich (1984), pp. 172–186; see also James J. Sheehan, "What is German History? Reflections on the Role of the Nation in German History and Historiography," *Journal of Modern History* 53 (March 1981), pp. 2 f., and now in much greater detail his magisterial *German History, 1770–1866,* Oxford (1990).

predicted an iron age of warfare and radical changes dawning.[29] An Austrian diplomat argued in a similar vein as early as 1871 that Prusso-German unification was creating a military monarchy menacing Europe.[30]

More recently, historians have come to question the *kleindeutsch*-oriented historiography that viewed German unification as the logical culmination in the trajectory of German historical development. In such a reading, the European order was gravely shaken by the violent formation of the German nation state. Even Michael Stürmer admits that with the formation of the German national state "a nucleus of power came about in the center of Europe" that was a threat to its neighbors. "The role of *Mitteleuropa* — which had been a guarantor of the European equilibrium through the balance between Prussia, Austria, and the third Germany — had changed in its basic features."

The U.S. historians, not nourished on the mother milk of German nationalism, seem to be more clear-headed on these issues. Roy Austensen has advocated an interpretation that sees continuity of traditional Metternichian concepts to be the hallmark of Austrian foreign policy in the post-Metternichian period between 1848 and 1866. Metternich's successors on the *Ballhausplatz* tried "to preserve Austria's traditional influence among the German states and to prevent any unification schemes which would exclude Austria, divide Austria's own territories, or provide a magnet for Austria's German population." Because Metternich's successors saw "German affairs in the context of maintaining a stable European system," they knew that "if Austria were to lose her position in Germany, it would significantly lessen her ability to play a stabilizing role in European affairs and would very likely bring about a major shift in the relations among the great powers." Austria acted with restraint. It "tried to exert a moderating influence on European affairs." Prussia's methods were violent. Thus "it was only after two world wars involving German aggression that it became respectable to have second thoughts about Bismarck's methods and to see a connection between his successful *Machtpolitik* and German militarism in the twentieth century." Austensen's conclusion: One tends "to suspect that the militarism and aggressive nationalism were necessary to hold the empire together, that it was a state mortgaged from the very beginning by the methods of its founding."[31]

The highly respected Stanford historian James Sheehan addresses the

29. Stürmer, *Die Reichsgründung*, p. 172.

30. Quoted in Schröder, "Austro-German Relations," p. 303.

31. For Stürmer see his *Die Reichsgründung*, p. 93; Austensen, "Austria and the 'Struggle for Supremacy in Germany,' 1848–1864," pp. 198, 225 f.; see also Austensen, "Einheit oder Einigkeit," pp. 41–57.

problem from the historiographical perspective. He deems it "remarkable" that "the historiographical preeminence of the nation persists even after the historical existence of the nation has been disrupted." He notices how in both successor states "German historians have continued to accept the *kleindeutsch* definition of their nation." He then makes a plea not to consider the *Kaiserreich* "the only, natural, and inevitable answer to the question, What is German history?" Instead he wants to see the *"kleindeutsches Reich"* removed "from its unique and privileged position as *the* subject of German history and put in its place the persistent struggle between cohesion and fragmentation." One of the upshots of this concentration by German historians on the *kleindeutsches Reich* is the unfortunate fact "that the defeat of Austria in 1866 resulted in the exclusion from German historiography." And this is as regrettable, argues Sheehan, as the political partition of North America, which "resulted in the scholarly separation of Canada from 'American history.' "[32]

These questions raised by a new generation of U.S. historians are important ones. Characteristically, they are issues thrown into the hot historiographical debates on Germany's *Sonderweg* from the safe distance of the trans-Atlantic ivory towers. It will be pointed out at the end of this chapter that a number of Austrian historians have recently raised similar questions for post-World War II Austro-German historiography, but with much more fervor than their American colleagues.

How did the Germans fare, then, with their new nation state? Bismarck — the man who, in David Calleo's words, "began as Cavour and ended as Metternich" — had contributed most to creating the monster that was the *Reich*. But as long as he masterfully kept all the strings in his hands, the powerful new German *Reich* was relatively tame. He precipitated a crisis now and then, but he usually kept it under control and presided over keeping the general peace.[33] He managed the continental European balance almost single-handedly with his intricate system of alliances, designed to keep France isolated. Bismarck had learned from Metternich in declaring Prusso-Germany "saturated." But his alliance system proved to be too clever by half for his successors and for Emperor William II. The *Reich* without Bismarck's consummate diplomatic skills and with William's bluster and arrogance fulfilled its potential of becoming a serious threat to the European balance. Or, as Andreas Hillgruber has put it:

---

32. All quotes from Sheehan, "What is German History?," pp. 22 f., 18, and Sheehan, *German History*.

33. David Calleo, *The German Problem Reconsidered: Germany and the World Order, 1870 to the Present,* Cambridge (1978), p. 12; for the "Krieg-in-Sicht" crisis and the Congress of Berlin see Stürmer, *Die Reichsgründung,* pp. 98–106.

Bismarck's premise was that the preservation of Germany's great power status required keeping the general European peace. After 1890, this axiom was replaced by another that supposed rigid fronts and unbridgeable differences between certain great powers and was concerned with strengthening the German position through clear alliances. Foreign policy thereby became increasingly one-dimensional and acquired, more or less necessarily, an ever stronger strategic, and at length, narrowly military, emphasis.[34]

The men who followed Bismarck set Germany on its aggressive path toward expansion by demanding a "place in the sun." The Germany of Emperor Wilhelm II entered *Weltpolitik* with a vengeance. Wilhelmine Germany's powerful economy demanded world markets, its domestic social problems and the noisy nationalists called for participation in the global scramble for colonies. Even though the German *Reich* accepted the constraints of the international system, its governments demanded a territorial sphere in the world comparable to those of Britain, Russia, and the United States. With the building of the "risk fleet" by Tirpitz, imperial Germany challenged England, the premier world power. This brought about the triple entente, which in turn caused those irrational German fears of "encirclement" and the planning for preventive war. The Schlieffen Plan calculated the risks of a two-front war against France and Russia and became one of the principal causes for the local July 1914 Balkans crisis balooning into a global war.[35]

In the dual alliance, Austria-Hungary was forced to countenance German preponderance in central Europe. This foreshadowed the relative inequality that the monarchy was forced to accept willy-nilly during World War I. Bismarck may have designed the dual alliance to prevent Austrian revanchism for Königgrätz, or, the wily German chancellor may have sensed a growing German isolation in Europe. The dual alliance helped to keep the *Reich* from being left "alone with Russia and France," as Chancellor Holstein put it. But it was clear that Bismark intended to be in the driver's seat, or as the "Iron Chancellor" noted: "Within an alliance, there is always a horse and a rider."[36] The court in Vienna failed to discern that Berlin was dictating the

---

34. Andreas Hillgruber, *Germany and the Two World Wars,* Cambridge and London (1981), p. 6.

35. For summaries of imperial German foreign policy see Fritz Fischer, *Germany's Aims in the First World War,* New York (1967), pp. 3–49; Paul Kennedy, *The Rise and Fall of the Great Powers,* New York (1988), pp. 194–256; for the "German sphere" see Calleo, *The German Problem Reconsidered,* p. 21.

36. Holger H. Herwig, "Disjointed Allies: Coalition Warfare in Berlin and Vienna, 1914," *Journal of Military History* 54 (July 1990), pp. 265–280 (here p. 269); Herwig adds: "There can be no question which Bismarck intended to be."

terms in the dual alliance. Emperor Wilhelm forced Austria to adhere to his anti-Russian and anti-French policy. The *Kaiser's Flottenpolitik* and German blundering in Morocco and elsewhere pulled the Habsburg monarchy more deeply into the resentments building up against Germany in Europe.

Archduke Rudolf, the maverick Habsburg crown prince, was one of the few prominent figures in Vienna who questioned the value of the unequal dual alliance. Rudolf despised Emperor "Willy's" noisy bluster and arrogance and saw Austria's antagonism vis-à-vis France and Russia as unnatural and as a direct result of Bismarck's devious arm-twisting. Rudolf argued that the "Prussian-Punic" Machiavellian Bismarck "forces Austria into dire straits, leading through the morass or ridicule directly to the precipice." Bismarck, argued the crown prince, forced the bad company that was Italy on Austria "to use it for his own ends against France." Rudolf predicted that future generations of historians would not be able to resist laughing when they addressed Austria's alliances: "This page of history, drowned in blood and tears, will be read like bitterly ironic funny pages."[37] But Rudolf was a lonely critic and had to hide his view from his father, Emperor Francis Joseph, who refused to consult him on political matters.

Before the outbreak of World War I, the central powers became increasingly dependent on each other in the international arena. Austria-Hungary constituted the only reliable ally Berlin had. Both central powers were facing increasing international isolation. Austria needed German backing both against Russia in the Balkans and for keeping a lid on the explosive nationality problem. A false sense of *"Nibelungentreue"* chained the two central European powers inextricable together. Mainly because of its domestic problems, Austria increasingly turned into the weaker partner in the Austro-German Alliance. The German economy continuously outpaced the Austrian monarchy. The proportion of military strength in relation to Germany deteriorated for the Habsburg Empire from 3:4 in 1879 to 1:3 in 1917. With the growth of German economic might and the progressive domestic decline of the dual monarchy, the Austro-German relationship turned more to Germany's favor every day.[38]

---

37. On Rudolf's bitter frustrations with the dual alliance, which may have contributed to his suicide, see the fascinating biography by Brigitte Hamann, *Rudolf. Kronprinz und Rebell,* Munich and Zurich (1987), pp. 313–343, 348–356 (here p. 351).

38. Much of the information in this paragraph – including the proportions of military strength – is from Lothar Höbelt's essay "Österreich-Ungarn und das Deutsche Reich als Zweibundpartner," in Lutz and Rumpler (eds.), *Österreich und die deutsche Frage,* pp. 256–281; I am also grateful to Höbelt for a manuscript copy of his "Die Handelspolitik der österreichisch-ungarischen Monarchie gegenüber

In the early 1910s, both Austrian and German general staffs, without keeping each other informed, started to seriously consider "preventive war" as a desperate option to solve their domestic problems. The German military wanted a "decision" before Russia became too strong. In Vienna, "one project for preventive war chased the next." Because of personal antagonism between the Austrian and German military leadership, however, the Berlin and Vienna general staffs failed to start joint-operations planning for any future war.[39]

The stage was set for the swift events of July 1914 after the assassination of Archduke Francis Ferdinand in Sarajevo on June 28. Berlin wanted quick and decisive action against Serbia and a general "settling of accounts." Germany promised to support the monarchy "through thick and thin." And on 5 July, Wilhelm issued the famous "blank check" to Vienna. Germany "would regret it if we [Austria-Hungary] let this present chance, which was so favorable for us, go by without utilising it," reported the Austrian ambassador from Berlin.[40] Austria thus was encouraged to deliver its unacceptable ultimatum to Serbia. At the end of July 1914, the world was at war; but the "disjointed allies" were not prepared for war.

Even though Germany bore the brunt of the action on the eastern and western battlefields during World War I, it could not have held on for as long as it did without Austria-Hungary. The wartime alliance was strangely uneven. Paul Kennedy has observed that "the alliance with Berlin not only kept Vienna in the war, it also prevented the Habsburg Empire after 1916 from getting out of it." One historian has characterized the wartime alliance between Germany and Austria-Hungary as one between "secret enemies." In the course of the war, the alliance ties had became iron chains. Separate Austrian peace feelers were firmly cut off by the German army high command once they became public. The Habsburgs, at last, had lost their room to maneuver vis-à-vis Germany. The monarchy would stand or fall with the

---

dem Deutschen Reich," which covers Austro-German trade relations in the same period. For a comparative statistical analysis of the respective strength of the Great Powers see Kennedy, *Rise and Fall of the Great Powers*, pp. 198–203. Still the best study on the Austro-German triple alliance with Italy is Fritz Fellner's *Der Dreibund. Europäische Diplomatie vor dem Ersten Weltkrieg*, Vienna (1960).

39. For Germany see Fischer, *Germany's Aims*, pp. 29–38; Höbelt quote in "Zweibundpartner," p. 277; for failure to prepare for war see Herwig, "Disjointed Allies," pp. 269–280.

40. All quotes from Fischer, *Germany's Aims*, pp. 52–54; for a good discussion of the calculated risk the German leadership took in July 1914 see Hillgruber, *Germany and the Two World Wars*, pp. 22–40.

twists and turns of German fortunes on the battlefield.[41]

This also meant that Austria-Hungary not only fought for its own survival, but also for German war aims. Those war aims, however, were becoming increasingly unrestrained and expansionist as the war progressed. Even though some historians see Chancellor Bethmann-Hollweg's famous "September Program" as an attempt at trying to curb the expansionist ambitions of the German military, it nevertheless envisioned a German continental hegemony of sorts. The least the German leadership demanded was an economically integrated *Mitteleuropa* controlled by Germany. Poland, the Low Countries, Northern France, Italy, Scandinavia, and, of course, Austria-Hungary were intended to be part of such a *Mitteleuropa*. A colonial empire in *Mittelafrika* should have provided raw materials and markets for such an autarkic European common market dominated by Germany.[42]

In 1918, Ludendorff's Third Army Command made a quantum jump in extending German war aims. Before the war ended, the German leadership demanded "the creation of an eastern sphere ruled by Germany alone." The design was no less than keeping the giant Russian Empire, now plagued with civil war and revolution, in a state of permanent dependency. The Peace Treaty of Brest-Litovsk (1918) presents the clearest of indications of Germany's expansive aims in the east, with the Ukraine and the Crimea in German hands and much of the Balkans and the Baltic states controlled by the Germans as well. Hillgruber and those historians that see a continuity in Germany's expansionist foreign policy seem to be right when they argue that "Germany's Eastern Imperium" had been a reality for a brief time in 1918 and clearly pointed the way toward some of Hitler's principal foreign policy goals.[43]

---

41. There is massive evidence on the disruptive alliance "partnership" in Fischer, *Germany's Aims*. Kennedy's quote is from "The First World War and the International Power System," *International Security* 9 (Summer 1984), pp. 7–40 (here p. 11); Gary W. Shanafelt, *The Secret Alliance: Austria-Hungary and the German Alliance, 1914–1918*, New York (1985).

42. For the "September Program" see Fischer, *Germany's Aims*, pp. 103–106, and Calleo, *The German Problem Reconsidered*, pp. 42–45; for a critique of Fischer, namely that Bethmann-Hollweg's secretary Kurt Riezler accumulated these war aims as a "provisional catalog of possible war aims drawn up for negotiating purposes" but not as an annexation "program," see Wayne C. Thompson, "The September Program: Reflections on the Evidence," *Central European History* 11 (December 1978), pp. 348–354 (here p. 353).

43. Hillgruber, *Germany and the Two World Wars*, pp. 46 f.; see also Hillgruber, *Kontinuität und Diskontinuität in der Deutschen Außenpolitik*, Düsseldorf (1969), and Klaus Hildebrand, *The Foreign Policy of the Third Reich*, Berkeley and Los Angeles (1973).

It goes without saying that such an expansionist German foreign policy revolutionized the international system and led to the complete breakdown of the balance of power that Metternich and the Congress of Vienna had so carefully constructed. Austria-Hungary had no input in the formulation of the German war aims, and Austrian attempts for a separate peace, once exposed, were brutally suppressed. In this sense Austria-Hungary had become a puppet of the German high command, a truly unequal partner for the first time in its long relationship with Germany. Instead of providing wise council and putting restraint on Germany, as it had so often done before 1866, the Habsburg Empire was entrapped by the Prussian military autocracy. In the latter part of the Great War, Austria-Hungary was fighting for Germany's goal of establishing European hegemony, instead of concentrating on its own numerous domestic economic and nationality problems.

The disintegration of the Habsburg monarchy in 1918, of course, was not a direct result of Germany's uncompromising strategy during World War I. There were many domestic problems that the sullen and old Emperor Francis Joseph had been unwilling or incapable of resolving for an entire generation. Germany's refusal to respond to Western peace offers, which refused to accept Germany's extensive war aims, however, led to the same *"alles oder nichts"* approach that is more prominently associated with Hitler. In this sense Wilhelmine Germany contributed much to the dissolution of the Habsburg Empire and the vacuum of power resulting therefrom in eastern central Europe.

The Anschluß Era

Before 1914, the international system *and* the determination of the Habsburgs to save their monarchy against the centrifugal pulls of the nationalities allowed Austria some room to maneuver vis-à-vis Germany.[44] After the break-up of the monarchy in the last days of the war, the Habsburgs were gone as a strong integrating factor in central European politics. At Versailles and Saint-Germain, the Western powers prohibited the *Anschluß* — the incorporation of the new Republic of Austria into the German *Reich*.[45] Once the German-Austrians had lost their role in the monarchy, only the interna-

44. For the "pull" of the nationalities see Oscar Jaszi, *The Dissolution of the Habsburg Monarchy,* Chicago and London (1929).

45. Fritz Fellner, "The Genesis of the Republic," in Kurt Steiner (ed.), *Modern Austria,* Palo Alto (1981), pp. 1–20.

tional system could stop them from joining Weimar Germany voluntarily.[46] The victorious Western powers, however, did not want to see the defeated Germany augmented with the prize of Austria.

Among the German-Austrians, the desire for *Anschluß* was all-pervasive after 1918. The new Austrian Republic, first proclaimed as "German-Austria," was a state against its will. It was the artificial creation inhabited by most of the leftover German-speakers of the monarchy. Cut off from its traditional markets and suppliers in the east, the new state was not economically viable. Not only the German National party — the Trojan horse of German nationalists similar to its predecessor, the Schönererites — but also the Socialists and Christian Socials saw their only salvation in a union with Germany.[47] Moreover, in 1921, two provinces — 90 percent of the Tyrolese and 75 percent of the Salzburgers — voted heavily in plebiscites in favor of an annexation to Bavaria or Germany.[48]

Shelves of books have been written on the complicated question of the *Anschluß*. A British observer has caught the inherent ambiguity of the *Anschluß* as well as anybody when he called it "the seduction of the Austrian coquette." He noted:

> People now speak of the rape of Austria as if her virtue was above suspicion, and Austrians like to imagine that they only submitted to Germany after their abandonment by Britain and France ... It should be remembered that Austria yielded with so little opposition and afterwards accepted her violator with such enthusiasm that it was legitimate to wonder whether it was a case of rape or seduction.[49]

---

46. Katzenstein calls the pattern of Austro-German relations from 1918–1938 "voluntaristic." See Katzenstein, *Disjoined Partners,* pp. 133–162.

47. For the varieties of *Anschlußdenken* see Gerhard Botz, "Das Anschlußproblem (1918–1945) – Aus österreichischer Sicht," in Kann and Prinz (eds.), *Deutschland und Österreich,* pp. 179–198, and Andreas Hillgruber's equally revealing, "Das Anschlußproblem (1918–1945) – Aus Deutscher Sicht," pp. 161–178.

48. For the results of the plebiscites, see Botz, "Das Anschlußproblem," p. 186. The strong local consciousness (*"Landesbewußtsein"*) of individual Austrian federal provinces (*Bundesländer*) has to be neglected in this chapter, even though provinces like Tyrol and Vorarlberg claim long-standing common historical ties with their neighboring German territories Bavaria and Alemania/Swabia; see Anton Staudinger, "Landesbewußtsein und Gesamtstaatsverständnis in Österreich nach den beiden Weltkriegen," *Austriaca* (special issue), *Deux Fois l'Autriche* 3 (1979), pp. 121-134. For the "special relationship" between Tyrol and Bavaria, see Michael Forcher, *Bayern – Tirol: die Geschichte einer freud-leidvollen Nachbarschaft,* Vienna (1981).

49. Public Record Office (PRO), Kew, London, Foreign Office (FO) 371/93597/CA 10113/28.

Keeping this ambiguity in mind, there seem to be two basic views of the *Anschluß*, one blaming the loss of Austrian independence on Austria itself, the other on Nazi Germany.[50]

One view holds that the Austrians finally got what they deserved. After all, they had pushed hard for such a union with Germany in the 1920s (less so in the 1930s). The casual observer may remember those madly cheering Austrians and their enthusiastic welcome of Hitler on 12 March 1938. Gordon Craig, the grand old man of German historians in the United States, has summed up this view:

> In the photographic record of the entry of the German troops into Vienna there are no anguished and tear-streaked faces as was true in the case of the similar action in Prague a year later. The *Anschluß* was approved by 99.7 percent of the respondents to the *Volksabstimmung* of April 1938, with notables like the former Socialist chancellor Karl Renner and Cardinal Innitzer urging approval.[51]

There exists, then, a popular view of the *Anschluß* that sees most Austrians out in the streets in March 1938, wildly jubilant over the *"Heimkehr ins Reich."* Hitler indeed was welcomed overwhelmingly in Austria. Few have expressed this feeling with more pathos — from today's perspective, bathos — than the historian Heinrich von Srbik, an ardent admirer of National Socialism. On 19 March 1938 he wrote:

> The deep German longing for one empire, which has been living for so many generations in millions of German souls, was fulfilled at last. German-Austria is again united with the maternal soil from whence she sprang. The center of Europe no longer is the home of two separate German states of one people, but of one empire of 75 million Germans.[52]

---

50. See, for example, Stanley Suval, *The Anschluss Question in the Weimar Era: A Study of Nationalism in Germany and Austria, 1918–1932*, Baltimore and London (1974); and Jürgen Gehl, *Austria, Germany and the Anschluß 1931–1938*, London (1963); for a useful bibliography see Botz, "Das Anschlußproblem," pp. 532–536.

51. This is quoted from an exchange of letters between Gordon Craig and Gerald Stourzh in the pages of the *New York Review of Books*, 26 February 1987, following the publication of Craig's review "The Waldheim File," *New York Review of Books*, 9 October 1986, pp. 3–6.

52. "Das großdeutsche Sehnen nach dem einen Reich, das seit vielen Geschlechtern in Millionen deutscher Herzen lebte, ist erfüllt worden. Deutschösterreich ist mit dem Mutterboden, aus dem es entsprungen ist, wieder vereint, und die Mitte Europas beherbergt nicht mehr zwei getrennte deutsche Staaten des einen Volks, sondern nur ein Reich von fünfundsiebzig Millionen Deutschen." See the *"Nachwort"* to Srbik's second edition of his essay "Mitteleuropa," p. 41.

The dreams of this highly respected Austrian historian, "a true believer in a great pan-German state,"[53] had finally come to fruition. Hitler accomplished what Schwarzenberg had failed to do almost 90 years earlier. An "empire of seventy million" of sorts — the Third *Reich* — had been created under the guise of an evil genius, as it turned out. In the ups and downs of the interwar *Anschluß* movement, this is the interpretation that sees Austria as the culprit by stressing Austria's initiative in joining Germany.

Yet there is a second side to the *Anschluß*. Was it not the renegade Austrian Adolf Hitler who pushed for a quick *Anschluß* once he had seized power in Germany? Hitler's motivation may have been his desire to settle accounts with the Viennese, who had failed to see his artistic "genius" in his youth. It more likely was his program for hegemony in Europe and Nazi Germany's need for the Austrian economic resources that made the *Wehrmacht* march into Austria. In such a reading of history, the Austrians were discarding the *Anschluß* idea in the 1930s and were constructing an "Austrian national identity." The Austrian Nazis assassinated Chancellor Dollfuß because he resisted Hitler's desire to engineer a quick *Anschluß*. Such a reading of history stresses the fact that a vast majority of Austrians stayed at home during Hitler's triumphant return to the city of his youthful failures. While the masses cheered Hitler's appearance, "not so few others stayed away fear-stricken," as Gerald Stourzh has noted.[54]

Viewing the *Anschluß* from the vantage point of the German perspective, one recognizes economic and geostrategic motives often overlooked. In his massive study on the *Anschluß*, the Austrian historian Norbert Schausberger has reconstructed the continuity of Germany's economic *Mitteleuropa* plans that included Austria. In these plans, Austria provided important raw materials for the German war economy (iron ore, magnesium, oil, and timber). Austria also had a well-trained work force and unused industrial capacity. Austria, in this view, constituted the jumping board into southeastern Europe with all of its old economic and transportation ties into the Balkans. Austria would become the missing link for German expansion into the Balkans. Nazi brochures already claimed as early as 1932: "Whoever owns Austria, controls

---

53. See the interesting observations on the characteristics of "Austrian" history writing in Thomas A. Brady, Jr., "Imperial Destinies: A New Biography of the Emperor Maximilian I," *Journal of Modern History* 62 (June 1990), pp. 311–314 (here p. 312).

54. Gerald Stourzh in his exchange of letters mentioned in note 51; for the two sides of the *Anschluß* movement see Gerhard Botz, "Eine Deutsche Geschichte 1938–1945? Österreichische Geschichte zwischen Exil, Widerstand und Verstrickung," *Zeitgeschichte* 14 (October 1986), pp. 19–38 (here p. 21).

Mitteleuropa!"[55]

Austria figured as one among many territorial ambitions of "Hitler's Program," the German step-by-step plan (*"Stufenplan"*) to become a world power. Hitler tried to achieve what Ludendorff had failed to accomplish in 1918. The German dictator first wanted to establish continental mastery and add "living space" (*"Lebensraum"*) in the vast expanses of Russia, inhabited by the "inferior" Slavic race. Once this continental base would be secured, Germany would expand overseas to become a world power through colonial possessions. One day the German Empire would have to confront the United States to complete this mad program of world conquest. Hitler did add the new and horrendous racist dimension to German foreign policy — part of it undoubtedly stemming from his Austrian background. Compared with Wilhelmine designs for Great Power status, Hitler's fierce racial hatreds added a new dimension to traditional German expansionism. Nevertheless, there is an unmistakable continuity in German expansionism from 1870 to 1945.[56]

In "Hitler's program" Austria was only a small pawn in a large chess game. Naturally the post-World War I history of Austrian *Anschluß*-desires played into Hitler's hand. The Nazi putsch to seize power in Austria in July 1934 failed. The Austrian Nazis assassinated Chancellor Dollfuß, the leader of Austrian clerical fascism. This made Dollfuß a martyr and paradoxically one of the first "victims" of "Hitler's program."[57] Hitler subordinated the *Anschluß* problem to his larger plans for a continental empire. But Dollfuß's

---

55. Norbert Schausberger, *Der Griff nach Österreich. Der Anschluß,* Vienna (1978); for a convenient summary see his "Anschlußideologie und Wirtschaftsinteressen 1918–1938," in Lutz and Rumpler (eds.), "Österreich und die deutsche Frage", pp. 282–299; the quote is from Gottfried-Karl Kindermann, *Hitler's Niederlage in Österreich. Bewaffneter NS-Putsch, Kanzlermord und Österreichs Abwehrsieg,* Hamburg (1984), pp. 9 f.

56. For "Hitler's program" see Hildebrand, *Foreign Policy of the Third Reich,* pp. 20 f., and Hillgruber, *Germany and the Two World Wars,* pp. 49–55; both these books make strong arguments for the continuity in German foreign policy from Bismarck to Hitler, as does Calleo, *The German Problem Reconsidered,* pp. 85–121. Calleo speculates on the influence of "Austrian" racism on Hitler's program, ibidem, pp. 120 f.; for sophisticated critiques of the "continuity problem," see Thomas Nipperdey, "1933 und Kontinuität der Deutschen Geschichte," *Historische Zeitschrift* 227 (August 1978), pp. 86–111; and Konrad H. Jarausch, "From Second to Third Reich: The Problem of Continuity in German Foreign Policy," *Central European History* 12 (March 1979), pp. 68–82.

57. Gottfried-Karl Kindermann has made the argument that Austria's fight against Nazi Germany in 1933–1934, which culminated in Dollfuß's assassination, represented "the first European resistance against the expansion of the Third Reich;" see Kindermann, *Hitlers Niederlage in Österreich,* p. 15.

and Schuschnigg's authoritarian regimes, with their determination to develop an ideology of Austrian national identity, always nettled Hitler.[58] Hitler responded with economic warfare, political pressure, across-the-border terrorist raids by Austrian Nazi exiles, and considerable propagandistic din.

Behind the scenes, however, Hitler announced his military-strategic solution to the Austrian and Czech problems to a small group of military leaders. Hitler's short-term goals are clearly outlined in the famous "Hoßbach Protocol" of November 1937: "For the improvement of our politico-military position our first objective, in the event of our being embroiled in war, must be to overthrow Czechoslovakia and Austria simultaneously in order to remove the threat to our flank in any possible operation against the West."[59] Five months later the German troops marched into Austria.

Hitler's cold-blooded power-political calculus should be part of any *Anschluß* discussion. His geostrategic design must be juxtaposed with the romantic-emotional pan-German perspective of a Srbik. Whereas for a great number of Austrians the *Anschluß* meant the fulfillment of a long-standing desire to be brought "home into the *Reich*," for Hitler and the Nazi power elite the annexation of Austria was based on purely economic, strategic, and geopolitical factors. Austria constituted a valuable economic asset for a Nazi Germany starved of financial assets and raw materials. Austria represented only a small step on Nazi Germany's road to continental hegemony.

In March 1938, from the international point of view, Austria became an appendix to the German problem. After the German *"Einmarsch"* (invasion and annexation/occupation), Austria ceased to exist as an independent state. Western appeasement quietly accepted the incorporation of Austria into Germany. Sir Alexander Cadogan of the British Foreign Office summed up Western reasoning for pacifying Hitler in Austria: "We may argue about the percentages in Austria that wanted or did not want the 'Anschluß' with a Germany Nazi or pre-Nazi, but we are always left with a more or less considerable residue that did want it."[60] On 10 April, in a plebiscite well engi-

---

58. For an incisive discussion of the *"Österreichideologie"* see Fritz Fellner's essay: "Die Historiographie zur Österreichisch-Deutschen Problematik als Spiegel der nationalpolitischen Diskussion," in Lutz and Rumpler (eds.), "Österreich und die deutsche Frage," pp. 33–59.

59. "Minutes of the Conference in the Reich Chancellery, Berlin, 5 November 1937," *Documents on German Foreign Policy 1918–1945*, ser.D (1937–1945), vol. 1, Washington (1949), pp. 29–39 (here p. 35); for a discussion see Hillgruber, "Das Anschlußproblem aus deutscher Sicht," in Kann and Prinz (eds.), *Deutschland und Österreich*, p. 171; for the Austro-German cold war see Kindermann, *Hitler's Niederlage in Österreich*.

60. Minute Sir Alexander Cadogan, PRO, FO 371/C 1866/132/18; see also Günter

neered by the Nazis, 99 percent of the Austrian population voted for the *Anschluß*.[61]

The Question of Austrian "Responsibility" for Nazi War Crimes

Interpreting Austro-German relations during World War II is a tricky business because Austria ostensibly did not exist and Austrians were transmuted into "Germans" overnight. From March 1938 to April 1945, Austria's presence as a geographic and political entity was suspended. It did not take German Nazi officials long to complete the administrative incorporation of Austria into the Third *Reich*. With its absorption (*"Gleichschaltung"*), "Austria" no longer existed on maps but only in the minds and memories of people who did not feel "German." Berlin objected even to the old historical term *"Ostmark."* In 1942, the Nazis renamed it the "Danube and Alpine districts" (*"Donau- und Alpengaue"*) of Nazi Germany. This was the era of total German tutelage over Austria. Only in the woes of World War II did Austrians come to long for the reestablishment of an independent Austria, realizing that they definitely did not want to be part of a German state in any shape. During World War II, when Austro-German relations reached a nadir of complete inequality, historians have come to see the turning point in the development of an Austrian national consciousness. In the dark hours of the war, Austrians discovered their desire for an "Austrian nation," independent of Germany. It took the iron heel of Nazi mastery to come to the recognition that a separate Austria was necessary.[62]

Though many Austrians discovered a new sense of national identity during World War II, others made a considerable contribution to the German war machine and to Nazi war crimes. After the war, the Austrian government developed an official view stressing the "rape" of Austria in March 1938. Government officials constructed a legal theory that aimed at clearing Austria of any legal responsibility for Nazi war crimes.[63] According

---

Bischof, "Between Responsibility and Rehabilitation: Austria in International Politics, 1940–1950," (Ph.D. diss., Harvard University, 1989), pp. 1–14.

61. Botz, "Eine Deutsche Geschichte 1938–1945?," p. 24.

62. Botz, "Das Anschlußproblem," pp. 195 f.; Radomir Luza, *Austro-German Relations in the Anschluss Era,* Princeton, NJ (1975).

63. The Austrian historian Oliver Rathkolb has discovered convincing documentation that reveals the official argumentation in the conscious construction of the

to this view, Nazi Germany occupied Austria in 1938. Since Austria did not exist as a state during World War II, the Austrian state that was reestablished in 1945 could not be made responsible for the crimes of Nazi Germany, nor should Austria pay reparations. Stephan Verosta, a legal adviser in the postwar Austrian foreign ministry and a principal proponent of the "occupation theory," has carried it toward its logical conclusion. Verosta has argued that Hitler did the Austrian people a great service: "As a result of 13 March 1938, and from the perspective of international law, Germany took on the entire responsibility for everything that subsequently happened on Austrian territory."[64] The Allied powers ultimately accepted the Austrian version when they agreed to drop a paragraph from the preamble of the Austrian draft State Treaty, which posited Austrian responsibility (*"Verantwortlichkeit"*) for its participation in Hitler's war.[65]

In short, the offical Austrian postwar view argued that, no matter what war crimes Austrians committed in the Nazi war machine, Germany would have to suffer the consequences. These Austrians made it easy for themselves by cheating their way around mastering the past (*"Trauerarbeit"*). "As 'victims' they distanced themselves from the 'Prussian' *Kriegsschuld* and from their responsibility for the National Socialist war of aggression and the Holocaust."[66] Obviously, the Germans did not agree with such a one-sided interpretation of events.

Such a perspective facilitated the whitewash of a difficult chapter in Austrian history and added a peculiar twist to Austro-German relations. It supported the notion that Austrians merely "did their duty" during the war. Germans, of course, remember well that some Austrian Nazis participated eagerly in every aspect of Hitler's killing-machine — be it the notorious *"Einsatzgruppen"* in the east, or the Holocaust. Like so many other European

---

"occupation theory;" see his unpublished paper "Die Wiedererrichtung des Auswärtigen Dienstes nach 1945," Vienna (1988).

64. Quoted in *Die Furche*, 24 July 1987, p. 2. It is quite astounding to what length respected jurists went to plead for Austrian innocence. In June 1955 the well-known legal scholar Franz Gschnitzer argued in a parliamentary debate that Austria was as responsible (for the war) "as a lamb, devoured by the wolf that wants to build up his strength" ("Wie konnte es sich da verantwortlich machen? Höchstens wie das Schaf, das der Wolf frißt, um sich dadurch zu kräftigen"). For further legal details see the chapter by Hanspeter Neuhold in this volume.

65. For dropping Austrian responsibility in the preamble of the State Treaty see Gerald Stourzh, *Geschichte des Staatsvertrages 1945–1955. Österreichs Weg zur Neutralität*, 3d ed., Graz, Vienna, and Cologne (1985), p. 167.

66. See the introduction to the perceptive collection of essays, Oliver Rathkolb, Georg Schmid, and Gernot Heiss (eds.), *Österreich und Deutschlands Größe. Ein schlampiges Verhältnis*, Salzburg (1990), p. 7.

peoples that were occupied by the Germans, Austrians also collaborated with the Nazis. After the war, Austrians preferred to dwell on their resistance to the Nazi regime. They fabricated what the British historian Robert Knight has called a "victim-cum-resister mythology."

More recent historical research has been uncovering the transparency of the rigidly legalistic "occupation theory." Jurists have presented a very complicated historical record in overly simplistic terms; they have partially falsified history to clear Austria of any legal responsibility for German war crimes. This strategy was understandable in 1945, when Austria was poor and desperate, but it was transparent and morally callous.[67]

Here is only a partial summary of the historical record of Austrians aiding and abetting Nazi Germany during World War II: Hitler was Austrian; the concept of "national-socialism" was first sported in the Bohemian rim of the old Monarchy;[68] Hitler's anti-Semitism was largely Austrian-inspired; after the *Anschluß*, "the persecution of Jews in the *Ostmark* ran ahead of the Jewish policy in the '*Altreich*' and radicalized it," as the Austrian historian Gerhard Botz has asserted; anti-Semitism gained further popularity with aryanizations (of 36,000 Jewish businesses and 70,000 flats in Vienna); the '*Reichskristallnacht*' was excessively brutal in Austria; Austrians certainly were not underrepresented in executing the killing of the Jews in the Holocaust;[69] the "Danube and Alpine *Gaus*" had a concentration camp of their own in Mauthausen (in the vicinity of Hitler's "hometown," Linz), and the civil population around the camp was in no way ignorant of the horrors committed inside the camp; Hitler and Göring built up huge war industries in the Danube and Alpine *Gaus*; forced labor was put to work there; in fact, German investments sped up Austrian industrialization and thus contributed to the quick economic recovery of the country after the war.[70]

---

67. For recent critical analyses by historians of the "occupation theory," see Robert H. Keyserlingk, *Austria in World War II: An Anglo-American Dilemma*, Kingston and Montreal (1988); Robert Knight, "Besiegt oder befreit? Eine völkerrechtliche Frage historisch betrachtet," in Günter Bischof and Josef Leidenfrost (eds.), *Die bevormundete Nation. Österreich und die Alliierten 1945–1949*, in Rolf Steininger (ed.), *Innsbrucker Forschungen zur Zeitgeschichte*, vol. 4, Innsbruck (1988), pp. 75–91; Bischof, "Between Responsibility and Rehabilitation," pp. 623–726; Rathkolb, "Die Wiedererrichtung des Auswärtigen Amtes."

68. Botz, "Eine Deutsche Geschichte 1938–1945?" pp. 24 f.; see also Bruce F. Pauley, *Hitler and the Forgotten Nazis: A History of Austrian National Socialism*, Chapel Hill (1981).

69. Botz, "Eine Deutsche Geschichte 1938–1945?" pp. 24–28.

70. On Mauthausen, see Gordon Horwitz, *In the Shadow of Death: Living Outside the Gates of Mauthausen*, New York (1990); for the industrial buildup during

I am not asking for collective guilt here. But postwar Austria must bear responsibility for the crimes committed by the inhabitants of the Danube and Alpine *Gaus*, who on 27 April 1945 were once again magically transmuted into "Austrians," when the establishment of the provisional Renner government was proclaimed. Austria is culpable in the broad sense of a nation's duration over time, as the U.S. historian Charles Maier has insightfully argued: "Insofar as a collection of people wishes to claim existence as a society or nation, it must thereby accept existence as a community through time, hence must acknowledge that acts committed by earlier agents still bind or burden the contemporary community."[71]

The crimes of Austrians in the Nazi regime are part of the historical record and are a burden on postwar Austria, whether the government is prepared to admit responsibility or not.

The broad involvement of many Austrians in all aspects of the Nazi regime ironically indicates an unprecedented intensity in Austro-German relations never experienced before or after the war. Though Austria was absorbed into the Third *Reich* on the state level and therefore without a political will of its own, in the personal sphere, Austro-German relations were highly intimate. Many Danube and Alpine *Gauers* welcomed the jobs in the German war economy and their role in Hitler's revisionist policies. Austrians, after all, were interspersed throughout the German armed services, and many Germans from the *"Altreich"* sat in the higher echelons of political, social, and economic administration in the Danube and Alpine *Gaus*.

Viewed from the perspective of the Allied powers during World War II, the "Austrian question" was part of the German problem. When the Western powers started their wartime planning for postwar Austria, they initially included Austria in their plans for German dismemberment — another indication that they had accepted the *Anschluß* as a fait accompli. The basic point of reference for the planners was a weaker multiunit Germany that

---

World War II, see Herman Freudenberger and Radomir Luza, "National Socialist Germany and the Austrian Industry, 1938–1945," in William E. Wright (ed.), *Austria Since 1945*, Minneapolis (1982), pp. 73–100, and Günter Bischof, "Foreign Aid and Austria's Economic Recovery after World War II," in Werner J. Feld (ed.), *New Directions in Economic and Security Policy*, Boulder and London (1985), pp. 79–91; see also Evan Burr Bukey, *Hitler's Hometown: Linz, Austria, 1908–1945*, Bloomington-Indianapolis (1986); the recent scholarship of a younger generation of historians is summarized in Emmerich Talos et al. (eds.), *NS-Herrschaft in Österreich 1938–1945*, Vienna (1988); for a critical analysis of Austria's role during World War II, see Robert Knight, "The Waldheim Context: Austria and Nazism," *Times Literary Supplement*, 3 October 1986.

71. Charles S. Maier, *The Unmasterable Past: History, Holocaust, and German National Identity*, Cambridge, Mass. (1988), p. 14.

posed no imminent threat to its neighbors, namely a sort of preunification Germany. For many Anglo-American planners German dismemberment began with reestablishing Austria's independence, after they had thrown various other options overboard, such as an Austria part of a South German or a Danubian Confederation.

The Moscow Declaration of 1 November 1943 stated that Austria had been "the first free country to fall victim to Hitlerite aggression;" therefore it should "be liberated from German domination." Designed as a statement of psychological warfare encouraging resistance in wartime Austria against the Nazi regime, the Moscow Declaration nevertheless served as a principal prop for the above-mentioned "occupation theory," which stressed Austria's role as a "victim" of Nazi Germany.

Such an interpretation practically obviated the third paragraph of the Moscow Declaration that reminded Austria of its responsibility "for participation in the war on the side of Hitlerite Germany," a view that stressed Austrian participation in Nazi war crimes.[72] A high British diplomat held a view that was not unrepresentative of many informed observers on the Allied side: "Were it not for the strategic importance of keeping Austria separate from Germany, we could let this flabby country stew."[73]

The reestablishment of an independent Austria gave the Allied powers an instrument for cutting up an oversized Germany. To make Austria politically and economically viable, the powers promised postwar Austria a favored international status. It was declared a "liberated" country, whereas Germany was treated as a "defeated" country. The liberation of Austria constituted the price the Allies were willing to pay for instilling in Austrians a will to live in their own nation. Next to such a favorable Allied approach, the wartime experience of suffering the arrogant and condescending tutelage of the "Prussians" did more than anything to kindle a new sense of Austrian identity in the inhabitants of the Danube and Alpine *Gaus*. The realization of grave exploitation during the German occupation in economic, political, and cultural terms fostered a strong desire in the Austrians to reestablish their

---

72. On the origins of the Moscow Declaration see Keyserlingk, *Austria in World War II*, pp. 123–156; Bischof, "Between Responsibility and Rehabilitation," pp. 26–54; 840–844; Gerald Stourzh, *Geschichte des Staatsvertrages 1945-1955*, pp. 1–5. Fritz Fellner has stressed repeatedly how the Austrian problem must be seen as a "by-product of the partition of Germany;" see "The International Problem of the Reestablishment of Austria's Independence After 1945," in Wright (ed.), *Austria Since 1945*, p. 5.

73. Minute J.M. Troutbeck, 4 July 1944, PRO, FO 371/38839/C 8260; Robert Knight has recently used this quote for his article "Dieses schlaffe Land," *profil*, 22 June 1987, pp. 16 f.

own nation, separate from Germany. This constituted the basic lesson of World War II for most Austrians (not the die-hard German nationalists in Austria, those most active in the Nazi elite organizations and probably responsible for the more shameful Austrian war crimes).

Austro-German Relations After World War II

Adolf Schärf, the respected Austrian Socialist, foreshadowed postwar Austro-German relations with his famous dictum of 1943: "The *Anschluß* is dead; the Austrians have been disabused once and for all of their love for a German Empire."[74] In the immediate postwar period, anti-German statements were popular among Austrian politicians. For one, the whole world had to be made aware that the *Anschluß* was indeed dead.

Fritz Fellner, one of the few Austrian historians working on Austro-German relations and Austria's "German" historical identity, has recognized a "frightening hatred of the Germans" on the part of the conservative propagandists of "the Austrian idea" (*"österreichische Idee"*) after the war. Fellner has argued that, when the war was over in 1945, some of them replaced the Germans as the new scapegoats in place of the Jews. Comparing 1918 and 1945, Fellner has maintained that "in the place of the desire to be part of the German *Reich*, now came the demand to be separated from Germany."[75] A good example of the official postwar Austrian *"Berührungsangst"* with all things German is the fact that the language Austrian children learned in school after 1945 was called the "language of instruction" — not German.[76]

In the immediate postwar years, the Allied occupation powers kept Austria and Germany at great distance. Until the early 1950s, Austro-German trade was greatly restricted by the Allies. There were few bilateral official visits between Austria and Germany in the occupation era. Although the

---

74. Quoted in Hillgruber, "Das Anschlußproblem," p. 176.

75. Fritz Fellner, "Das Problem der österreichischen Nation nach 1945," in Otto Büsch and James J. Sheehan (eds.), *Die Rolle der Nation in der Deutschen Geschichte und Gegenwart*, Berlin (1985), pp. 200, 194.

76. On this last point see Alfred Ableitinger, "Österreichisch-Deutsche Nachkriegsbeziehungen seit 1945," in Kann and Prinz (eds.), *Deutschland und Österreich*, pp. 199–219 (here pp. 199 f.). For discussions of a postwar "Austrian nation" and "identity" see Ernst Bruckmüller, *Nation Österreich. Sozialhistorische Aspekte ihrer Entwicklung*, Vienna, Cologne, and Graz (1984), pp. 192–199, and Emil Brix, "Zur Frage der österreichischen Identität am Beginn der Zweiten Republik," in Bischof and Leidenfrost (eds.), *Die bevormundete Nation*, pp. 93–104.

Anschluß was dead, it remained a sensitive issue throughout the ten-year occupation of Austria. The Allied powers demanded that the prohibition of any future *Anschluß* be written into the State Treaty (Article 4: *"Verbot des Anschlusses"*).[77] The Soviets frequently used the threat of a renewed *Anschluß* as a bogey to procrastinate signing the Austrian State Treaty, especially in the early-to-mid 1950s, when Austro-German relations started to be normalized again. During the Conference of Foreign Ministers in Berlin in 1954, Moscow linked the Austrian question to the successful conclusion of a German peace treaty. Unsettled by the Western attempts to integrate West Germany into the Western defense system, the Soviets frequently charged that the West and "German militarism" were preparing for an *Anschluß* of Austria to the Western defense system.[78]

The records of the West German Foreign Ministry show that the FRG was very careful in not giving the Soviets any grist for their propaganda mills on the matter of a renewed *Anschluß*. The West Germans were extremely sensitive in proving that they fully respected the new Austrian Republic. In 1954, for example, all the high-level visits planned by German officials to Austria were cancelled. At this time the British Foreign Office Research Department (FORD) argued perceptively: "Responsible spokesmen on both sides [Austria and the Federal Republic of Germany] have, however, been at pains to stress the importance of respecting the other's national rights, and, apart from a tiny extremist minority in Austria, and a perhaps larger one in Germany, it would seem true to say that the idea of a fresh *Anschluß* is not held worthy of consideration."[79]

Official Austro-German relations were developed with great caution by both sides. In November 1945, four years before the establishment of the Federal Republic, the Austrians elected a government. After World War II, the powers allowed the liberated Austrians to develop their statehood ahead of the defeated Germans (*"Vorsprung an Staatlichkeit"*).[80] In 1945, the very first contacts across the border occurred during barter deals between Tyrol/

---

77. For the exact text see Stourzh, *Geschichte des Staatsvertrages*, p. 246.

78. Ibidem, pp. 116–129.

79. For quote see FORD on "Austro-German Relations in the Post-War Period," December 1954, PRO, FO 371/112995/WR 10318/1; this is a very useful survey of the development of the political and economic relationships between Austria and the Federal Republic. This paragraph is based on the records on "Austro-German" relations in the "Politisches Archiv des Auswärtigen Amtes" in Bonn; see also Engelbert Washietl, *Österreich und die Deutschen*, Vienna (1987), pp. 59–88.

80. The phrase is Ableitinger's, "Österreichisch-Deutsche Nachkriegsbeziehungen," p. 201.

Vorarlberg and Bavaria. Next to rebuilding Austro-German relations on a local basis, first contacts between Austrian and German politicians took place at international conferences, such as at the Hertenstein Conference on a united Europe in 1946 and at various political party congresses. First official contacts occured at the Organization for European Economic Cooperation (OEEC), the Paris institution that coordinated the Marshall Plan. Both the Bizone (the later West Germany) and Austria were represented in the OEEC and during the General Agreement on Tariffs and Trade (GATT) talks held between 1948 and 1950. In November 1950, Austria and the FRG signed a trade agreement that became operational in 1951.

The rebuilding of official diplomatic relations proceeded with great caution and subterfuge. In 1950, Austria instituted an "Austrian Contact Bureau" ("*Österreichische Verbindungsstelle*") in the FRG. The importance of the *Verbindungsstelle* to rebuild bilateral relations can be deduced from the fact that it was headed by the top diplomat Josef Schöner. During the visit of Austria's foreign minister Karl Gruber in Bonn in May 1953, the two sides agreed to install a "German Economic Delegation" ("*Deutsche Wirtschaftsdelegation*") in Vienna. Adenauer sent Carl-Hermann Müller-Graaf as an envoy (*Gesandter*) to open up the bureau. For all practical purposes, the *Wirtschaftsdelegation* was Bonn's diplomatic representation in Vienna, and it reported to the foreign ministry in Bonn. Official diplomatic relations were finally restored on 20 December 1955 after Austria had regained its independence.[81]

The most spectacular aspect of Austro-German relations was the quick growth of economic ties in the 1950s. Whereas Austria took 10 percent of its imports from Germany in 1948, three years later this figure tripled to 31 percent. A detached British report still noted that "it is not thought that, under the present conditions, Austria is economically dependent on Germany to an abnormal or dangerous degree." Not overly exercised by a renewed threat of *Anschluß*, the British concluded: "Neither the economic nor the political circumstances of either country at the present time seem to suggest any reason why either should desire a change in the *status quo*."[82]

---

81. Reinhard Bollmus provides a useful survey of the origins of postwar relations; see his "Die Bundesrepublik Deutschland und die Republik Österreich 1950–1958," *Christliche Demokratie* (Schriften des Karl Vogelsang Instituts) 1, no. 3 (October 1983), pp. 9–23. This issue on postwar Austro-German relations contains a number of useful essays. See also Washietl, *Österreich und die Deutschen*.

82. FORD report, December 1954, "Austro-German Relations in the Post-War Period," PRO, FO 371/112995/WR 10318/1; for German investments in Austria, see Wilhelmine Goldmann, "Kapitalverflechtung Österreich-Deutschland. Öster-

Serious strains in the budding bilateral relationship developed over the signing of the Austrian State Treaty. For its independence, Austria was willing to pay the price of permanent neutrality. But West German Chancellor Konrad Adenauer and the Western powers in the spring of 1955 feared that the Soviets wanted to neutralize Austria to block German rearmament. Geoffrey Wallinger, the British ambassador in Vienna, summarized the Western point of view in March 1955:

> The basic Soviet objective appears to be the creation of a belt of neutral states consisting of Sweden, Germany, Austria and Yugoslavia. In view of the apparent recent trend in Yugoslavia towards neutralism, the creation of a situation in which Germany would be the only missing link in this chain must have great attractions for the Soviets. We therefore consider it possible that the Soviets are prepared to conclude the Austrian treaty if neutralization, or something closely approaching neutralization, of Austria can be achieved. The prevention of German rearmament is probably still their primary aim and they may consider that the neutralization of Austria would contribute thereto.[83]

Geoffrey Harrison, the head of the German desk in the Foreign Office, speculated in a similar vein that the Soviets were only using "Austria as a card of re-entry into talks about Germany."[84] In the spring of 1955, the Western powers still were reluctant to separate the Austrian and the German questions.

Adenauer was most upset about the freewheeling Austrian diplomacy in the spring of 1955. In speech after speech he propounded that West Germany, which was at the center of East-West tensions with its fifty million inhabitants and its strong economy, must not be compared with the small and geographically peripheral Austria. For Adenauer reunifying and neutralizing Germany threatened to bring it into the Soviet sphere of influence. Austro-Soviet bilateral negotiations leading to Austria's independence, therefore, were no example to follow for the FRG.[85]

reich als Partner oder Commis?" in Rathkolb et al. (eds.), *Österreich und Deutschlands Größe*, pp. 165–173.

83. Telegram No. 50, Wallinger to Foreign Office, 23 March 1955, PRO, FO 371/117786/RR 1071/55.

84. Harrison, "Record of Conversation with the Austrian ambassador (Schwarzenberg)," 25 March 1955, PRO, FO 371/117787/RR 1071/74. I have given a first summary of the contents of these newly opened British files dealing with the critical 1955 period in "Infiltration statt Okkupation. Britische Ängste anno 1955," *Die Furche*, 14 February 1986, pp. 4 f.

85. Adenauer speech given at Goslar, 22 April 1955, File Reden-Interviews-Aufsätze 1955, Adenauer Papers, Stiftung Bundeskanzler-Adenauer-Haus, Rhöndorf; on Adenauer and Austria, see also Bollmus, *Bundesrepublik Deutschland und Österreich, 1950–1958*, pp. 10–12; on Germany's response to the Austrian State Treaty,

In the late 1950s, strained Austro-West German relations were overcome once bilateral negotiations resolved the disagreements over "German assets". While the Federal Republic played an important role on NATO's central front in Europe, Austria practiced a respectable breed of active neutrality, frequently mediating in East-West tensions.

It is interesting to note that politicians on both sides continued to be easily irritated by each other. Adenauer liked to quip that if Austria had claims toward the FRG, he would gladly start by returning the bones of Adolf Hitler, if he only could find them. The former Austrian Chancellor Bruno Kreisky had various occasions to discover that Adenauer did not like Austria.[86] Bruno Kreisky himself proved capable of "pretty harsh diatribes" against Germany. Kreisky noted that "there were no gentle sentiments for Austria in Western Germany," and that "the Austrian Government was not 100 percent happy about future relations with Germany." The cultural arena was particularly sensitive, as Kreisky demonstrated when he was miffed over a demarche from Bonn protesting the performance of a play by Grillparzer as opposed to Goethe for the grand opening of the new Burgtheater.[87]

In a way, such piques indicated the return to normal relations between two equal countries. Both Austria and the FRG developed a healthy independence vis-à-vis each other. They settled down to what has been called a "sloppy" ("schlampig") relationship.[88] In the postwar era, the overbearing cultural and historical ties no longer held the formerly strong attraction and vanished into the past. Although political relations remained sensitive at least until 1955 and beyond, economic ties improved steadily since the early 1950s.

After World War II Austro-West German relations were characterized by mutual respect. The trend of the postwar relationship, then, was one toward true equality, which is rare in the history of Austro-German relations. Austria once again played an independent role in central Europe as it had done prior to 1866. The political pressures and the cultural pulls from Germany, which had been so characteristic for three quarters of a century after German unification, became a thing of the past. Instead of *"Großdeutschland"* and *"Kleindeutschland,"* "three Germanies" came into existence after 1945. Germany reverted back to a *"Trias"* of three states. The postwar Austrian

see Oliver Rathkolb, "Deutsches Unbehagen an der Neutralität Österreichs 1955 und 1990. Ein 'unhistorischer' Vergleich mit verblüffenden Parallelen," in Rathkolb et al. (eds.), *Österreich und Deutschlands Größe*, pp. 85–92.

86. Quoted in Bruno Kreisky, *Zwischen den Zeiten. Erinnerungen aus fünf Jahrzehnten,* Berlin and Vienna (1986), p. 449.

87. Letter, Wallinger (Vienna) to Harrison, 22 March 1955, record of conversation with Figl and Kreisky, PRO, FO 371/117786/ RR 1071/47.

88. Rathkolb et al. (eds.), *Österreich und Deutschlands Größe*.

"economic miracle" resulted directly from the "German economic miracle," and Austria's economic prosperity has been directly linked to the well-being of the West German economy. Austria nevertheless maintained a healthy independence and sense of "Austrian nationhood" vis-à-vis the FRG (and the GDR). Will this Austrian independence persist, however, now that the two Germanies are united?

A Postscript on German Unification

The amazing Eastern European revolutions of late 1989 have surprised and confounded pundits and politicians alike. For almost an entire year, predictions about the future of Germany have been overtaken by events, literally overnight. When Erich Honecker, the long-time leader of the GDR, visited West Germany in 1987, his position seemed unassailable. Few people would have cast much doubt on the political stability of the GDR; fewer still would have placed a bet on a quick reunification of Germany. The *New York Times* ran a story with the headline "One Germany? No Way, Say Moscow and Warsaw."[89] Germany's neighbors to the West savored their security resulting from the division of Germany. Both German states were firmly tied into and contained by their respective alliance systems — NATO and the Warsaw Treaty Organization (WTO). Even the distinguished editor of the German weekly *Die Zeit* predicted confidently that "a peaceful European order will more likely develop on the basis of [German] partition rather than reunification."[90]

Such smug predictions were quickly rendered obsolete by the breathtaking pace of German unification in 1989–1990, coming in the wake of Gorbachev's revolutionary policies in the Soviet Union and Eastern Europe. The East German demonstrations and Honecker's sudden fall in October 1989 were only outdone by the miraculous fall of the Berlin Wall in November. In March 1990 came the first free elections in East Germany. The pace of unification increased after the withdrawal of Soviet objections to an incorporation of a united Germany into NATO. After economic and social unification in July, both Germanies sped toward political unification, accomplished on 3 October 1990. Only a few weeks before unification, the "2 + 4 talks" were concluded successfully and German unity and independence were sanctioned

89. *New York Times,* 6 September 1987.

90. Theo Sommer, "Die Einheit gegen die Freiheit tauschen," *Die Zeit,* 26 June 1987.

by the occupation powers, fourty-five years after the end of World War II.
The two Germanies are united again!

As a result of German unification, Germany's neighbors and the world
are inclined to worry about the implications of one politically and economically overpowering Germany in the center of Europe. Are we to ponder seriously once again David Calleo's challenging question? "Whenever unified
into one state, Germans become a menace at home and abroad."[91] Is the
conservative U.S. pundit George Will correct when he muses: "Are the
Germans inherently, incorrigibly menacing? Is there some character trait
transmitted down the generations, some national chromosome, as it were,
that makes Germans not only different but dangerous?"[92] Or, are the editors
of the progressive U.S. weekly *The Nation* correct when they dismiss the idea
of an inherently militaristic Germany? "It's bigoted to believe that the Germans, because of some *völkisch* character quirk, are more prone to the abuse
of super power than anyone else. History holds too many nightmares all
around."[93] Whatever the lessons of the past may be, the world is once more
anxious about German economic might and the looming German political
predominance in the unified Western Europe of 1992.[94]

Some Austrians are asking the question: Will a unified Germany once
again behave like the bull in the china shop vis-à-vis Austria? Even before
German unification, 45 percent of Austrian trade was with Germany. Will an
intensifying Austrian dependency on the German economy lead to new political pressures as well? Nobody can tell. But apart from the die-hard pro-
German nationalists in the Austrian "Freedom Party," there are few indications that Austrians would welcome closer ties with Germany beyond their
ties in the EC, which Austria would like to join after 1992. Austrians have
developed a strong sense of support for their state in the postwar era
(whether it is a "nation" is a different question).[95] But given the trajectory of

---

91. Calleo, *The German Problem Reconsidered*, p. 2.

92. "Europe's Banner Unfurled," *Newsweek*, 26 February 1990.

93. "Editorial," *The Nation*, 12 March 1990; for a summary of U.S. views about
    German unification see Günter Bischof, "Die Amerikaner, die Deutsche
    (Wieder)Vereinigung und Österreich," in Rathkolb et al. (eds.), *Österreich und
    Deutschlands Größe*, pp. 224–234.

94. For a brilliant discussion of the "lessons of the past" in the case of Germany
    (also applicable for Austria), see Charles S. Maier, *The Unmasterable Past:
    History, Holocaust, and German National Identity*, Cambridge, Mass. (1988).

95. For a broad and critical reassessment of the present state of Austro-German
    relations, see the challenging collection of essays in Rathkolb et al. (eds.), *Öster-
    reich und Deutschlands Größe*.

unified Germany's hegemonic behavior toward Austria between 1871 and 1945, the world ought to closely monitor Austro-German relations for any signs of German expansionist itches. After all, Germany's bilateral relationship with its small neighbor to the south is a good indicator for revisionism in German foreign policy.

A Note on Recent Historiography

A final point needs to be made on the recent historiography of Austro-German relations. Though the politicians on both sides of the border have discarded most of the chips on their shoulders, some historians of Austro-German relations have gone to the trenches again. There is quite an interesting *"Historikerstreit"* raging over what is already an academic question, namely the thesis of the German historian Karl Dietrich Erdmann, who has included Austria in a project on a comparative postwar "German" history vis-à-vis the FRG and the GDR. Erdmann presented his ideas in a lecture entitled "Three States, Two nations, One People?" In an earlier book he had categorically stated that Austria could not be "left out of the German historical continuum."[96]

Austrian historians of "the younger generation" such as Rudolf Ardelt are getting "the creeps" (*"ein gelindes Grausen"*) from "once again being embraced" by the Germans. Ardelt sees the FRG "instrumentalizing" Austria for its "national-political" goals. He forcefully argues that the question of Austria's "Germanness" no longer plays as important a role as it played for earlier generations.[97] The highly respected Viennese historian Gerald Stourzh also sees a "tendency of *'Wiedervereinnahmung'* " in Erdmann's no-

---

96. "Ein vergebliches Unterfangen wäre es auch, das wiedererstandene selbständige Österreich aus dem deutschen Geschichtszusammenhang ausklammern zu wollen," see Karl Dietrich Erdmann, *Das Ende des Reiches und die Neubildung deutscher Staaten,* in Gebhardt, *Handbuch der deutschen Geschichte,* vol. 22, 4th ed., Munich (1984), p. 354; see also Erdmann, "Drei Staaten – zwei Nationen – ein Volk?" Überlegungen zu einer deutschen Geschichte seit der Teilung, Vorlesung in der Universität Kiel anläßlich des 75. Geburtstages am 29. April 1985; for a critique see Fritz Fellner and Georg E. Schmid, "Ende oder Epoche der Deutschen Geschichte? Bemerkungen zum Abschlußband des Gebhardtschen Handbuches," *Zeitgeschichte* 5 (January 1978), pp. 158–171.

97. Rudolf G. Ardelt, " 'Drei Staaten – zwei Nationen – ein Volk?' oder die Frage: 'Wie deutsch ist Österreich?'," *Zeitgeschichte* 13 (April 1986), pp. 253–268 (here pp. 258, 264).

tion of "three" German states, or the *dreigeteiltes Deutschland.*[98] It appears that some die-hard German historians of the old Prussian school cannot refrain from taking Bismarck's *Reich* as the central reference point. They refuse to see that a "non-German" Austria has developed quite a strong sense of its own national "Austrian" identity (in a 1964–1965 poll, for example, 47 percent of the Austrians felt that Austria was a "nation"; in a 1977 poll, 62 percent felt that Austria was a "nation"; in 1979 it was 68 percent).[99]

Fritz Fellner has argued sensibly that it is time for the German historians to discard the idea of German unity as the only framework in which to think about German history. Instead he offers to take the "rich variety of national life" (*"reichgestaltete Vielfalt des nationalen Lebens"*) as the main point of reference.[100] It was this variety of German history that was lost with Bismarck's unification, as James Sheehan has so convincingly shown.

Vereinnahmung by the academic establishment of the more powerful neighbor should be a familiar theme to Canadian historians. Is it not the case that Canadian history is often considered just a subcategory of "American" history? The United States, not known to be bashful when it comes to its historical "greatness," would like to claim exclusive rights for American history. Similarly some Germans like to gloss over Austria and its long contribution to "German" history. Even in the history books the Big Brothers like to spread out in elephantine sizes. It is left to the small neighbors to twitch and grunt to get their due.

---

98. Gerald Stourzh, "Vom Reich zur Republik," *Wiener Journal* (April 1987), pp. 17–19 (here p. 19), reprinted in Gerald Stourzh, *Vom Reich zur Republik. Studien zum Österreichbewußtsein im 20. Jahrhundert,* Vienna (1990), pp. 25–55; for a discussion of the controversy see Emil Brix, "Deutsche Frage mal drei. Im Fluß treiben viele Leichen," *Die Furche,* 21 March 1986, p. 4.

99. Georg Wagner, "Die Meinungsumfragen über die österreichische Nation (1956–1980)," in Georg Wagner (ed.), *Österreich. Von der Staatsidee zum Nationalbewußtsein,* Vienna (1982), pp. 126, 131, 140.

100 Fritz Fellner, "Problem der österreichischen Nation nach 1945," in Büsch and Sheehan (eds.), *Die Rolle der Nation,* pp. 193–229 (here p. 216), translated and reprinted as "The Problem of the Austrian Nation after 1945," *Journal of Modern History* 60 (1988), pp. 264–289. John W. Boyer has called this "Fellner's plea on behalf of a disjunctive pattern of German history," see his "Some Reflections on the Problem of Austria, Germany, and Mitteleuropa," *Central European History* 22 (1989), pp. 301–315.

5

English-Speaking Intellectual Defense of Canadian Nationhood

Joseph Levitt

Perhaps the most interesting question about Canada is why its English-speaking component has never wished to join the United States.[1] Had they spoken a different language from the Americans, as do the Mexicans, there might be little cause for wonder. But they lived next to an English-speaking people with whom they shared a common North American culture all along a four-thousand-mile border. Yet there have been very few movements by Anglophones to become part of the United States. The most celebrated advocate of Canadian annexation to the United States, Goldwin Smith, in his book, *Canada and the Canadian Question,*[2] published in 1891, maintained that the regions of Canada were merely northern extensions of American ones. The natural lines of trade flowed not east and west but north and south. Moreover, English Canadian social and economic life was becoming more like that of the United States. But Smith's book had little effect. Since then, no prominent Canadian has advocated accession. Clearly, English Canadians have had a deep emotional commitment to their country remaining separate from the United States. It may well be that their justification is largely a rationalization of what they have wished to do. Or perhaps the idea of a Canada separate from the United States has remained powerful among

---

1. See Joseph Levitt, *A Vision Beyond Reach: A Century of Images of the Canadian Destiny,* Ottawa (1982) for the response of twelve eminent Canadian intellectuals to this question.

2. For a modern version see Goldwin Smith, *Canada and the Canadian Question,* Toronto (1973).

English Canadians because over the generations it has made good sense. It is this point of view that this chapter will explore.

To begin with, the United States has never shown any interest in absorbing Canada. Since the Treaty of Washington in 1871, when it first formally recognized the new Dominion of Canada, the United States has never suggested or promoted an annexationist movement in Canada. No serious force has appeared on the American political scene that aimed to persuade or coerce Canadians into joining the United States. And, in fact, no serious initiative for any move in this direction has come from the Canadian side either.

Canada has evolved through two distinct periods. During the first, the major external political influence on Canada was exercised by Great Britain. However, World War II reduced Great Britain to a secondary power, and the United States replaced Canada's mother country as the dominant external force. Despite this change, the concepts of a separate identity, a superior political system, and a national economy that impelled the Fathers of Confederation to set up a separate British transcontinental state in 1867 still convince the great majority of Anglophones that retaining a separate country remains a good idea.

The British Period

In founding the new Dominion of Canada in 1867 the Fathers wished to ensure that Canadians would remain British. Disdaining the example of democratic republicanism south of the border, Canada was to be a constitutional monarchy. The Queen would reign over Parliament made up of a House of Commons and a Senate. Power would be exercised by the prime minister and a cabinet, the members of which would come from the party that held a majority of seats in the House of Commons. Finally, the Fathers aimed to build a transcontinental economy not only separate from that of the United States but also in competition with it.

Up to the beginning of World War II Canada's public figures, such as its politicians and journalists, agreed that what made Canada different from the United States was that it was British. Prime Minister John A. Macdonald spoke for the majority of his people when, in 1891, he declared that "a British subject I was born, a British subject I will die."

The next prime minister, Wilfrid Laurier, although a French Canadian, gladly went to London in 1897 to help Queen Victoria celebrate her Diamond Jubilee, an event that epitomized the power and splendor of the British Empire. In London, Laurier defined Canada as a "self-governing British kingdom." Two years later the implications of this phrase were brought home to him painfully when massive English Canadian public opinion compelled him to send Canadian troops to help the British subdue the Boers in South Africa.

It is true that English Canadian opinion split over the nature of the British tie. Some who called themselves imperialists believed that Canada would increase its stature by joining an organic union with Great Britain in a grand global Britannic confederation. Others, who referred to themselves as nationalists, argued that what made the empire great was its commitment to liberty and freedom, best expressed by its efforts to spread the blessings of parliamentary government. The nationalists felt that Canada's relationship to the mother country should be based on common values rather than on actual political links. The imperialists insisted that the empire possessed only one navy and that Canada should contribute to it financially; the nationalists maintained that Canada should have its own navy. They did agree, however, that in the case of a serious imperial conflict the Canadian navy should be turned over to the British admiralty. Both groups accepted the principle that when Britain was at war, Canada was at war. In August 1914, Canada found itself in conflict with Germany because of a British declaration, and Anglo-Canadians of all classes gave enthusiastic support; "No greater calamity," warned John Dafoe, editor of the *Manitoba Free Press*, "could overtake the world at this time than the break-up of the British Empire, the best expression yet obtained of freedom and democracy."[3] Almost half a million Canadians made up equally of British immigrants and of Canadians born of British extraction went overseas to defend the British Empire in some of the bloodiest battles of World War I.

World War I changed the British Empire into a Commonwealth in which, constitutionally, Great Britain was only one among equals. Canada had acquired the right to its own foreign policy. The Statute of Westminster in 1931 stated that Great Britain had no legal controls over the Dominion of Canada except the power to amend the constitution, which for internal political reasons Canada did not wish to receive. After Great Britain went to war in September 1939, Canada remained neutral for seven days before declaring war against Nazi Germany, thus demonstrating that only the Canadian Parliament and not the British government could legally place Canada in a state of war. This struggle for autonomy dominated Canadian foreign policy during the interwar period, but despite its nationalist flavor it did nothing to weaken the British tie. As war came closer, there was never any doubt that if Great Britain entered the war, Canada would follow.

---

3. *Manitoba Free Press*, 8 August 1914. Also cited in Levitt, *A Vision Beyond Reach*, p. 65.

Canada was British not only because of its loyalty to the Crown, however, but also because of its political system. Victorian imperialist writers like John Bourinot were convinced that the parliamentary system was far superior to the republican form.[4] The very existence of the monarchy guaranteed that the head of the empire would speak for the best values and traditions. Queen Victoria had attained her position as a matter of inherited right, not by being elected because she catered to the ephemeral mood of a fickle electorate. She was ideally placed to provide moral leadership and to ensure that the society developed through liberty and evolution rather than through license and concessions to the uneducated masses. Queen Victoria made her throne the rallying point of a vast outpouring of imperial sentiment in Canada around the turn of the century. Over the next decades, however, the fervency for monarchical rule diminished.

The U.S. example undermined the moral legitimacy of any kind of privilege based on birth. In North America, in principle, everyone was free to make his or her own way. Until 1939, there still remained a widespread conviction that the British parliamentary system was superior in that it avoided the deadlock between president and Congress that was such a marked feature of U.S. politics. George Wrong, a noted historian, could proclaim that "politically, Canada is Britain in America."[5] Dafoe believed that Canada's system of government made it distinct from the United States.

Another assumption that went into the making of a system of thought to resist the integration of Canada into the United States was that an independent Canadian transcontinental economy tied to London could vie successfully with that of the United States. During the 1880s, the Conservative government, headed by Macdonald, instituted a system of tariffs and built a transcontinental railway to ensure that trade would flow east and west. Reflecting the optimism of the business classes, Bourinot asserted that because of the wheat-growing potential of the as yet untapped Northwest, Canada could compete with the United States in attracting immigrants. Entrepreneurs played no small role in helping to defeat the Liberal opposition's proposal for what was in fact a commercial union with the United States in the election of 1891. With the opening of the British market to its agricultural products in the 1890s, Canada entered an era of unprecedented prosperity. Dafoe observed that "Canada was the happiest land in the world. It is a country without an unsolvable problem."[6] Another editor, John Willi-

---

4.   See Levitt, *A Vision Beyond Reach,* pp. 3 f.

5.   George Wrong, *The Canadians: The Story of a People,* Toronto (1938), p. 409. Also cited in Levitt, *A Vision Beyond Reach*, p. 118.

6.   John Dafoe, "Optimism as a Factor in Nation Building," in *Fort William Cana-*

son of the *Globe,* remarked that Canadians were seized with the idea of making "a great nation."[7]

All these opportunities colored the mood of Canadian businessmen. They were confident that a prosperous transcontinental economy was growing. In 1911, they helped the Conservative opposition defeat the Liberal government's proposal to allow the free entry of most natural products between Canada and the United States. They feared that such reciprocity would shift the direction of trade from east-west to north-south. In addition, such close commercial ties with Washington would gradually alienate the mother country and would cut off British capital and settlers.

Leading circles of businessmen continued to have faith in an economy separate from the United States, even after American investment in Canada began to overtake that of Great Britain. The Canadian Reconstruction Association (CRA), formed in 1917, spoke for big business and campaigned vigorously to prevent major revisions in the tariff demanded by an aroused farmers' movement. The CRA argued that unless industry grew in Canada, the country would be reduced to a "commercial adjunct" of the United States.[8] Whether Americans owned the industries, auto industries, for example, was irrelevant to this strategy; what counted was that as industry grew U.S. branch plants in Canada would be part of the Canadian economy. In December 1921, just before the federal election, the CRA was dissolved because its program was taken over by the Conservative party led by Arthur Meighen. In that election and in two subsequent ones, all of which he lost, Meighen's main economic plank was the protective tariff. Moreover, his successor as leader of the Conservative party, R.B. Bennett, won the election of 1930 on this issue.

Up to this time, leading entrepreneurs had supported the tariff, but the Great Depression of the early 1930s undermined their confidence in a separate economy. Their spokesman, Prime Minister Bennett, reversed his stance on tariff protection and began to initiate steps toward a trade agreement with the United States, which his Liberal successor, Prime Minister King, would finally sign in November 1935. From now on, Canada's economic relationship with Great Britain would be much less important than the one with the United States. Yet, from the days of Macdonald, the protective tariff, a necessity for a separate economy, had been a fundamental goal of Canadian entrepreneurs and of the Conservative party, which most closely reflected their interest.

dian Club (1911), p. 35. Also cited in Levitt, *A Vision Beyond Reach*, p. 41.

7. Quoted in Levitt, *A Vision Beyond Reach*, p. 41.

8. John Willison, "Agriculture," in *Canadian Club of Toronto,* 15 November 1920, p. 90. Also cited in Levitt, *A Vision Beyond Reach*, p. 82.

Since 1867, with Canada (except for Quebec) and the United States
sharing the common language of English, there has been no linguistic barrier
to the flow of U.S. culture into Canada. The 1920s and 1930s were an era of
unprecedented expansion in the amount of U.S. books and magazines entering the Dominion. American films monopolized the theaters, and American
radio dominated the airwaves. U.S. politics and sporting events headlined
Canadian newspapers. This wave of culture bore with it many American values. There was much more interest in acquiring consumer goods — many
more people were anxious to make money — equally, American movements
for social justice, such as trade unions and the women's movement, also
found Canadian adherents. Finally, the influence of U.S. business became
enormous. None of these developments, however, altered the political allegiance of Canadians. Their consumption of these cultural offerings and economic opportunities in no way disturbed their belief that Canada was a
British country.

The Continental Period

World War II strengthened the idea of Canadian nationhood among
Anglo-Canadians because it increased the country's self-confidence and
destroyed any vestige of colonial mentality. After all, among middle powers,
Canada emerged as one with the greatest military capacity. More than a half
million of its citizens joined the armed forces. Its armored vehicles helped
the British and the Americans drive the Germans out of Italy, France, and
Holland. It displayed enormous economic vitality, paid for its own war effort,
and had enough left over to grant Britain a credit of Cdn$ 1.2 billion.

Yet, Canada's newly found strength and national spirit failed to ease a
certain postwar anxiety among its people about its independence, for the
United States had emerged as a superpower. With the onset of the cold war,
the status of Canada as a freewheeling middle power was reduced to that of
a junior partner in the U.S.-dominated Western military alliance. More and
more the Canadian economy was coming under the sway of U.S. corporations. The coming of television only strengthened the already tremendous
impact of American cultural agencies on Canadian life. Of course, there
never was a time when any articulate element of the Canadian population
was emotionally drawn to be part of the United States. As we shall see, however, some of the intellectual rationale for staying apart from the U.S. had
been shattered by World War II.

Until 1939, the concepts of a British identity, a transcontinental economy,
and a parliamentary political culture underpinned the belief that Canada was

different from the United States. But World War II destroyed the first concept. The great attraction of Great Britain for Anglo-Canadians had been that it was a major power, but in June 1940 the British were chased off the European continent by the Nazis. Prime Minister Mackenzie King concluded that, from then on, Canada would have to depend on the United States for protection.

It is true that nostalgia for the British tie remained. Canada spent a good deal of energy in an attempt to elevate the Commonwealth into a great moral force that would bridge the gap between East and West. The accession of Queen Elizabeth II to the throne in 1952 stimulated a new interest in the monarchy, but now royal visits clearly were much less occasions for national introspection about political values than they were simply good entertainment. Although the Suez crisis in 1956 allowed some posturing by Conservative politicians about the British tie, it also revealed the military impotence of Great Britain — without U.S. support it was unable to make any major strategic moves. Finally, late in 1957, Great Britain's economic weakness was such that Prime Minister Diefenbaker was unable to shift at least 15 percent of Canadian trade to the United Kingdom (U.K.), as he had promised to do in the summer of 1957. The U.K. might still be a good friend and a valued partner in NATO but unlike the pre-1939 Great Britain and its empire, which had towered over world politics for so many years, it was no longer a world leader. There was no longer much point for Canadians, let alone the new waves of European immigrants who were flooding the country, to think of themselves as British.

After World War II, it became clear that many Canadian entrepreneurs had given up on an independent economy. The postwar Liberal government attempted to integrate the Canadian and U.S. economies. It encouraged the importing of U.S. manufactures and capital for which it proposed to pay by exporting raw materials. The result was an enormous U.S. penetration of the Canadian economy. To many business people, especially those whose living depended on their connection with U.S. corporations, the idea of a transcontinental economy separate from the United States made little sense.

Parliamentary forms, however, continued to constitute a distinctive difference. It is true that the old idea of a president paralyzed by a recalcitrant Congress seemed of little validity, when as the head of a superpower he emerged as the most powerful individual in the world. But the parliamentary system was essentially government by party. Unlike his congressional counterpart, a Canadian member of Parliament had either to toe the party line or else leave the caucus. Those with powerful convictions, either to the left or the right, were unable to stay within the two established mainstream parties. The 1950s and 1960s saw two minor parties, the Social Credit and the Co-operative Commonwealth Federation/New Democratic Party (CCF/NDP), participate in parliamentary life. Unlike the U.S. Congress, Canada's Parliament had developed a multiparty system.

The postwar period featured the celebrated search for the Canadian identity. In the 1950s, those who called themselves nationalists affirmed that Canadians had acquired a particular national character, not because they were a different biological type from their American neighbors, but because of the powerful influence of the northern climate and the British tradition. Being Canadian meant more than just being a citizen of a country called Canada; it also denoted that each inhabitant had a psychological and cultural dimension that made him or her dissimilar from the other Americans. This implied that all Canadians shared a common linguistic culture, an argument difficult to maintain in the face of not only the growing presence of ethnic groups but above all the rising movement in Quebec to make French the major language in that province and to set up an independent Quebec. Indeed, these nationalists found themselves in the impossible position of advocating force to keep Quebec in confederation in order to build a powerful nation able to stand up to the U.S. threat.

Another school of thought about Canadian identity, the liberals, denied vehemently that they were nationalists. They believed Canada was a nation because its citizens had voluntarily accepted a common political allegiance. Both French and English as well as those of other national extractions could all continue to be what they were because there was no such thing as a homogeneous Canadian cultural identity and no such person as the archetypical Canadian. But the liberals differed from the nationalists in another important way. The latter believed that if Canada were to remain separate from the United States, there must be a conscious attempt to strengthen the Canadian national spirit by appealing to the hearts and minds of Canadians to resist assimilation into a continental arrangement. Liberals, however, appeared to think that such a plea was unnecessary and even a little retrograde.

In the 1960s, many writers began to define Canadian society as one that was morally superior to U.S. society. Their most eloquent spokesman, George Grant, believed that the American way of life was dominated by a hunger for making money and a conviction that individuals should be restrained as little as possible from doing what they believed was in their best interests. He argued that since the days of the Loyalists a tradition had existed in Canada that led politicians to assume that the public good was more important than individual gratification and that, if necessary, the force of government should be used to achieve this result.[9] What differentiated

9. George Grant, *Lament for a Nation: The Defeat of Canadian Nationalism,*
    Toronto (1970), p. 71, p. 59.

Canada from the United States was that it was a more compassionate society, more concerned with helping those who for one reason or another were unable to help themselves. The 1960s were the decade of race riots in U.S. cities and the bombing of Vietnamese civilians by the U.S. air force. Meanwhile, Canada was instituting valuable social programs such as universal medicare and pensions designed to narrow the gap between the rich and the poor. At the same time, these moral standards of political action propounded by Grant and his supporters excluded no one from accepting their definition of the national identity because of language. Like the liberals, these new nationalists agreed that Canada could exist as a nation only if both French and English voluntarily accepted political allegiance to the national government. For the most part, they were ready to make any constitutional arrangement to allow the French to feel comfortable within the confederation. They, along with the great majority of liberals, rejected keeping Quebec in confederation by force. They differed from the liberals and resembled their older counterparts, however, in their belief that on all fronts, political, economic, and cultural, Canada must be militant in defending itself against U.S. encroachments.

Many English-speaking Canadians have felt that their society was different from that of the U.S. Americans for any one of the above reasons. But they have found it difficult to articulate this sentiment because of the similarity of the language and the culture. During the recent free trade talks with the United States, Canada demanded the preservation of something Canadian that negotiators referred to as cultural sovereignty. Much of the force behind this demand stemmed from the articulate lobby of the artistic community, which wished to preserve Canadian cultural institutions so that their members might continue to have work in Canada. The wide support for this proposal also suggests that many Canadians hoped that artists and writers would develop a culture that would reflect their distinctiveness from U.S. society and thus rationalize their emotional desire to remain separate from the United States. The current Conservative government signed a free trade pact with the United States, which only increased the anxiety of the cultural community. Because of the complexity of the agreement, at this time many do not know if they will be hurt economically. The agreement has done nothing to ease their concerns that this may happen nor to ease their determination to continue to stand on guard for the Canadian identity.

As we have seen, continental economic movements were drawing Canada closer to the United States. Foreign investment in Canada grew from Cdn$ 7 billion in 1945 to Cdn$ 17.4 billion in 1957; of this latter total, more than Cdn$ 10 billion represented direct rather than portfolio investment, and four-fifths of it came from the U.S. Americans who now controlled 70 percent of the Canadian petroleum and natural gas industries, 52 percent of mining and smelting, and 43 percent of manufacturing. Formerly, economic nationalists, who had advocated tariff protection, had displayed no concern about who owned Canadian industry as long as it was located in Canada. Now, however, a prominent businessman and member of the Liberal cabinet, Walter Gordon, warned that a U.S. takeover of Canadian industry would eventually lead to loss of political sovereignty.

Stimulated by two government reports drawn up under Gordon's direction that documented his concerns, a protest movement arose in the late 1960s against the U.S. domination of the Canadian economy. The previous movements to protect the Canadian economy had been led by the business class. Now their place was taken by intellectuals who agreed with Gordon that the influence of U.S. multinationals on Canadian life must eventually erode Canadian sovereignty. As the public debate continued, these economic nationalists won more and more popular approval and, consequently, support from both the NDP and the left wing of the Liberal party. Their opportunity came in 1972 when the minority Liberal Trudeau government, dependent on NDP support, set up a government-owned oil company as well as an agency to prevent any foreign investment that did not directly benefit Canada. After Prime Minister Trudeau regained his majority in 1974, he found himself confronted by the regional aspirations of Western businessmen and governments who wished to derive as much profit as possible from the oil boom. In fighting to raise Ottawa's share of the tax revenue, Prime Minister Trudeau was simultaneously confirming the need to keep in mind the needs of a national economy. On his return to office in 1980, he instituted the National Energy Policy designed to ensure Ottawa of a greater share of tax revenues from the oil industry and to raise to 50 percent the amount of Canadian control over it. Although he would not have said this, Prime Minister Trudeau was becoming something of an economic nationalist.

More recently the issue of an independent economy has again been joined by the Conservative government's decision to conclude a comprehensive free trade pact with the United States. Support for this measure stemmed from many sections of the business community and from the organizations that lobby on their behalf. But considerable opposition to the agreement has been voiced by labor, by intellectuals, and by some members of the business community who expect to be injured by free trade. There is also widespread concern that a free trade pact will result in Canada being integrated into a continental economy. The government has tried to allay these fears by stressing that Canadian-U.S. economic relations will be made more predictable and orderly as a result of the accord and its mechanism for dispute settlement without the sacrifice of Canadian political and cultural autonomy. At best, this would only allow Canada a measure of control over what would be a continental economy. Moreover, at this point in time there are signs that the economy is slowing down, and, fairly or not, many are blaming free trade. In any case, part of the growing skepticism about free trade demonstrates that considerable numbers of Canadians continue to believe that a national economy is still crucial to maintaining their independence from the United States.

Finally, that Canada's parliamentary system, inherited from Great Britain, has compelled social democrats to form their own party is important in helping to convince Canadians that their society is different from that of the United States. It is true that the Canadian federal election of 1988, won by the Conservatives, was a disappointing one for the NDP. Despite a growing popularity in the three previous years, the unusual and unlucky circumstances in the campaign concerning the free trade issue polarized the electorate, prevented the NDP from cutting into Liberal support, and kept their vote down to their traditional level of some 20 percent. Yet, the NDP message that Canadian social programs were absolutely vital was so popular that in order to win the Conservative party needed to argue that free trade would leave them intact. By so doing the Tories were bowing to the widespread sentiment that Canada ought to be much less individualistic and much less dominated by the exigencies of an uncontrolled market economy than was the United States. Social democratic influence, spread through years of active campaigning by a lively and respected political party like the NDP, had molded Canadian values into something different from those of the Americans.

Of the three concepts that make up the intellectual defense of Canadian nationhood, the parliamentary system is the most consistent because it is embedded in the constitution. The other two concepts, a separate identity and the vision of an independent economy, come much more under the influence of current political and social factors. During the British period, they appeared to be very stable; there seemed little reason to doubt that Canada would continue and thus little need for a nationalist movement. All this changed, however, with the disappearance of Great Britain as an important force in Canadian life. Without impugning any malign motive to the United States, in this new continentalist period, Canadian ability to maintain a separate identity and economy in the face of the massive attractions of an English-speaking superpower is now much more in question. Unlike the generations who lived during the British period, the present one will have to exert itself continually to maintain a separate identity and economy if it wishes Canada to remain independent; a nationalist movement that stands on guard against the inevitable pull of American society will now be a permanent feature of Canadian politics.

PART THREE

Political Relations

6

Political Relations Between Austria and the Federal Republic of Germany

Hanspeter Neuhold

It is stating the obvious to point out that Austria and Germany form a peculiar and interesting dyad of unequal and similar partners. It is therefore surprising that this relationship has received so little systematic attention by social scientists and rather has been analyzed mainly by historians.[1]

This chapter will focus on the relations between Austria and the "old" FRG; this means that an important dimension will be omitted that merits a separate study, namely Austria's relations with the other Germany, the former "socialist" German state, the GDR. A new page will be turned after the recent unification of the two German states.

The principal differences between the two countries under consideration in this chapter include:

1. geographic size (with an area of 248,715 square kilometers the FRG was until 1990 three times larger than Austria, with a territory of 83,853 square kilometers)
2. population (in the FRG about 62.2 million, including some 4.7 million foreigners, compared to Austria's 7.6 million or a ratio of approximately 8:1)

---

1. A notable exception is Peter J. Katzenstein, *Disjoined Partners: Austria and Germany since 1815,* Berkeley, Los Angeles, and London (1976). A more recent contribution to filling the gap in the literature on contemporary Austro-German relations was provided by Engelbert Washietl, the correspondent of the Austrian daily *Die Presse* in Bonn from 1979–1985. His book, *Österreich und die Deutschen,* Vienna (1987), also covers Austria's relations with the GDR.

3. economic potential (the GNP of the FRG exceeded that of Austria roughly by a factor of ten — US$ 1.131,265 million to US$ 117,644 million in 1988)[2]

4. military strength (the FRG's potential was clearly superior to that of Austria; for instance, West Germany's defense budget amounted to US$ 31.02 billion in 1990, whereas the corresponding Austrian figure was US$ 1.61 billion)[3]

5. the main foreign and security policy orientations (the Federal Republic was and is a member of NATO and the EC; Austria is one of the few permanently neutral states in the world and does not belong to either organization)

At the same time, the following similarities existed and continue to exist between Austria and the FRG:

1. German as the common language and resulting close cultural ties

2. geographic proximity between two neighboring countries sharing a long common border

3. similar political systems — both are Western, pluralist, market-oriented democracies with similar domestic political structures

4. close economic relations, with the FRG as *the* dominant partner for Austria, including such key sectors as trade, investment, monetary policies, and tourism[4]

5. a common history, which, however, has also been marked by frequent conflict[5]

This chapter will deal with the following aspects of the contemporary (in the broad sense of the term) political relations between Austria and the FRG:

1. the official interpretation of the *Anschluß* by Austria, the relevant provisions of the State Treaty, and Austria's neutrality, which set the stage for the development of those relations after 1955

2. various facets of recent Austro-West German relations, especially at the governmental and interregional level, and their assessment by public opinion

---

2. The figures quoted here are taken from Hanswilhelm Häfs (ed.), *Der Fischer Weltalmanach 1991*, Frankfurt am Main (1990), pp. 151, 459, 834.

3. The International Institute for Strategic Studies, *The Military Balance 1990–1991*, London (1990), p. 66, 89.

4. See Georg Winckler's contribution to this volume.

5. For a discussion of the concept of a shared history, see the chapter by Frederick Engelmann in this volume.

3. the role of the FRG in Austria's efforts to further develop its relations with the EC

4. the place of Germany in the discussion on *Mitteleuropa* (Central Europe) as a possible new main direction for Austria's foreign policy in order to counterbalance somewhat the West European orientation, which is bound to become even more pronounced if the above-mentioned EC option can be implemented

It should also be understood that relations between Austria and the Federal Republic will be presented mainly from an Austrian point of view. Moreover, for the purposes of the interdisciplinary approach adopted in this volume, a primarily descriptive and less theoretical approach seems to be preferable.

A New Beginning for Austro-German Relations

Because the history of Austro-German relations is discussed in two other chapters in this volume, the historical background of three interrelated factors on the Austrian side that paved the way for a new pattern of relations between Austria and Germany can be omitted here. Instead, the focus will be placed on the legal explanation of the *Anschluß*, the relevant articles of the State Treaty, and the impact of the permanent neutrality of Austria on its relations with the FRG.

The attempts to construe the meaning of the events of 1938 under international law are more than legalistic exercises of interest only to a small circle of experts;[6] they also have far-reaching political and sociopsychological consequences. According to the official Austrian view, Austria did not cease to exist as a subject of international law after the *Anschluß* but merely lost its capacity to act. Under this "occupation theory", Austria was not transformed into an integral part of Germany and therefore did not become a belligerent as part of the Third *Reich* in World War II. Consequently, it could bear no responsibility for that war and was not obligated to pay reparations for it afterward. Furthermore, international treaties concluded by Austria prior to the *Anschluß* remained in force, so there was no need to renew them after 1945; nor was it necessary to provide for a new citizenship for Austrian nationals after the war had come to an end.

---

6. Stephan Verosta, *Die internationale Stellung Österreichs 1938–1947. Eine Sammlung von Erklärungen und Verträgen,* Vienna (1947).

In line with these arguments, the Austrian government emphasized the term "State Treaty" for the international agreement that was to restore the country's full sovereignty: Because Austria had not taken part in World War II on the side of the defeated Axis Powers but rather, as stated by the Allies in their Moscow Declaration of 1943, had been "the first free country to fall a victim to Hitlerite aggression," a peace treaty with it would have been out of place.[7]

This Austrian reading of events was not accepted by those who endorsed the "annexation theory," according to which Austria did become part of Germany in March 1938. From this premise, they deduced opposite conclusions with respect to the above-mentioned effects of the *Anschluß*.

Given the complexity of the situation fifty years ago, it is hardly surprising that factual and legal evidence can be adduced to support either interpretation. That the Austrian government opted for the occupation theory in light of its much more favorable consequences for the country and its people in a particularly difficult period should be understandable. Austrians ought to have been better aware, however, than many of them were willing to acknowledge, that this was a somewhat too neat and simplistic legal strait-jacket for ambivalent facts.[8] They should have realized that there were influential groups in quite a few foreign countries that — not without reason — continued to bear a grudge against Austria and felt that it had gotten away too easily after 1945 under the "victim theory." One may also criticize many Austrians for failing to look thoroughly enough into and to face up to those unpleasant aspects of their country's recent history. All this would probably have at least reduced the image problems that Austria has recently been confronting, in particular in the wake of the events surrounding the 1986 presidential election. Whether all the accusations Austria has been faced with in this context are well-founded is another matter.

Issues involving Germany were among the main stumbling blocks on the road to the State Treaty. It will be recalled that the USSR in particular regarded the Austrian question as part of the German problem.[9] It should

---

7. The text of the Moscow Declaration can be found in Gerald Stourzh, *Geschichte des Staatsvertrages 1945–1955. Österreichs Weg zur Neutralität.* Studienausgabe, 3d. ed., Graz, Vienna, and Cologne (1985), p. 214.

8. The legal explanation of the fate of Germany after 1945 and the emergence of the FRG and the GDR causes even more difficulties. See Ignaz Seidl-Hohenveldern, *Völkerrecht,* 6th ed., Cologne, Berlin, Bonn, and Munich (1987), pp. 160–165, and the literature quoted on pp. 150 f.; Michael Bothe, "Deutschland als Rechtsproblem," in Hans-Jürgen Schröder (ed.), *Die deutsche Frage als internationales Problem,* Stuttgart (1990), pp. 39–69.

9. As late as 1954, Soviet Foreign Minister Molotov insisted on the continued pres-

also be borne in mind that the recovery of the so-called German assets —
above all, industrial installations — and the compensation to be provided by
Austria to the Soviet Union for them was another major point of discord.

In the Preamble to the State Treaty, a rather contradictory approach to
the interpretation of the *Anschluß* is adopted.[10] On the one hand, there is a
reference to the 1943 Moscow Declaration in which the annexation of Austria by Germany was declared null and void. On the other hand, mention is
made of "the participation of Austria in the war as an integral part of Germany."

The key provision concerning future relations between Austria and Germany is to be found in Article 4 of the State Treaty. It prohibits the direct or
indirect, political or economic union between the two states. Compliance
with this prohibition by Austria was closely watched by the USSR after 1955.
From time to time, Soviet warnings were addressed to Austria, in particular
against too close economic ties with the Federal Republic. The USSR also
referred to the *Anschluß* prohibition as an additional argument against Austrian membership in the EC.

Other provisions relevant in the present context include a ban on the
acquisition of war material of German manufacture, origin, or design
(Article 14 of the State Treaty) and on civil aircraft of German design or
embodying major assemblies of German or Japanese manufacture or design
(Article 16). Moreover, Article 22, paragraph 13, does not allow Austria —
subject to minor exceptions — to return to German ownership former German assets transferred to it. Under Article 23, Austrian governmental or private property in Germany is to be restored to its owners.[11] In the same provision, however, Austria — again subject to some exceptions — on its own
behalf and on behalf of its nationals waives all claims against Germany and
German nationals that existed at the end of World War II on 8 May 1945.
Austria pointed out that this was a heavy sacrifice imposed on it, given its

---

ence of troops of the Big Four in Austria even after the entry into force of the
State Treaty. Until the conclusion of a peace treaty with Germany, these forces
were to serve as a safeguard against a new *Anschluß*. Stourzh, *Geschichte des
Staatsvertrages*, pp. 122–125; Audrey Kurth Cronin, *Great Power Politics and the
Struggle over Austria, 1945–1955*, Ithaca and London (1986), p. 132.

10. English text in the Austrian *Bundesgesetzblatt* (Federal Law Gazette) 1955,
    no. 52.

11. In light of the recent fundamental changes in Europe, in particular the unifica-
    tion of Germany with the consent of the Big Four, Austria (thus following a
    similar step by Finland) declared Articles 12–16 (with the exception of the pro-
    hibition concerning weapons of mass destruction) as well as Article 22, para-
    graph 13, obsolete in November 1990. *Österreichische außenpolitische Doku-
    mentation*, December 1990, pp. 28–32.

enormous claims against Germany for damages caused by the *Anschluß* and by World War II.

Austria had to pay a political price to the USSR for the unprecedented voluntary release of a sizeable piece of territory under Soviet control — the adoption of the status of permanent neutrality. Austria took pains to avoid the image of a neutralized country, one on which neutrality was imposed by other states. Therefore, the State Treaty remained silent on the issue of permanent neutrality to which Austrian political leaders had agreed in the Moscow Memorandum.[12] Austria preferred to declare its perpetual neutrality in a constitutional amendment on 26 October 1955 — the day following the deadline for the withdrawal of all foreign soldiers from its soil.[13] The subsequent notification of this declaration of neutrality to all states with which Austria entertained diplomatic relations at that time, and their express or implicit recognition of it, provided this originally solely internal and unilateral act with a foundation that is binding under international law.

Nevertheless, the political linkage between the State Treaty and Austrian neutrality is obvious. The main effect this deal has on Austria's foreign policy are the limitations on the options open to it. Permanent neutrality did not require Austria to abandon its Western ideological orientation, to cease to be a pluralist, marked-oriented democracy; however, that status did and does not allow Austria to base its security policy on a military alliance with those countries with which it shares its basic political values, in other words, within NATO or — during the cold war — in some West European mutual defense system. Nor can Austria participate fully and simply in the process of nonmilitary integration in Western Europe, first and foremost in the economic field. For instance, like the FRG, Austria was thus free, on the one hand, to join the Council of Europe, *the* West European regional political organization, whose limited powers[14] appear almost tailored to the needs of a permanently neutral state. Yet, on the other hand, permanent neutrality has been considered an obstacle to an application by Austria for unqualified membership in the supranational EC.[15]

---

12. This "gentlemen's agreement" was initialled by an Austrian and a Soviet governmental delegation on 15 April 1955; Stourzh, *Geschichte des Staatsvertrages*, pp. 226–229.

13. English text in Alfred Verdross, *The Permanent Neutrality of Austria*, Vienna (1978), p. 28.

14. From which matters relating to national defense are expressly excluded (Article 1, paragraph d) of the Council's Statute.

15. See below, pp. 126–132, and the chapter by D. Mark Schultz in this volume.

To sum up, the points of departure for Austria and Germany were the same in 1945. Both were divided into occupation zones by the Big Four. However, Austria benefited from a brief thaw in the cold war after Stalin's death to regain its full sovereignty, that is, above all, to obtain the withdrawal of all foreign forces and full national unity in 1955. The State Treaty and permanent neutrality erected a twofold legal and political barrier that obligates Austria to keep a certain distance vis-à-vis Germany on the bilateral level, as well as within a multilateral framework.

By contrast, Germany remained partitioned until 1990, and foreign troops are still stationed there, although their purpose will change. The Federal Republic became a full-fledged member of the Western camp. It joined NATO in 1955 and turned into a key ally of the Western bloc leader, the United States. The FRG also was one of the six founding members of the EC, already as a party to the 1951 Treaty of Paris, which created the ECSC, and, later on, to the Rome Treaties of 1957 establishing the EEC and the European Atomic Community (Euratom).

Recent Developments in the Political Relations Between Austria and the FRG

Austrian foreign policy after 1955 can best be conceptualized in three circles: relations with neighboring countries, the all-European circle, and the worldwide dimension. The FRG is a key partner for Austria with respect to both the first and the second circle.

What must strike a North American observer in particular about the countries surrounding Austria is their diversity, above all in political terms. This diversity, however, is becoming less far-reaching than in the past.[16] Two of these neighbors — Hungary and Czechoslovakia — were separated from Austria by the iron curtain, which was removed in 1989–1990. After practicing "real socialism" for four decades, these countries have moved toward Western democracy and market economy. It was a painful irony of history that Hungary and Czechoslovakia were the countries with which Austria had had the closest ties over many centuries.

Yugoslavia adopted its peculiar brand of socialism, which among the Yugoslav Republics has now been abandoned most unequivocally in Slovenia

---

16. Andreas Khol, "Österreichs Beziehungen zu den Nachbarstaaten," in Renate Kicker, Andreas Khol, and Hanspeter Neuhold (eds.), *Außenpolitik und Demokratie in Öster-reich. Strukturen − Strategien − Stellungnahmen,* Salzburg (1983), pp. 371–409.

and Croatia, and opted for membership in the Non-Aligned Movement. Switzerland and Liechtenstein are most similar to Austria in that they are Western in their political and economic systems and permanently neutral, Switzerland legally and Liechtenstein de facto. Finally, the FRG and Italy, the two biggest[17] adjacent countries (especially in their economic importance) are members of NATO and the EC. Among all of its neighbors, West Germany is the most important partner for Austria. Its economic preponderance cannot but spill over into the political relations between the two countries.

Although as a matter of principle Austria has tried to be on good terms with all neighboring countries, the quality of its actual relations with them differed and still differs.

Until the "velvet revolution" in late 1989, Austria's relations with Czechoslovakia were notoriously strained — due to historic reasons but also because of a hard-line foreign policy that the Communist hawks evidently favored as long as they were in power in Prague.

Today, relations with Yugoslavia pose a serious problem. The Austrian government and the Austrian population sympathize with Croatia, Slovenia, and Bosnia-Herzegovina. Political support for one conflicting party is bound to antagonize the other, the Serbian side. A negative historical legacy prior to and after the assassination of Archduke Francis Ferdinand in Sarajevo in 1914 further complicates the Austro-Serbian relationship.

By contrast, in light of historic burdens, factual asymmetries, and partially divergent political orientations, Austria's relations with the FRG may even appear surprisingly good. In the annual Foreign Policy Report issued by the Austrian Ministry for Foreign Affairs, the relations between Austria and the Federal Republic have been described as good-neighborly and undisturbed.

The intensity and quality of these relations can be gauged by the frequent official visits in both directions and on various levels (including that of the heads of state) and by the results of these encounters.[18] FRG Presidents Walter Scheel and Richard von Weizsäcker visited Austria in 1979 and 1986, respectively. Their Austrian counterpart, Rudolf Kirchschläger, paid a state visit to the FRG in 1982. Austrian Chancellor Bruno Kreisky traveled on an official visit to the Federal Republic in 1980; his West German colleague,

---

17. The geographic size of Yugoslavia (255,804 square kilometers) slightly exceeded that of the (old) FRG (248,678 square kilometers).

18. After certain hesitations during the first years after 1955, these contacts were intensified in the 1970s. Khol, "Österreichs Beziehungen," p. 383. As regards West German resentments concerning Austrian neutrality and the provisions of the State Treaty on the prohibition of another *Anschluß* and on German assets, see Washietl, *Österreich und die Deutschen*, pp. 59–88.

Helmut Kohl, came to Austria as an official visitor in 1983. Chancellor Franz Vranitzky, Vice-Chancellor and Foreign Minister Alois Mock, and his successor as Vice-Chancellor, Josef Riegler, visited the FRG several times — both officially and unofficially — from 1987 to 1990. The heads of various ministries in Vienna and Bonn also exchanged invitations quite often. Furthermore, mention should be made of regular trilateral meetings between the Austrian, FRG, and Swiss ministers of Economics and Finance, of Transportation, and of Environmental Protection.

In addition to official visits, less formal exchanges between ministers and their officials take place rather frequently. For example, the annual Salzburg Festival provides an almost ideal opportunity for such casual encounters. Chancellor Kohl is not deterred by the proverbial rain in that part of Austria from spending his summer vacation at St. Gilgen near Salzburg each year. His regular presence there has facilitated meetings with leading Austrian politicians.

Austro-German contacts are not only close at the governmental level but also at the party level. In this context, the highly similar political structures of the two countries are of course relevant. For instance, until the German elections in December 1990, the same four political parties were represented in the parliaments in Vienna and Bonn for several years: the Social Democrats, the Christian Democrats,[19] the Liberals, and the Greens.[20] It is quite normal for delegates from those parties to attend and address conventions of their respective sister parties. What is more, their leading representatives also try to support each other by appearing in election campaigns in the other country. As a rule, this is not considered intervention in the internal affairs of the country in which the electoral confrontation takes place.

In addition to bilateral contacts, the parties mentioned above cooperate within their respective international institutions, above all the Socialist International, its conservative counterpart, the European (and the International) Democratic Union (EDU and IDU), and the Liberal International. The EDU is currently headed by Austrian Foreign Minister Alois Mock. The late Bruno Kreisky, who shaped Austrian policy as chancellor from 1970 to 1983, belonged, together with Willy Brandt and the late Olof Palme, to the famous

---

19. Their party is called Austrian People's Party (*Österreichische Volkspartei* – ÖVP) in Austria.

20. A closer analysis of the similarities but also of the rather interesting differences between the domestic political systems of the two countries is beyond the scope of this chapter, which focuses on the relational aspects of the Austro-German dyad.

triumvirate of the Socialist International that was also held together by personal friendship.

It can be safely asserted that good and intensive Austro-West German relations are also supported and promoted by numerous economic groups and by other pressure groups that have a vested interest in close cooperation between the two countries.

The federal character of both states — which is more marked in the FRG than in Austria — adds another dimension to the dense network of contacts linking them. As a result, these contacts include meetings between the governors and the prime ministers of the Austrian and West German *Bundesländer*. In this connection, the recent trend toward international subregional and regional cooperation in Central Europe is of particular interest.[21]

Working communities (*Arbeitsgemeinschaften*) have been formed by adjacent territorial units of Western, (formerly) "socialist," neutral, and nonaligned states alike. They include Swiss Cantons, Italian Provinces and Regions, Hungarian Comitats, Yugoslav Republics, and Austrian and West German *Bundesländer*. For instance, the "ARGE Alp" (*Arbeitsgemeinschaft Alpenländer*), which was established in 1972, comprises the Swiss Cantons of Graubünden, St. Gallen, and Ticino, the Italian Provinces of Trentino and South Tyrol, and the Region of Lombardy, the "Free State" Bavaria and the Land Baden-Württemberg as observer, as well as the Austrian *Länder* Salzburg, Tyrol, and Vorarlberg.

The legal aspects of such international cooperation have caused a number of headaches to constitutional and international lawyers. Despite the legal problems, these *Arbeitsgemeinschaften* have clearly proven their worth in practice. They try to solve common problems together — from traffic problems to pollution problems, from economic matters to health matters, and from cultural activities to sports and youth exchanges. In their formulation of cooperative solutions, these working communities make do with a minimum of institutions and bureaucracy, an approach that may not diminish but may even enhance their efficacy.

The intensity of relations between Austria and the FRG is also reflected in their mutual importance as treaty partners. It is perhaps less astonishing that the Federal Republic ranked first for Austria in this respect. According to the World Treaty Index compiled by Peter H. Rohn, Austria concluded almost 10 percent (9.8 percent) of its bilateral agreements from 1946 to 1975 with West Germany, followed by two other neighboring states, Yugoslavia

---

21. Fried Esterbauer, *Regionalismus: Phänomen – Planungsmittel – Herausforderung für Europa*, Munich (1978); Renate Kicker, "Föderalismus in der österreichischen Außenpolitik. Initiativen der Bundesländer," *Österreichische Zeitschrift für Politikwissenschaft* 17 (1988), pp. 133–144.

(5.8 percent) and Switzerland (5.7 percent).[22] What is more surprising is that Austria held third place for the FRG with 3.9 percent, preceded only by the United States (4.8 percent) and France (4.4 percent). Recently, matters requiring regulation by agreement between Austria and the Federal Republic have become more and more specific, if not exotic: They have come to include the transit of police and prisoners and the border control of gliders and balloons.[23]

Mutual Popular Perceptions

The assessment of public opinion in regard to the development of Austro-German relations after World War II is of considerable interest, especially in Western democracies whose governments have to take account of the views expressed by the common citizen. In light of the ambivalent common past, the choice of West Germany as their country's favorite partner by a clear majority of Austrians should not be accepted as a foregone conclusion. Yet, when asked with which country Austria should entertain particularly close and good relations, 83 percent of a representative sample of Austrians interviewed in 1978 named the FRG; 71 percent chose Switzerland, 58 percent the United States, 43 percent Italy, and 42 percent opted for international organizations.[24] A poll published almost ten years later, in July 1987, revealed the same top two preferences — 68 percent for West Germany and 62 percent for Switzerland.[25] A 1989 opinion survey in which Austrians were asked,

22. Peter H. Rohn, *World Treaty Index*, 2d. ed., vol. 1, Santa Barbara and Oxford (1984), p. 386; Wolfram Karl, "Die Verträge der Republik Österreich – Bedeutung, Vertragsbestand und Vertragsprofil," *Jahrbuch der Universität Salzburg 1983–1985* (1987), pp. 105–121.

23. Bundesministerium für Auswärtige Angelegenheiten, *Außenpolitischer Bericht 1985*, Vienna (1986), p. 495.

24. Rudolf Bretschneider, "Das außenpolitische Bewußtsein des Österreichers," *Österreichische Zeitschrift für Außenpolitik 19*, Sonderheft (1979), pp. 37–48 (here p. 44).

25. Obviously due to a number of recent controversies involving, above all, the placing of President Kurt Waldheim on the U.S. "watchlist," however, sympathy for the United States in Austria declined drastically – down to 38 percent, as compared with 31 percent for Hungary and 29 percent for the Soviet Union. *Die Presse*, 22 July 1987.

inter alia, to indicate the country for which they felt the greatest sympathy confirmed these results.[26]

This priority accorded to close ties with the Federal Republic, however, should not be equated with the expectation of nor the desire for another *Anschluß*. In point of fact, the results of another poll were unambiguous in this respect: In 1981, only 1 percent believed such an event to be absolutely certain; merely 3 percent considered it rather probable. In contrast, 55 percent ruled it out categorically and 27 percent thought it unlikely or rather unlikely.[27] In this connection, it is also quite significant that in the 1970s only 7 percent held that the Austrians were not a nation.[28]

Furthermore, it is worth mentioning that average Austrians are not concerned with the close economic ties between their country and the Federal Republic. In the 1981 opinion survey, 63 percent replied that Austria's economic relations with the neighboring FRG were normal, although they were told by the interviewers that in 1980 more than 40 percent of Austria's imports came from the FRG and more than 30 percent of its exports went to this country. However, only 9 percent regarded these links as too close.[29]

The results of a poll taken in July/August 1988 revealed other interesting aspects of the West German image as perceived by the average Austrian. Austrians had the highest degree of personal experiences with the FRG. 74 percent of the Austrians interviewed had been to the Federal Republic (followed by Italy with 69 percent and Yugoslavia with 53 percent). West Germans received the highest ratings for being hardworking (62 percent) and progressive (69 percent), with the Swiss in second (62 percent and 42 percent) and, interestingly, the Swedes (25 percent and 32 percent) in third place. When it came to enjoying life, however, Austrians considered the citizens of the FRG less successful (30 percent) than the Italians (55 percent), the Spaniards (35 percent), and the Greeks (31 percent); Austrians also gave themselves a higher score in this respect (35 percent).[30]

The results of the previously mentioned 1989 poll underscores the contention that this was a typical assessment. Austrians identified "purposeful,"

---

26. Twenty-nine percent opted for (West)Germany, 22 percent for Switzerland, 11 percent for Italy. (Only one choice was possible.) Sixty-four percent felt the highest inner affinity with (West)Germany, surprisingly 16 percent with Hungary, 10 percent with Italy.

27. Kicker, Khol, and Neuhold (eds.), *Außenpolitik und Demokratie,* pp. A118 f.

28. Ernst Gehmacher, "Meinungen des Österreichers zur Außenpolitik," *Österreichische Zeitschrift für Außenpolitik* 19, Sonderheft (1979), pp. 49–62.

29. Kicker, Khol, and Neuhold (eds.), *Außenpolitik und Demokratie,* pp. A116 f.

30. *IMAS-report* no. 23, Linz (1988).

"successful," "modern," and "sociable" as the most salient qualities of the West Germans. By contrast, the nationals of the FRG mainly characterized Austrians as "sociable," "likable," "peace-loving," and "merry."[31]

Recent Conflicts Between the Two Countries

In light of all these facts, one can subscribe in principle to the official positive assessment of Austro-West German relations by both sides. However, the occasional conflicts that flare up between the two countries should not be swept aside. Moreover, such differences of opinion increased in number and intensity in the recent past. It is also interesting to note that at times the main conflicting party on the German side was not the FRG as a whole but the Free State of Bavaria. The geographic size of Bavaria alone (70,554 square kilometers), however, almost equals that of the whole of Austria (83,856 square kilometers); furthermore, Bavaria's population of 11.2 million considerably exceeds the total of 7.8 million Austrian nationals.

One main point of discord between Austria and the FRG concerned the project to build a nuclear reprocessing plant near Wackersdorf in Bavaria, only about 160 kilometers off the Austrian border. Many inhabitants of the adjoining Austrian *Bundesländer* of Upper Austria and Salzburg were worried in particular about the possible consequences of a nuclear accident across the frontier. Their anxieties were shared by many in the rest of the country and were also taken up by the Austrian government.[32] Yet, the German side rejected Austrian efforts to prevent the realization of the Wackersdorf project and argued that the construction of the plant was a matter of its sovereign decision. The conflict with Bavaria came to a head in the summer of 1986 when about 350 Austrians who wanted to take part in an anti-Wackersdorf demonstration were turned back at the border. To mention just one other episode of the conflict, the late Bavarian Prime Minister Franz Josef Strauß did not allow two members of his cabinet to take part in a television debate in Salzburg in the spring of 1987.[33]

---

31. See also note 26.

32. In this connection, one must bear in mind the opposition to the nuclear reactor about to go into operation at Zwentendorf near Vienna by a close majority of those Austrians who voted on it in a referendum in 1978, the subsequent renunciation of nuclear energy by Austria, as well as the aftermath of the Chernobyl disaster.

33. *Die Presse*, 9 April 1987.

Vienna and Bonn took pains to play down the nuclear issue as an open question between two friends that should not be allowed to seriously damage the otherwise excellent relations between the two governments. An agreement on mutual information about reactor safety and assistance in the event of nuclear accidents was close to signature in 1987.[34] Yet, disagreements over the geographic application of the treaty led to a deadlock. After the cancellation of the Wackersdorf project had removed the sticking point, Austria proposed to resume the negotiations. At long last, a rather original solution is now being envisaged: The 1988 Agreement between Austria and the GDR on the Exchange of Information and Experiences in the Field of Protection Against Radiation is to be extended to the FRG as a whole.

What probably irritated Austrians as much as the issue of the controversy was the contemptuous tone adopted by the Bavarian authorities in dealing with their grievances. The Austrians were given to understand that they did not know enough about nuclear safety. Many Austrians suffer from a more or less latent inferiority complex vis-à-vis their Big Brothers to the north anyway. They feel that Germans tend to regard them as nice and friendly people, who turn out to be not very competent, however, when it comes to serious organizational and technical matters. Austrians, therefore, are particularly sensitive when this point is expressly made by their German neighbors, as it was on the occasion of the Wackersdorf affair.[35]

Ultimately, however, domestic and international pressure paid off. In 1989 the Wackersdorf project was abandoned; instead, a French plant will take care of reprocessing West German nuclear waste.

Emotions were again running high in February 1987 when the Bavarian Council of Ministers announced that Austrians, like all other non-EC citizens, would have to undergo compulsory acquired immune deficiency syndrome (AIDS) tests before receiving a residence permit in the Free State.[36]

---

34. Interestingly enough, Austria signed the first agreement of this kind in 1982 with Czechoslovakia, the neighboring country with which relations, in general terms, were most strained. On the shortcomings of the agreement see Bruno Simma and Günther Handl, "Der österreichisch-tschechoslowakische Vertrag über grenznahe Kernanlagen im Lichte des völkerrechtlichen Nachbarrechts," *Österreichische Juristenzeitung* 40 (1985), pp. 174–178.

35. One of the ironies of this dispute was the fact that the Christian Democratic governors of Upper Austria and Salzburg who added their voices to those who expressed their misgivings were rebuked and almost ridiculed by the *Christlich Soziale Union* (CSU) government in Munich, which is a member of the same conservative political family. By contrast, they were supported by the West German Socialists and the Greens.

36. *Wiener Zeitung* and *Die Presse*, 26 and 27 February 1987. The decision was even-

Bavarian authorities invoked West German federal legislation as the basis for this discriminatory requirement, which was also criticized within the Federal Republic. Objections were raised not only by the opposition parties there, but even by the CDU health minister Rita Süssmuth. She referred to the Bavarian measures as an erroneous approach; experience had proven voluntary steps more efficacious in the fight against the disease.

Franz Josef Strauß and his supporters, in turn, felt seriously offended by another protest demonstration, this time opposite the Vienna State Opera (where the Bavarian prime minister attended the Opera Ball in 1987) and by the coverage of this event by the Austrian media. His deputy, Karl Hillermeyer, wrote a letter to Austrian Chancellor Vranitzky in which, inter alia, he called on Vranitzky to dissociate himself from rather tasteless remarks in the *Neue Kronen Zeitung,* the Austrian daily with the largest circulation.[37] In the eyes of many Austrians, this move indicated a strange understanding of the freedom of the press on the Bavarian side.[38]

Another conflict broke out between the two countries when Austrian Minister of Economics Robert Graf launched the idea of requiring the payment of a toll for the use of all Austrian express freeways (*Autobahnen*) in April 1987. This measure was envisaged in order to raise funds necessary for the extension of the Austrian freeway network. This time, both the governments in Munich and Bonn reacted strongly. Both threatened to take countermeasures. A CSU member of the Bavarian *Landtag* even referred to the Austrian plan as "robber-knight methods."[39] After a study had revealed that the disadvantages of implementing the toll project would outweigh the benefits, Minister Graf eventually abandoned his scheme, which had been equally controversial in Austria from the outset.

Another Austro-German conflict was caused by the Austrian decision, after lengthy discussions, to prohibit the use of certain Austrian transit routes by all heavy (more than 7.5 tons) and noisy trucks during the night (from 10 P.M. to 5 A.M.) as of 1 December 1989. This step was taken to protect the population and the environment in the Alpine regions against growing noise and increasing pollution. The FRG retaliated by imposing a similar ban only on Austrian trucks and on all West German roads one month later; Italy responded in the same way. Austria criticized these sanctions as discrimina-

---

tually modified as a result of Austrian protests.

37. *Die Presse,* 5 March 1987. The text of the letter and the Austrian reply to it can be found in Washietl, *Österreich und die Deutschen,* pp. 20–24.

38. One should bear in mind, however, that Franz Josef Strauß and his CSU were at times also involved in intra-German controversies, including disputes with their sister party, the CDU.

39. *Die Presse,* 3 April 1987.

tory measures directed exclusively against Austrian transports and therefore as violations of the GATT, the 1972 free trade treaties with the EC and a bilateral transport treaty. Strong language was used this time by Austrian spokesmen: Helmut Kukacka, secretary-general of the ÖVP, referred to West German "gunboat diplomacy"; according to his opposite number in the SPÖ, Central Secretary Josef Cap, the minister of transport of the FRG, Friedrich Zimmermann, acted "like a *Reichstransportminister*."[40] In February 1990, Austria took legal action against the West German countermeasures within the GATT framework.[41]

Recent controversies that have pitted Austria and the Federal Republic against each other appear to confirm the truism that geographic proximity tends to breed conflict as well as to lead to cooperation. What is less self-evident is the failure of similarities in the national characters of Bavarians and Austrians to check this negative trend; instead, additional disputes broke out between the Free State and its neighbor to the south. As a matter of fact, the mentalities, dialects, and cultures of these two neighboring populations resemble each other rather closely and, in some respects, more strongly than those of the Bavarians and northern Germans.

These events justify the conclusion that Austro-West German relations are not quite as good as they appear on the basis of official statements and quantitative indicators. Below the surface of the assumption of parallel interests and mutually favorable clichés, some potential for conflict may be hidden. It could also be argued that, especially on the mass level, tourism does not provide a remedy. Those numerous German tourists who come to Austria each year more often than not may merely find their prejudices confirmed. By contrast, rather few Austrians spend their vacations in the FRG. Consequently, the average Austrian's knowledge of Germany is not based on direct personal observation but on second-hand reports in the media that are frequently under West German domination. Hence, one observer spoke of two peoples who pass each other sitting in separate corridor trains.[42]

Economic Dependence Without Political Dominance?

A key question concerns the degree of influence that the more powerful partner wields over the weaker one and the extent to which the latter is

---

40. *Die Presse* and *Salzburger Nachrichten*, 18 November 1989.

41. *Die Presse*, 21 February 1990.

42. Washietl, *Österreich und die Deutschen*, p. 167.

dependent on the former in a dyad between two unequal States. That Austria's economy depends heavily on that of the Federal Republic and that this diagnosis also applies to the cultural field, and above all the media sector, is demonstrated in other contributions to this volume.[43]

In the political field, the same amount of dependence does not seem to prevail between the two countries. This fact can be ascribed to at least two reasons: First, unlike, for example, Canada and the United States, Austria as a permanent neutral, and the FRG, a member of NATO and the EC, do not pursue a joint security policy, nor do they operate within the same principal institutional frameworks; yet, one could raise the objection that a multilateral framework is apt to dampen or dilute pressure by a more powerful state on a weaker actor, whereas a purely bilateral relationship offers less protection. Second and more important, although the Federal Republic ranks among the economic Great Powers, it was prevented, principally by the two superpowers, from playing a corresponding political part in world affairs during the cold war. German political leaders have also emphasized that a united Germany would not embark on power politics.

One, admittedly problematic, indicator measuring the similarity of the foreign policies of two states are their respective voting patterns in the United Nations (UN) General Assembly.[44] If these records between a powerful and a weak country are closely parallel, this would at least suggest a relationship of dependence; GNP figures could be used as a meaningful yardstick to quantify the elusive concept of power.[45] The results of an analysis of the 1978 session of the General Assembly may be quoted as a relevant illustration in this connection because they are typical of the general pattern. The FRG was not among those ten UN members whose voting records most closely resembled that of the Austrian delegation: They were not unexpectedly led by Sweden, followed more surprisingly by New Zealand, Denmark, Finland, Norway, Ireland, Iceland, Australia, the Netherlands, and Portugal; the Federal Republic was only to be found in eighteenth place (and Canada in thirteenth place).

Finally, the Austrian position on the unification of the two German states and its effects on Austria ought to be mentioned in this context. Austrian political leaders by and large welcomed German unity. They argued that the

---

43. See the chapters by Georg Winckler, Adolf Haslinger, and Hans Heinz Fabris in this volume.

44. Because the resolutions of the General Assembly are not legally binding, the majority of UN members, which consists of small states from the Third World, enjoy more freedom of action vis-à-vis the Great Powers than they would otherwise.

45. A.F.K. Organski, *World Politics,* 2d ed., New York (1968), pp. 207–215.

right to self-determination had also to be granted to the Germans. Chancellor Vranitzky was not afraid that history would repeat itself because he believed in the ability of peoples to learn from past mistakes and in the efficacy of guarantees provided by democratic institutions and by European integration in its various forms.[46] Austrian politicians also emphasized that there was no question of Austria becoming a "third (or rather second) German state." Austria's firmly established identity was said not to be threatened. According to Foreign Minister Mock, Austria will be a small neighboring country next to Germany, just like Switzerland and the Netherlands.[47] Some comments added the need for diversifying Austria's political and economic relations. A recent poll revealed that Austrian public opinion also strongly supported German unification: Seventy-eight percent of those interviewed by telephone in March 1990 declared themselves in favor of German unity.[48]

A few critical voices pointed out, however, that Austria was burying its head in the sand by claiming not to be affected by the emergence of an even more powerful single Germany, although this effect was denied by 73 percent of a representative sample of Austrian public opinion according to the previously mentioned poll in early 1990. Instead of ignoring the changes brought about by this turn of events, the Austrian government was urged to develop an adequate strategy to cope with them.[49]

The FRG: An "Honest Broker" Helping Austria to Solve its Problems with the EC?

The FRG is a key country to consider in the discussion of two Austrian foreign policy orientations. The first issue, the question of EC membership, has received more attention by Austrian public opinion than has usually been paid to international issues. It should be remembered that the status of permanent neutrality was generally regarded as ruling out membership in those supranational organizations, in particular in the EEC.[50] In a worst case scenario, however, which has to be taken into account in deciding the member-

---

46. *Der Standard,* 21 February 1989.

47. *Die Presse,* 12 February 1990.

48. *Kurier,* 18 March 1990.

49. See the Viennese journalist Hans Rauscher, *Wochenpresse,* 27 April 1990.

50. See, for example, Verdross, *Permanent Neutrality,* pp. 60–65.

ship issue, the constituent treaties of the Communities might entail obligations contrary to those under the international law of neutrality. For instance, the EC Council could impose an embargo on the export of war material against a state involved in a war. Participation in such sanctions — regardless of whether a Community member is a party to the conflict or not — would run counter to the principles of impartiality that a permanent neutral has to observe by virtue of its special international legal status. Because, under the constituent treaties, such an EC measure could be decided by a majority vote, opposition to the decision by a permanently neutral member would not prevent that member from being bound by it. Consequently, the member state could confront an insoluble dilemma: either fulfill its duties as an EC member and violate the norms of neutrality or vice versa.

Hence, after a "Long March to Brussels," which lasted more than ten years, Austria, like the three other European neutrals, initially settled for mere free trade arrangements with the EEC and the ECSC. Those agreements, signed in 1972, contained special provisions designed to permit full compliance with neutrality obligations.[51]

Austria, however, encountered another political and legal roadblock in its search for a satisfactory regulation of its relations with the EC.[52] The USSR not only objected to close ties between Vienna and Brussels because of Austria's neutral status, it also brought up the German issue by pointing to the *Anschluß* prohibition in Article 4 of the State Treaty. The Soviet Union argued that the Federal Republic, in fact, dominated the EC as the economically most powerful member country. Therefore, an *"Anschluß* through the backdoor" had to be prevented. Although this argument appeared rather farfetched, Austria could not simply brush it aside, because it could not ignore the realities of power politics in Europe.

For about a decade, the neutral states of Europe considered their free trade arrangements of 1972[53] an adequate basis for their relations with the Communities. However, they could not but view subsequent progress in EC

---

51. For instance, each contracting party is free to take those measures that it considers essential to its security in times of war or in the event of grave international tensions; Article 21, paragraph c, of the Agreement between Austria and the EEC; *Bundesgesetzblatt* 1972, no. 466.

52. Heinrich Haymerle, "Die Beziehungen zur Großmacht im Osten," in Erich Bielka, Peter Jankowitsch, and Hans Thalberg (eds.), *Die Ära Kreisky. Schwerpunkte der österreichischen Außenpolitik*, Vienna (1983), pp. 143–193 (here pp. 173–180); Hanspeter Neuhold, "Austria and the Soviet Union," in Bo Huldt and Atis Lejins (eds.), *European Neutrals and the Soviet Union*, Stockholm (1985), pp. 83–118 (here pp. 96–98).

53. Finland signed its agreements with the Communities in 1973.

integration with mixed feelings. The admission of Spain and Portugal doubled the initial membership figure. More important, integration and cooperation were extended to new sectors, such as research and technological development or environmental protection. The prospect of the completion of the internal market of the twelve member states by the end of 1992 in accordance with the Single European Act (SEA) of 1986 raised the specter of increasing discrimination and exclusion of the neutrals. The Single Act also placed cooperation among the EC countries in the area of foreign policy on a formal legal foundation. In addition, the question of an eventual political — and military — union into which the EC could develop began to loom large on the European horizon.

These developments were followed with particular alarm in Austria. One reason for this concern could be the economic difficulties in which the country found itself in the mid-1980s. Moreover, among the European neutrals, Austria has the highest share of the total exports that go to the EC countries. Another explanation might be the shattered, or at least weakened, self-confidence of many Austrians as a result of the image problems their country is faced with abroad. These feelings of insecurity and nagging doubts may make it more attractive than ever to move closer to, if not completely join, the big family of West European nations.

Austria and the other members of EFTA initially tried to cope with the new challenges by adopting a three-level approach aimed at closer ties with the Community: first, arrangements between all EFTA states and the EC; second, bilateral sectoral agreements between the Communities and individual EFTA countries; and third, the autonomous implementation of EC measures by the latter.

Unlike its EFTA partners, who until recently appeared more or less satisfied with the results of this strategy and ruled out membership in the Communities, Austria soon concluded that this triple approach could not accomplish the objective of the grand coalition government that was formed in 1987 by the two major political parties, the SPÖ and the ÖVP. The EC made it quite clear that Austria's declared goal — full participation in the substance of the internal market — was only open to members that accepted all Community obligations as well. Austria therefore eventually applied for EC membership on 17 July 1989, on the condition that its permanent neutrality be safeguarded and that its neutrality policy as Austria's specific contribution to peace and security in Europe could be continued.

An often heated public debate preceded the decision to hand over the famous "letter" (of application) in Brussels. The main points in this discussion may be summarized and divided into four issues.[54]

---

54. Waldemar Hummer and Michael Schweitzer, *Österreich und die EWG. Neutrali-*

First, on the legal level there was widespread consensus in Austria that the dilemma of the compatibility of Community membership with the obligations of neutrality could be solved, provided that the EC also accepted this solution. Above all, the EEC Treaty contains two relevant "escape clauses." Under Article 223, a member is allowed to take steps it deems necessary to its security interests with regard to the production and the trade of war material. Article 224 exempts member states from their Community duties if, inter alia, they fulfill obligations undertaken for the maintenance of international peace and security. If the EC recognized Austrian neutrality as serving this purpose, Austria could invoke these provisions to avoid the implementation of Community measures contrary to its neutral status, notably the above-mentioned restrictions on the export of war material to a belligerent party. Furthermore, steps taken by Austria to safeguard its neutrality should not be subject to the jurisdiction of the EC Court.[55]

The second controversy revolved around Austria's participation in European Political Cooperation (EPC). Those who saw no obstacles put forth four arguments: (1) the fact that EC cooperation in the field of foreign policy was limited to mere information and consultation; (2) that it operated by consensus, which conferred a veto power on each member; (3) that EPC was limited to the political and economic aspects of security, but did not include military defense, which would be really problematic for a neutral; and (4) that the final goal of a political union had still to be defined. As an EC member, Austria therefore could make sure that the union would be shaped in conformity with the requirements of neutrality by exploiting the consensus rule.

The skeptics contested each of these arguments. In their opinion: (1) a relatively weak dissenter in political reality often had no choice but to follow

---

tätsrechtliche Beurteilung der Möglichkeit der Dynamisierung des Verhältnisses zur EWG, Vienna (1987); Karl Zemanek, "Österreichs Neutralität und die EG. Rechtliche Voraussetzungen zur Wahrung der dauernden Neutralität Österreichs im Falle eines Beitritts zur EG," *Economy* 1, no. 4 (1989), pp. 59–65; see also Manfred Rotter, "Soll Österreich der EG beitreten?" *Österreichische Zeitschrift für Politikwissenschaft* 17 (1988), pp. 169–181; Thomas Nowotny, "Warum Österreich nicht EG-Mitglied werden wird. Sicherheits- und außenpolitische Gegebenheiten, die einen EG-Beitritt verhindern," *Österreichisches Jahrbuch für Politik '88* (1989), pp. 79–109; Andreas Khol, "Warum Österreich EG-Mitglied werden wird," ibidem, pp. 779–810.

55. In its 1991 *"avis"* on the Austrian application, however, the EC rejected the Austrian argument based on Article 224. The Commission called for a redefinition of its neutrality by Austria or an exception from the constituent EC Treaty in the act of accession. *Österreichische außenpolitische Dokumentation,* Sonderdruck (special issue) 1991, pp. 26–28.

the technically nonbinding wishes of the majority; (2) the consensus principle was balanced in the SEA by the commitment to refrain, as far as possible, from impeding the formation of a consensus; (3) the line between nonmilitary security and armed defense was thin; and (4) a genuine political union was bound to include a common security policy and to be governed by majority decisions.

With regard to the third issue, the *policy* of neutrality, the measures aimed at enhancing the credibility and attractiveness of a neutral's special status, one side stressed that the activities in this field were at the exclusive discretion of that state. Moreover, if Austria joined the Community, it could contribute its main foreign political assets, its experience with "bridge-building" toward Eastern Europe, to the *Ostpolitik* of the EC.

The critics of this view agreed that a neutral country was indeed free to conduct its *Neutralitätspolitik* as it deemed fit. The achievement of the objective of this policy, however, depended on the response of the other countries to it. Only they decided how credible and attractive a neutral's special status was in their eyes. Austria would also be ill-advised to jettison the political capital accumulated by its third-party services between the blocs over the years, for example within the group of neutral and nonaligned (N+N) countries in the CSCE process.

Finally, in a still broader perspective, it was pointed out that a sovereign and neutral Austria had become a universally recognized and appreciated element of European stability. The advocates of Austrian EC membership retorted that, due to "harmonization pressure," nonparticipation in West European integration would entail even heavier losses of sovereignty than would membership. A member would at least have a vote in EC decision making; a nonmember simply had to implement measures adopted by the Community if it wanted to remain economically competitive. The traditional neutral objective of economic autarky had become an anachronism.

The decisive step now lies with the EC, and it ought to be seen in the broader perspective of the Community's future political orientation. If the members of the EC opt for a strong political union with a common security policy, the admission of an applicant that demands a special status because of its neutrality obligations appears rather unlikely. If, however, no further substantial limitations on the sovereignty of member states are eventually agreed on or a common security policy is shifted to a separate institution, for instance the Western European Union, and placed on a voluntary basis, then Austria stands a much better chance of being accepted.[56]

---

56. The 1992 Maastricht Treaty on European Union into which the EC is to grow leans in this second direction. The key provisions on a common foreign and security policy are, however, subject to revision in 1996; text in *International Legal*

In the meantime, the other neutral states of Europe have reconsidered their position on EC membership.[57] Sweden followed the Austrian example and applied for admission to the Communities in 1991, Finland and Switzerland in the first half of 1992. In October 1991, the EC and the member states of EFTA reached political agreement on the European Economic Area (EEA), which is to extend the four freedoms of the EC internal market (the free movement of goods, persons, capital, and services) to the members of EFTA, without, however, giving them a say in EC decisions by which they would be bound.[58] In any event, the EEA is increasingly seen in EFTA countries as a transitional phase on the road to membership and not as a permanent solution.

With regard to the topic of this volume, it is a fine question whether closer ties between Austria and the EC or the eventual admission of Austria to the Community will result in a less marked Austrian orientation toward the (enlarged) FRG as the country's principal economic partner. Conceivably, Austria's external relations could become more diversified and balanced because other EC members could gain in importance for Austrian trade, as sources of foreign investment, in tourism, and so on. The example of Ireland, which reduced its economic dependence on Great Britain after its entry into the Community, is quite encouraging in this respect.[59]

In its attempts at reaching a new comprehensive arrangement with the EC as well as common solutions to certain specific problems, Austria used to consider the FRG the principal advocate for its concerns and claims within the Community. Leading West German politicians in fact frequently expressed their sympathy for Austria's difficulties with the EC and promised to support the Austrian position. However, doubts have been raised in Austria every now and then as to the wisdom of relying too heavily on the FRG as the spokesman for Austrian interests vis-à-vis the other EC members.

There are certain misgivings (as a rule, misgivings not officially admitted to) in some EC countries caused by the prospect of strengthening German preponderance in the EC by the addition of seven million German-speaking Austrians.

Moreover, friendly words from Bonn were not necessarily followed by similar deeds, especially if and when they had financial implications. For

---

Materials 31 (1992), pp. 253–373.

57. For a comparative perspective see Paul Luif, *Neutrale in die EG. Die westeuropäische Integration und die neutralen Staaten,* Vienna (1988).

58. The EEA Treaty was signed on 2 May 1992.

59. See Paul Sharp, *Irish Foreign Policy and the European Community,* Aldershot and Brookfield (1990).

example, the West German government showed particular verbal understanding for Austria's transit problems but no readiness to support Austrian requests for EC assistance. The above-mentioned retaliatory measure against the Austrian ban on truck traffic during the night is hardly a token of sympathy for Austria's environmental plight. The FRG also blocked an agreement on increased cheese exports from Austria to the EC.[60]

Germany and the Austrian Discussion on "Mitteleuropa"

A few remarks may also be added on the recent reemergence of the debate on Central or rather "Middle" Europe (if the term *Mitteleuropa* is translated literally into English) and first concrete steps to implement one variant of this concept. Closer cooperation among the Central European countries — excluding Germany — is sometimes conceived as a counterweight against the preponderant influence that a united Germany is expected to wield, even if official spokesmen do usually not admit this strategic goal. Some Austrians also view it as a concept to balance, at least to some extent, their country's predominantly West European orientation.

The discussion that started on both sides of the iron curtain in the mid-1980s was initially limited to intellectuals.[61] Its common denominator was a growing feeling of frustration and apprehension, as well as an increasingly positive assessment of the past shared by the nations concerned.

The controversy over NATO's dual-track decision and the deployment of US intermediate-range nuclear forces (INF) to match their Soviet counterparts, the SS-20s, once again drove home two sobering lessons: That Europe had become a mere object of power politics conducted by two superpowers, which were increasingly perceived by some Europeans as extra- and non-European. Moreover, that new turn of the spiral of the arms race raised the specter of the Old Continent becoming the battlefield of a limited nuclear war, the disastrous effects of which could in the main be restricted to the European allies of the United States and the USSR.

---

60. *Die Presse*, 20 July 1987.

61. See, for example, György Konrád, "Der Traum von Mitteleuropa," *Wiener Journal* no. 45 (June 1984), pp. 9–11; Milan Kundera, "Die Tragödie Mitteleuropas," *Wiener Journal* no. 46/47 (July/August 1984), pp. 18–21; H.P. Burmeister, F. Boldt, and G. Mészarós (eds.), *Mitteleuropa: Traum oder Trauma? Überlegungen zum Selbstbild einer Region,* Bremen (1988); Sven Papcke and Werner Weidenfeld (eds.), *Traumland Mitteleuropa. Beiträge zu einer aktuellen Kontroverse,* Darmstadt (1988).

With the advent of the new East-West detente in the wake of Gorbachev's accession to the leadership of the Soviet Union, the *Mitteleuropa* debate focused on steps to bring the peoples on both sides of the divide between the two blocs in the heart of Europe closer together.

For the then "socialist" countries Hungary, Poland, and Czechoslovakia, the principal aim was more independence from the USSR and the assertion of their common Western cultural heritage. Supporters of the idea of *Mitteleuropa* in Northern Italy associated it with more autonomy for their region and increased cooperation with neighboring countries.

The interest in *Mitteleuropa* in Austria may be explained by the search for an active role to play that is worthy of its past.[62] It was reinforced by the humiliating experience of being excluded from full participation in the integration process of the EC; moreover, some Austrians were disenchanted with the Community, which appeared to them as a bureaucratic and undemocratic monster.

At that time, the concept of Middle Europe boiled down to making the iron curtain more penetrable. The negligible economic relations across the East-West divide were to be intensified, cultural cooperation was to be improved, and the common cultural heritage was to be preserved. Humanitarian measures along the lines set forth in Basket Three of the Helsinki Final Act and subsequent documents of the CSCE were considered particularly important. The *Arbeitsgemeinschaften* can be seen as institutional frameworks to implement this variant of *Mitteleuropa* on the level of "low politics."

In the FRG, the discussion took a different turn. Leftist groups and intellectuals who were worried about the nuclear threat, who felt increasingly alienated from the United States, and who wanted to overcome the arbitrary division of Europe in general, and of Germany in particular, considered their version of *Mitteleuropa* a solution to all these problems.[63] They advocated the withdrawal of the FRG from NATO and the adoption of a neutral and nonnuclear status by their country. Others did not plead for such a far-reaching new orientation of West German foreign and security policies, but merely called for a shift from the strong Western course to closer ties with the nations of Central Europe.[64]

---

62. Wendelin Ettmayer, "Plädoyer für Mitteleuropa," *Schriftenreihe Sicherheit und Demokratie* no. 9/10, Vienna (1985); Erhard Busek and Emil Brix, *Projekt Mitteleuropa*, Vienna (1986); see also the various contributions to "Mitteleuropa im Visier," *Europaeische Rundschau* 14, no. 2 (1986), pp. 99–136.

63. Jochen Löser and Ulrike Schilling, *Neutralität für Mitteleuropa. Das Ende der Blöcke*, Munich (1984).

64. Karl Schlögel, *Die Mitte liegt ostwärts. Die Deutschen, der verlorene Osten und Mitteleuropa*, Berlin (1986).

Some advocates of *Mitteleuropa* in other countries registered these German aspirations with misgivings. They recalled the "classical" German notion of *Mitteleuropa* developed by Friedrich Naumann and others — a euphemistic cloak for German hegemony (and by the German-speaking population of the disintegrating Habsburg Empire) over the peoples of eastern and southeastern Europe to be established after World War I.[65]

Therefore, prominent intellectuals from the eastern half of Europe, like the Polish Nobel Prize winner Czeslaw Milosz, the Czech novelist Milan Kundera, or the Hungarian writer György Konrád, tended to exclude Germany from their Middle European concepts. Similar views were held in Austria by some of the strongest supporters of the *Mitteleuropa* option, such as Erhard Busek, former deputy mayor of the city of Vienna and currently vice-chancellor and federal minister of science and research,[66] and former ambassador Hans Thalberg, who headed the Austrian Institute for International Affairs from 1983 to 1988.[67]

True enough, all those designs often met with strong objections in Austria and elsewhere. The principal points of criticism regarding the Austrian variants of a Middle or Central European revival were summarized by ÖVP member of Parliament Andreas Khol, director of the Political Academy of his party and professor of public law at the University of Vienna.[68] He warned against the use of a term fraught with a negative historic legacy. Khol felt Austria should refrain from unnecessarily antagonizing the Great Powers and Germany by putting that label on its policy of seeking and improving good-neighborly relations with the countries of the Danubian region. Instead, he urged Austria simply to continue its pragmatic *Ostpolitik*, which had already been initiated in the second half of the 1960s, earlier than its more widely publicized West German counterpart. Khol also emphasized that, by no means, must Austrian foreign policy be distracted by Central European ambitions from the need to participate in West European integration to the fullest extent possible.

---

65. Peter Theiner, " 'Mitteleuropa'-Pläne im Wilhelminischen Deutschland," in Helmut Berding (ed.), *Wirtschaftliche und politische Integration in Europa im 19. und 20. Jahrhundert*, Göttingen (1984), pp. 128–148.

66. Busek and Brix, *Projekt Mitteleuropa*, pp. 42–57.

67. According to Thalberg, Austria, Hungary, and Yugoslavia are to be the core countries of *Mitteleuropa*; whereas he sees no place in it for Germany, he would like to see Switzerland included as an important bridge to Western Europe. Hans Thalberg, "Zentraleuropa: Die Kunst des Möglichen. Eine Gedankenskizze," *Europaeische Rundschau* 14, no. 1 (1986), pp. 3–8.

68. Andreas Khol, "Mitteleuropa – Gefahren eines politischen Begriffes," *Österreichisches Jahrbuch für Politik* '86 (1987), pp. 137–143.

As a result of the fundamental transformation processes in Eastern Europe and the dismantling of the iron curtain, the original modest objectives of Central European cooperation have, to a large extent, been overtaken by events. The initiative for quadrilateral cooperation launched by Austria, Hungary, Italy, and Yugoslavia in November 1989 should be viewed against the background of new opportunities; they were joined by Czecho-Slovakia in May 1990 and Poland in 1991 and came to form the Pentagonal and later the Hexagonal Initiative.[69] In 1992, Bosnia-Herzegovina, Croatia, and Slovenia were admitted; the name of the cooperation scheme was changed to Central European Initiative. This time, not only border provinces but entire countries are involved. Initially, working groups were established on the level of civil servants and other experts in order to identify concrete possibilities for joint action in the fields of transport, environment, culture, education and youth exchange, telecommunications and information, and small- and medium-size enterprises. In the meantime, scientific and technological research, as well as tourism and migration, have been added as fields for cooperation. The first phase of the Pentagonal Initiative culminated in a summit of the prime ministers and foreign ministers in Venice from 31 July to 1 August 1990. On this occasion, the five heads of government adopted a policy document and a message to the other thirty states participating in the CSCE process, as well as a program of work for 1990–1992.

Projects already agreed on include the improvement of four road and six railway corridors linking member countries, the establishment of an environmental data center, the launching of a magazine of the Initiative, as well as cooperation between universities and news agencies.

Moreover, the Initiative spilled over from concrete schemes in various areas of low politics into high politics. At the Copenhagen Meeting of the CSCE Conference on the Human Dimension in June 1990, the five member countries submitted a joint proposal on minority problems to which they attached understandable importance; they also drafted a concluding document together. To some extent, for Austria the Initiative was thus beginning to replace the N+Ns as caucusing group.[70] Along similar lines, it was agreed

---

69. Gianni de Michelis, "Stability and Integration in Mitteleuropa," *The NATO Review* 38, no. 3 (1990), pp. 8–13; Ernst Sucharipa, "Die Pentagonale," *Europaeische Rundschau* 18, no. 3 (1990), pp. 25–34; see also Jacques Rupnik, "Central Europe or Mitteleuropa?" *Daedalus* 119, no. 1 (1990), pp. 249–278; Hanspeter Neuhold, *The Pentagonal/Hexagonal Experiment: New Forms of Cooperation in a Changing Europe*, Vienna (1991).

70. The group consists of Austria, Cyprus, Finland, Liechtenstein, Malta, San Marino, Sweden, Switzerland, and Yugoslavia; see Hanspeter Neuhold (ed.), *CSCE: N+N Perspectives: The Process of the Conference on Security and Co-oper-*

at the Venice summit conference to exchange views regularly on political matters and to take joint initiatives "within the latitude permitted by the international obligations of each member state in this respect."

On the institutional level, the Initiative is characterized by informality and flexibility; it does not yet have a permanent secretariat. In each field, one member acts as coordinator, whereas overall coordination rotates on an annual basis.

In terms of underlying political concepts, the members are motivated by evident common interests but also by somewhat divergent objectives. It makes sense to build a unified Europe from below and to preserve one of Europe's main assets, its diversity, by an emphasis on regionalism. There also exists an obvious need to fill the power vacuum left by the withdrawal of the Soviet Union from Central Europe and to jointly work toward stability in this region. The priority accorded by the Initiative to minority issues has to be seen in this light. In addition to the advantages of economic cooperation, the former "socialist" member countries hope to derive support for their domestic reforms and for their opening to the West from the Initiative. Italy in particular is sometimes supposed to regard the (former) *"Pentagonale/Esagonale"* as a counterweight under its leadership against a united Germany, although this orientation is usually denied or at least downplayed by officials.[71] For Austria, the Initiative constitutes an updated multilateral variant of its traditional policy of goodneighborliness and its general *Ostpolitik.*

However interesting the new cooperation scheme may be, its limits ought to be obvious. Because the main goal of the former "socialist" countries is also association with and an ultimate membership in the EC, Central European economic cooperation is, at best, an intermediate step. For Austria, this regional strategy is certainly not a substitute for full participation in West European integration. Useful results no doubt can be achieved in the current (and perhaps additional) areas of cooperation. Many problems faced by Austria and the other members, however, have a dimension transcending the framework of a small group of neighboring small or medium-sized powers. It is also doubtful whether this scheme for regional cooperation in sectors that are undoubtedly important for the peoples concerned, but that are of secondary overall political significance, is apt to establish even a limited counterbalance against German preponderance in Central and East Central Europe; some would also doubt whether such a course, which may lead to conflict, is desirable within the framework of a genuinely new European architecture.

ation in Europe from the Viewpoint of the Neutral and Non-Aligned Participating States, Vienna (1987).

71. For instance by Austrian Foreign Minister Alois Mock; *Die Presse,* 1 August 1990.

Moreover, the tragic events in former Yugoslavia have dealt a blow to the hopes once staked on the Initiative.

Conclusion

The Great Power deal of 1955 seems to have cut the Gordian knot of the Austrian question very successfully. Austria's new international identity as a small, ideologically Western, and militarily neutral state was quickly approved and internalized by the Austrian people. "The state that nobody wanted," as Austria was referred to in the interwar period, has indeed become the state behind which all Austrians have rallied. This is all the more remarkable because the solution agreed on in 1955 entailed a fundamentally new position for Austria in its international affairs. Yet, as early as 1972, an Austrian opinion poll revealed that 90 percent of those interviewed felt that the benefits of their country's permanent neutrality outweighed the drawbacks.[72]

One of the cornerstones of the "Austrian deal" was the regulation of Austria's future relations with Germany. After the mutual attempts at predominance and the disastrous moves toward integration, the clear-cut legal and political separation of Austria from Germany appears to provide a workable solution. Against the historic background, it is also surprising how rapidly the majority of Austrians developed the feeling of forming a nation of their own. West German President von Weizsäcker was right in pointing out during his state visit to Austria in 1986 that no identity problems existed between the two states and peoples.[73] In the same vein, his Austrian counterpart, Kirchschläger, stated on the same occasion that Austro-German relations were not overshadowed by complexes any more. He added that Austrians openly acknowledged their manifold historic and cultural links with the Germans as well as the differences that separated the two nations.[74]

The Anschluß prohibition and the partially divergent foreign policy orientations have indeed not prevented but rather have set the stage for a normal, relaxed, good-neighborly relationship between Austria and the FRG. Austria, at least until recently, has acted with a degree of self-confidence and success in world affairs that may have filled some Germans with envy.

---

72. Hanspeter Neuhold and Franz Wagner, "Das Neutralitätsbewußtsein des Österreichers," *Österreichische Zeitschrift für Außenpolitik* 13 (1973), pp. 67–94.

73. Österreichisches Jahrbuch für Internationale Politik 1986 (1987), p. 240.

74. Ibidem, p. 239.

However, there is no reason for complacency, especially not on the Austrian side. Austria's economic and cultural dependence on the Federal Republic ought to be watched closely and should not be allowed to increase substantially. Moreover, although this is the most banal truism of all, nevertheless, it is a momentous fact of life, to be ignored only at one's own peril, that even solutions envisaged as permanent do not last indefinitely. The political, military, and economic situation in Europe is more in flux today than it has been for a long time. In addition to the application for EC membership, Austria may sooner or later have to make other difficult decisions; on many of them the German factor will probably have a major direct or indirect impact.

7

The Political Dimension of Canadian-U.S. Relations

David Leyton-Brown

Canada and the United States form an unequal partnership with both unique and comparable features. Although many Canadians may be convinced that their situation is without parallel, they may find that a comparative examination of other unequal partnerships helps them better to understand their own.

This chapter seeks to analyze the political dimension of the Canadian-U.S. unequal partnership in ways that invite and enable comparison with the Austrian-FRG relationship. Though some of the observations may seem trite and obvious to Canadian analysts, it is hoped that they will be refreshingly new and relevant to European readers.

The chapter will first examine several major characteristics of the Canadian-U.S. relationship and then address the management of the relationship, the origins of inevitable problems on the bilateral agenda, the consistent categories of issues to be managed, and recent patterns of management style. Finally I will assess the century-long Canadian ambivalence concerning relations with the United States. Since the formation of their country, Canadians have been torn between the desire for the benefits (primarily economic) of closer relations with the United States and the fear that a closer relationship could threaten the loss of Canadian policy autonomy, cultural identity, and even political independence. After several abortive attempts to enter into a closer economic relationship with the United States, all of which have failed because of a fear of the anticipated political, social, and cultural (as well as economic) effects, the current Canadian government has negotiated and is now implementing a Canadian-U.S. FTA. The receptivity of the Canadian public to this initiative and their reaction to the short-term and eventual long-term results, whatever they may be, can only be understood in terms of this inescapable ambivalence.

Characteristics of the Relationship

Distinctive aspects of the Canadian-U.S. relationship fall in four areas: asymmetry, similarity, interdependence, and alliance.

Asymmetry

As might be expected given this book's theme of unequal partners, the predominant feature of the Canadian-U.S. relationship is the asymmetry between the two countries. Geographically the two countries are of comparable size (with Canada actually slightly bigger), but by virtually every other measure the United States is much the larger. The U.S. population is approximately ten times Canada's 25 million, and despite Canada's vastness, over three-quarters of the Canadian population lives within 100 miles of the U.S. border. (This makes Canada the demographic equivalent of Chile — 3,500 miles long and only 200 miles wide.) Though Canada's economy is one of the ten largest in the world and Canada is a member of the Group of Seven industrialized economies whose leaders meet annually in the economic summit, the U.S. GNP of almost US$ 4 trillion is more than ten times Canada's approximately US$ 300 billion.

The United States is an economic, military, and political superpower with worldwide responsibilities and interests, among which Canada has traditionally ranked low. It is preoccupied with alliance leadership, East-West relations, and political-strategic considerations, as well as with a principal determination of the norms of the international economic system. Its relationship with the Soviet Union, the rival superpower, was — at least until the latter's dissolution — the most important element in its foreign policy. Canada, though of considerable influence in world affairs, is not involved at the same level of responsibility and power as the United States. Its highest foreign policy priority is the management of its relationship with the United States.

Asymmetry is also characteristic of the attention and information in each country concerning the other. Canadians care more about the United States and are better informed about it than are Americans about Canada, though they can often be misinformed as well.

Similarity

There are enormous similarities between Canada and the United States, but the two countries are not identical. Both emerged, though in different ways, from the British colonial tradition. As a result of this common historical heritage, they share similar political values and structures. Both countries are representative democracies with similar legal systems. Nevertheless, concentration on the similarities can mask the existence and importance of differences in the political structures and processes.[1]

Social and cultural similarities are also pronounced. Apart from the francophone population of Canada, the majority of Canadians speak and read the same language as Americans. Citizens of both countries tend to watch the same films and television programs, read the same books and magazines, and cheer for teams in the same professional sports leagues. Because of Canada's small population and geographical proximity to the United States, as well as the availability and attractiveness of U.S. culture and entertainment, Canadian governments have been concerned to maintain and develop a distinctive Canadian cultural identity in the face of the danger of cultural homogenization.

Interdependence

The relationship between Canada and the United States continues to be marked by high and complex interdependence.[2] The two countries share the world's largest two-way trade flow, amounting in 1988 to more than Cdn\$ 185 billion (or US\$ 155 billion).[3] Each is the other's largest trading partner, with Canada selling 78 percent of its exports to and buying 70 percent of its imports from the United States, while the United States sends 22 percent of its exports to and receives 19 percent of its imports from Canada. Canada and the United States are also each other's foremost destination of foreign investment, with over US\$ 46 billion of U.S. direct investment in Canada and US\$ 26 billion of Canadian direct investment in the United States at the end

1. David Leyton-Brown, "The Domestic Policy-Making Process in the United States," in D.H. Flaherty and W.R. McKercher (eds.), *Southern Exposure: Canadian Perspectives on the United States,* Toronto (1986), pp. 34–41.

2. Robert O. Keohane and Joseph S. Nye, *Power and Interdependence,* Boston (1973).

3. External Affairs and International Trade Canada, *Canada's Merchandise Trade,* 19 September 1989.

of 1985.[4] These extensive economic transactions are complemented by a panoply of cultural flows, tourism and immigration, joint environmental issues, and the like. This heavy volume of interactions does not in itself constitute interdependence, but simply enables it to exist. Though the term interdependence is given different definitions or connotations by different analysts, its essence is a policy relationship with two features:

1. (Domestic) policy actions by one government inevitably have effects in the other country, whether intended or not.
2. One government or other on many issues is unable to achieve its (domestic) policy objectives unilaterally without the cooperation of the other.

Because of the asymmetry in the relationship, the U.S. impact on Canada is normally greater than the reverse, as is the constraint on Canadian rather than U.S. policy action, but the phenomenon of interdependence truly flows in both directions.

Charles Doran has criticized the characterization of the Canadian-U.S. relationship as interdependent. He disagrees, however, not with the concept itself but with some of the assumptions and implications commonly attached to the term, such as presumptions of cooperation rather than conflict, equality of national capability, structural necessity, the absence of the use of power, and irreversibility.[5] His preferred concept of "intervulnerability," involving the cost to partners of one's own domestic policy choices, corresponds quite closely to the definition of interdependence offered here. Whatever the label, the reality of Canadian-U.S. relations is that both governments affect and are affected by the other and are dependent on the other's actions for the attainment of some policy objectives.

Alliance

Canada's defense policy is an alliance policy. Canada lacks the population and resources to defend its vast territory against all potential threats or to secure international peace alone. What is more, as Canada's 1987 white paper on defense reaffirms, Canada is not neutral between East and West,

---

4. United States Information Service, *The United States and Canada: General Information on Bilateral Affairs,* Ottawa (1987), pp. 1–3.

5. Charles F. Doran, *Forgotten Partnership: U.S.-Canadian Relations Today,* Toronto (1984), pp. 48–53.

but aligns its values and interests with the other countries of the Western Alliance.[6]

Canada's closest ally in functional as well as geographical terms is the United States. Since the end of World War II, Canada's military cooperation has shifted focus from the traditional British connection to an institutionalized relationship with the United States. As partners in the multilateral NATO and in bilateral arrangements such as the Permanent Joint Board on Defense (PJBD) and the North American Aerospace Defense Command (NORAD), Canada and the United States jointly pursue continental defense and participate in the wider alliance.

There is little immediate military threat against Canada. The only country that could realistically mount an effective invasion of Canadian territory is the United States itself. Canada's defense policy of alliance membership is aimed at preventing the outbreak of a nuclear confrontation between the superpowers or a global conflict in which the prospect of direct attack on Canada could become a reality. In that light, Canada's alliance membership has been both a military priority, to ensure Canadian security, and a political convenience, to gain access to alliance councils where Canadian military, arms control, economic, and political objectives can be furthered. Membership in the multilateral alliance also conforms to a common Canadian policy of preferring to interact with the United States in a multilateral forum, buffered by other partners of comparable size, rather than dealing with the United States one-on-one, where the asymmetry of size and power could allow the United States to act in more arbitrary fashion.

There is, however, an interesting irony in Canada's alliance relationship with the United States. On the one hand, the United States is Canada's most important ally, on whom the security of NATO, North America, and Canada itself depends. On the other hand, the greatest threat to Canada's survival as a distinct and independent entity may also come from the United States. This threat is most certainly not a military one. Canadians and Americans alike are justifiably proud of the world's longest undefended border. Some Canadians, however, consider that the United States poses a threat to the autonomy of the Canadian economy, given the level of U.S. investment in Canada and the concentration of Canadian trade with the United States. Other Canadians fear the submergence of a distinctive Canadian identity in an irresistible tide of American culture.

---

6. Department of National Defense, *Challenge and Commitment: A Defense Policy for Canada*, Ottawa (1987), p. 5.

Management of the Relationship

Management of the relationship with the United States is Canada's highest foreign policy priority. Management is necessary because of the recurrent and inevitable emergence of problems to be managed. These problems in turn result from developments in the international environment, different political philosophies and cultures in the two countries, different political systems, and the adoption of dissimilar policies on similar issues. The international environment thrusts problems on the Canadian-U.S. agenda because of the changing structure of the international system and because of the different and changing international roles played by the two countries and hence the different interests and perspectives they address. The United States is a military, economic, and political superpower, whose interests are affected by developments in any part of the world. Canada, whether described as a middle power,[7] a foremost nation,[8] a regional power without a region,[9] or a principal power,[10] is not a superpower, though in many ways its power is growing and it responds to developments abroad in a less personalized fashion.

Also, many bilateral problems between Canada and the United States stem from different national responses to common problems in the changing international environment.[11] Structural changes in the international division of labor and intervention by other governments to alter trading patterns through protectionism or export subsidization compel the Canadian and U.S. governments to act on behalf of their domestic industries. Although some Canadian-U.S. disputes arise from actions by one of the two governments aimed at the other, more result from a "sideswipe" phenomenon in which Canada finds itself negatively affected by U.S. actions aimed at other trading partners such as Japan or the EC.

Despite all the cultural similarities and common history, Canada and the United States are constructed on some different philosophical assumptions

7. John W. Holmes, *The Better Part of Valour: Essays on Canadian Diplomacy*, Toronto (1970).

8. Norman Hillmer and Garth Stevenson, *Foremost Nation: Canadian Foreign Policy and a Changing World*, Toronto (1977).

9. Attributed to Dean Acheson.

10. David B. Dewitt and John J. Kirton, *Canada as a Principal Power*, Toronto (1983).

11. David Leyton-Brown and John Gerard Ruggie, "The North American Political Economy in the Global Context: an Analytical Framework," *International Journal* 42 (Winter 1986–1987), pp. 3–24.

and have in some ways developed along different lines. There is a revealing contrast between the U.S. political ideal of "life, liberty, and the pursuit of happiness," and the Canadian constitutional goal of "peace, order, and good government." Most importantly, the two societies have different conceptions of the appropriate role of government in the economy. In the United States, government intervention has traditionally been accepted only for the purpose of creating the opportunity for wider private participation in the free market. Because of Canada's enormous transportation distances and scattered population, the Canadian government has been expected to meet social and economic objectives not realizable by the free market system. These different philosophical positions can be responsible for incompatibility of motives of the two governments and for exacerbation of tensions, as occurred over Canada's National Energy Program in the early 1980s.[12]

Differences in the political systems of the two countries can complicate the handling of bilateral issues. The two domestic political systems respond to different pressures and work through different processes. A parliamentary government with standards of cabinet solidarity and secrecy functions very differently than a presidential system with separation of powers and checks and balances between branches.

Each government finds its freedom of maneuver in bilateral relations constrained by another domestic political actor — Congress in the United States and provincial governments in Canada. Canada finds the increasing role of Congress on many issues of Canadian-U.S. relations to be a particular difficulty. This can arise when the U.S. Constitution assigns a specific role to Congress, such as in the treaty ratification process. Canada, like other foreign countries, can be faced with the need for what amounts to a second round of negotiations with Congress over possible amendments to a proposed agreement, after a deal has already been struck with administration negotiators (as happened with the Fisheries and Maritime Boundaries Treaties of 1979). It can also arise when matters on the domestic political agenda, such as clean air legislation, affect issues in Canadian-U.S. relations, such as acid rain.

Regularly scheduled elections in the United States, in contrast to Canada's irregular elections called at the pleasure of the government (within a constitutionally specified maximum time), impose deadlines and domestic pressures on bilateral interactions.

The combination of different political philosophies and different political systems, along with particular interests and immediate objectives, inevitably

---

12. David Leyton-Brown, *Weathering the Storm: Canadian-U.S. Relations, 1980–1983*, Toronto (1985), pp. 23–42; Stephen Clarkson, *Canada and the Reagan Challenge*, Toronto (1982), pp. 6–82.

means that some of the two federal, ten provincial, and fifty state governments will adopt dissimilar policy responses to similar problems. Even when
the governments involved are pursuing compatible or identical objectives,
lack of synchronization of policy changes is an inevitable source of friction.

There is a remarkable consistency in the agenda of bilateral issues that
have arisen between Canada and the United States over the decades.
Although the specific issues, of course, are always changing, they fall in constant categories. It is instructive to compare the "questions of past and future
friction" enumerated in the famous memorandum on relations between
Canada and the United States written from the Canadian legation in Washington by Hume Wrong in 1927[13] with the agendas of issues dealt with by
Prime Minister Mulroney and President Reagan at their summit meetings.
With very few timebound exceptions (such as liquor smuggling from Canada
during Prohibition in the United States), the categories are still the ones in
which frictions must be managed sixty years later. Wrong's questions
included: tariff policies, conservation of Canadian natural resources, boundaries (with particular reference to the Arctic and to territorial waters), international waterways (including the export of power), smuggling, continental
air routes, law enforcement, immigration, defense issues, and radio broadcasting. Today's major issues of trade and investment, energy relations, Arctic sovereignty, defense cooperation, environmental protection, and cultural
sovereignty can all be related to that list.

Through the years, there have been identifiably different patterns in the
management of the relationship. The post-World War II era could be
described as having evolved from personalized diplomacy in the context of a
"special relationship," through a period of ad hoc management of issues, to
the recent experience of "semi-institutionalized consultation."[14] The special
relationship involved quiet diplomacy, institutionalization of economic and
defense cooperation, and exemptions for Canada from U.S. policies toward
other countries. It was effectively terminated by the Nixon shocks of August
1971 and was explicitly declared to have ended a year later in President
Nixon's address to Canada's Parliament, which called for a new, mature
relationship between equals. The period of ad hoc issue management
foundered during the tensions of the early 1980s and gave way to an effective
pattern of regularized consultations at the head of government, ministerial,
and official levels.

---

13. Hume Wrong, "The Canada-United States Relationship 1927/1951," *International Journal* 31 (Summer 1976), pp. 532–537.

14. Joseph T. Jockel, "The Canada-United States relationship after the third round:
the emergence of semi-institutionalized management," *International Journal* 40
(Autumn 1985), pp. 689–715.

A Break with the Past?

Canada has always been ambivalent about its relations with the United States. From the very beginning, Canadians have recognized the existence of the economic interdependence with the United States and have sought the economic benefits of closer relations with the United States. On the one hand, economic transactions would flow more naturally north-south than east-west across great distances and geographical barriers. Secure access to the U.S. market, ten times as large as that of Canada, would promise benefits of economies of scale and specialization. On the other hand, Canadians have worried about the loss of Canadian distinctiveness, autonomy, and even independence that might result and so have been reluctant to move too close.

Since the U.S. abrogation of the 1854 Reciprocity Treaty in 1866, the history of Canadian-U.S. relations has been a succession of cautious moves toward free trade and more open economic relations, followed by retreat from the brink before the action was finally taken.[15] A draft treaty on free trade in a wide range of manufactured goods was not approved for ratification by the U.S. Senate in 1874. Since then, the reluctance has been on the Canadian side.

In 1911, a free trade treaty was negotiated, but the Canadian government of Sir Wilfred Laurier was defeated in an election fought on the issue before it could be implemented. In 1947–1948, secret talks on free trade were held and the detailed framework of an agreement was drawn up, but Prime Minister Mackenzie King decided not to proceed. In the ensuing period, trade between Canada and the United States has been progressively liberalized through successive rounds of multilateral trade negotiations held under the GATT. Sectoral trade agreements of a variety of kinds have been developed to cover such matters as automobiles, agricultural machinery, and defense equipment. An initiative to pursue other sectoral trade agreements was undertaken by the government of Prime Minister Trudeau in 1983.

Canada's relationship with the United States was systematically reviewed in the early 1970s in the context of the overall foreign policy review con-

---

15. J.L. Granatstein, "Free Trade Between Canada and the United States: The Issue That Will Not Go Away," in Denis Stairs and Gilbert Winham (eds.), *The Politics of Canada's Economic Relationship with the United States,* Toronto (1985), pp. 11–54; Richard G. Lipsey, "Canada and the United States: The Economic Dimension," in Charles F. Doran and John H. Sigler (eds.), *Canada and the United States: Enduring Friendship, Persistent Stress,* Englewood Cliffs (1985), pp. 69–108; Simon Riesman, "The Issue of Free Trade," in E.R. Fried and P.H. Trezise (eds.), *U.S.-Canadian Economic Relations: Next Steps?,* Washington, D.C. (1984), pp. 35–51.

ducted by the newly elected Trudeau government. The statement on policy toward the United States did not appear as a part of the foreign policy white paper, *Foreign Policy For Canadians*. Rather it appeared as a special issue of the government-sponsored magazine, *International Perspectives*,[16] in the aftermath of the Nixon shocks of August 1971, which imposed a tariff surcharge on imports from Canada and other countries without prior consultation or Canadian exemption. This policy review identified three options that Canada might pursue in its relations with the United States and which came to be known imaginatively as the first option, the second option, and the third option. Each option offered a different response to the Canadian ambivalence mentioned above.

The first option involved "maintaining more or less the present pattern of our economic and political relationship with the United States with a minimum of policy change."[17] This meant the maintenance of the general thrust of industrial and multilateral trade policies and the ad hoc management of Canadian-U.S. issues within the context of a special relationship. This option was rejected because, though it did not foreclose other options, it was essentially reactive and because it ignored the underlying continental pull and so could have resulted in Canada being drawn more closely into the U.S. orbit.

The second option was to move deliberately toward closer integration with the United States over a range of possible closer economic ties, including sectoral arrangements, free trade, or a customs union.[18] This option would be aimed explicitly at the attainment of economic benefits from closer relations. It too was rejected, however. It was felt that such a move would be irreversible for Canada, but not for the United States. More importantly, it was felt that this option would involve an unacceptable cost to Canadian identity because there would be inevitable pressures to move toward political union in order to protect Canadian interests.

The third option was to pursue a comprehensive long-term strategy to develop and strengthen the Canadian economy and other aspects of its national life and, in the process, to reduce the present Canadian vulnerability to external factors, including, in particular, the impact of the United States.[19] This option certainly included a dimension of trade diversification, but it went far beyond that. It involved a complex of domestic and foreign policies to develop a balanced and efficient economy and a more confident sense of

---

16. Department of External Affairs, "Canada-U.S. Relations: Options for the Future," *International Perspectives* (Autumn 1972).

17. Ibidem, p. 13.

18. Ibidem, pp. 14 f.

19. Ibidem, p. 17.

national identity. As such, it encompassed trade policy, industrial policy, investment policy, energy policy, cultural policy, and the like. This option was the one adopted, at least nominally, by the Canadian government of the day. Attempts to implement it resulted in considerable tension between Canada and the United States in the early 1980s.[20]

Many prominent policy initiatives of the 1970s and early 1980s can be seen as consistent with the third option. The Foreign Investment Review Agency to screen incoming foreign investment to ensure significant economic benefit to Canada, the National Energy Program to capture the revenues resulting from rising oil prices and Canadianize the oil and gas industry, and cultural policy initiatives to ensure the existence of financially viable broadcasters and publishers to disseminate Canadian cultural products, all were measures to strengthen the Canadian economy and identity and to reduce Canadian vulnerability to external factors. The third option, however, was never wholeheartedly and consistently pursued by the entire cabinet. The hoped-for comprehensive strategy was never designed or adopted; instead a disconnected series of individual policies was put in place. In practice, the Canadian government continued to follow the first option of ad hoc management and business as usual, while giving lip service and only occasional substance to the third option. And all the while, the business community continued to increase the proportion of Canada's economic dealings with the United States, swamping any efforts at trade diversification in a tide of continental trade concentration.

The Mulroney government embarked on an effort to negotiate a comprehensive FTA with the United States, which was essentially a return to the second option, rejected earlier. Prime Minister Mulroney gambled his own political future and that of Canada and its relationship with the United States on the conviction that closer personal, official, and economic relations with the United States would yield economic and other benefits for Canada, without threat to Canada's identity or interests.[21]

The reason for his different calculation regarding the costs and benefits of closer economic relations with the United States than in 1972 can be found in a different assessment of the strength of Canada's identity. A consistent theme in the speeches of Prime Minister Mulroney and his cabinet ministers during their first term of office was confidence in Canada — a belief that Canada had matured economically, politically, and socially to such an extent that its identity and independence would not be jeopardized by

20. Clarkson, *Canada and the Reagan Challenge;* Leyton-Brown, *Weathering the Storm.*

21. David Leyton-Brown, "The Mulroney Gamble," *International Perspectives* (September/October 1985), pp. 27–30.

closer relations with the United States. By this calculation, the traditional Canadian ambivalence could be resolved by pursuing the benefits without fear of the costs, since a more prosperous Canada would be more independent and influential than a poorer one.

Judging whether the FTA is a fundamental breakpoint in Canada's relationship with the United States or a logical progression in the conduct of those relations depends on whether one poses the question in political or economic terms. For over a century, Canada's foreign policy has been designed to seek autonomy from the dominant partner — first Britain and then more recently the United States. Multilateral rather than bilateral arrangements have been preferred because they diluted the bilateral asymmetry and buffered the potential bilateral dominance. In these political terms, the FTA is a departure, marking not an attempt to escape from the U.S. orbit, but an embracing of that bilateral relationship. It is a turning point that creates new bilateral mechanisms and from which all aspects of the relationship, whether directly and explicitly covered by the agreement or not, will be conducted in a different context.

In economic terms, however, the FTA appears much more consistent with the long-term thrust of Canadian policy. Again for over a century, Canadian commercial policy has been directed to securing favorable access to markets. Postwar multilateral trade negotiations were a means to that end but so were bilateral agreements with the United States, such as the Defense Production Sharing Agreements and the Canadian-U.S. Automotive Agreement. Even the major GATT rounds of multilateral trade negotiations had as their main importance for Canada the reduction of barriers to bilateral Canadian-U.S. trade. Inevitably the cornerstone of Canadian trade policy is an agreement (bilateral or multilateral) with the country with which Canada conducts over 75 percent of its trade and which represents by far its largest and most important market. As market forces led to more and more trade concentration with the United States, the logic of a bilateral trade agreement became more compelling to the Canadian government, though more frightening to some other Canadians.

Despite the fears of some vocal critics of the FTA, Canada's distinctive social programs and cultural policies were not on the negotiating table and were not bargained away. There may be reason to wonder, however, if there could be long-term pressures under free trade to harmonize Canadian policies (such as corporate taxes or regulatory controls) with those in the United States, to minimize any incentive for industry to locate in the United States rather than in Canada, with equal access to the entire North American market.[22] Advocates of free trade argue that these harmonization pressures were increasingly evident already and could better be moderated in a negotiated and structured relationship.

The FTA was the principal issue in the November 1988 election. The Mulroney government was reelected with a majority of seats in the House of Commons (thus making possible the implementation of the agreement beginning in 1989) but without a majority of the popular vote. Supporters of the FTA applauded its anticipated economic benefits, emphasizing its success in insulating Canada from U.S. protectionism and giving Canada a voice in future negotiations concerning subsidies and trade remedies, its opportunity for rationalization and increased international competitiveness, and its secure and enhanced access to the U.S. market for exports and the U.S. economy for investment.

Opponents made three different arguments. Some argued that while free trade was desirable, the FTA itself was a bad deal in which Canada had given up too much and received too little in return. Others were simply opposed to this or any other free trade treaty, preferring instead some combination of managed trade and industrial policy. A third group saw the FTA as a threat to Canadian autonomy and independence. They characterized it as giving the United States a voice or a veto over future Canadian policy, thus endangering Canadian social and regional development programs, as imposing pressures for increased harmonization of policies, thus making Canada more and more like the United States, and as leading to the erosion of Canada's cultural identity.

The country was deeply divided over the free trade issue, and that division will continue at least into the next election as implementation proceeds. The ultimate judgement of the Canadian public will not rest solely on the criterion of economic costs and benefits. A fundamental assessment will concern whether or not the assumptions underlying the Mulroney gamble were correct. Even if economic benefits are evident, Canadians will want reassurance that their identity and independence have not suffered in consequence, in the short or long term. Over a century of Canadian ambivalence ensures that Canadians will be highly sensitive to any appearance of restricted autonomy or distinctiveness. These questions will continue to be asked long after the immediate effects of the FTA are but a memory.

The FTA will shape the course of Canadian-U.S. relations for many years to come. Irreversible changes will result for the Canadian economy — for the better, in the minds of FTA supporters, but potentially for the worse, in the minds of opponents. Even more important, though, will be the impact on

22. Denis Stairs, "Free Trade: Another View," *International Perspectives* (May/June 1987), pp. 3–8.

political relations with the United States. External perceptions of Canada as closely tied to the United States and internal expectations of opportunities and constraints resulting from this more institutionalized closer relationship will provide a context in which all aspects of the bilateral relationship will be affected.

If the FTA fails, objectively or subjectively, and is abrogated as was the Reciprocity Treaty in 1866, its negotiation, implementation, and termination could not be ignored, and no future Canadian government would be likely to embark again on the perilous journey toward closer economic relations, despite the underlying pressures of continental and international markets. If it succeeds, then Canada and its relationship with the United States will never be the same again. The Canadian preoccupation will shift from whether closer relations with the United States *would be* a good idea to whether they *have been* and to how to preserve autonomy and distinctiveness in the context of economic association with an unequal partner. Regardless of the outcome and the public evaluation of it, Canada will continue to find itself in the position of smaller partner in an unequal partnership, which matters more to the smaller than to the larger partner.

PART FOUR

Economic Relations

8

The Impact of the Economy of the FRG on the Economy of Austria*

Georg Winckler

Since the early 1950s, it is striking how closely the path of Austria's economy has followed West German economic development. Many Austrian and West German macroeconomic variables exhibit the same time pattern. Yet it is interesting to note that these comovements of variables cannot be explained by direct economic linkages between the two countries with respect to the flows of goods or capital. Hence, the comovements of real and financial variables seem to be more the result of Austria's policy orientation toward the FRG. This Austrian policy orientation, however, is not reflected in the political programs of its parties but rather is the outcome of a pragmatic approach.

Two statistical accounts should illustrate how closely Austria's macroeconomy has followed economic development in the FRG with respect to real aggregates and monetary variables.

The Statistical Record, Real Aggregates

Real GNP

An important and, for our analysis, representative aggregate figure is the real growth rate of GNP. In order to evaluate how closely Austria followed

*   I thank Wolfgang Müller, Peter Rosner, and D. Mark Schultz for comments on this chapter.

the path of West German real GNP, Belgium's and Denmark's economies are used for comparisons. Both countries are almost equal in economic size to Austria (Belgium is a little bigger, Denmark a little smaller than Austria); both are neighbors of the FRG as well.

Looking at the annual growth rates of real GNP from 1955 to 1985, the following correlations are found (see Table 8.1).

TABLE 8.1

Correlation Coefficients of Annual Growth Rates of Real GNP in the FRG, Austria, Belgium, and Denmark, 1955–1985

	Austria	Belgium	Denmark
FRG (lag 0)	+0.81	+0.61	+0.44
FRG (lag 1)	+0.58	+0.28	– 0.00
FRG (lag 2)	+0.28	+0.08	– 0.07

Source: International Monetary Fund, *International Financial Statistics,* monthly publication (various issues)

In this table, lagged variables, that is variables pertaining to previous time periods, are used to take account of possible delays in the effect of West German real growth rates on the neighboring small economies. As one can see, Austria's real growth rates correlate much more strongly with the FRG's than those of Belgium or Denmark.

This phenomenon is striking because for about half of the period being considered (1957–1972) Austria was subject to the EC's trade-diverting effects, but not so Belgium. What makes the strong correlation even more remarkable is that after 1973, when Austria's free trade treaties with the EEC and the ECSC came into effect, the correlation coefficients for Austria decrease in contrast to those of Belgium and Denmark (see Table 8.2).

This decrease contradicts what one would expect because important trade-creating effects have increased Austria's export dependence on the FRG considerably since 1973 (see Table 8.4). For the most part, the decrease is attributable to the fact that in the 1970s Austria experienced significantly higher real growth rates than the FRG because Austria was then less dependent on the West German business cycle.[1] In contrast, the economies of

---

1.   Thus after the first oil price shock, the unemployment rate in the FRG increased considerably from 1.3 percent (1973) to 4.7 percent (1975); Austria's unemploy-

Belgium and Denmark grew more independently of the FRG in the 1950s and 1960s, yet in the 1970s they increasingly followed the FRG's cyclical pattern of economic development; however, there are differences in the 1980s due to different stabilization policies.[2]

TABLE 8.2

Correlation Matrix of Annual Growth Rates of GNP, 1973–1985 (lag 0)

	Austria	Belgium	Denmark	FRG
Austria	1			
Belgium	+0.76	1		
Denmark	+0.50	+0.47	1	
FRG	+0.75	+0.77	0.70	1

Source: International Monetary Fund, *International Financial Statistics,* monthly publication (various issues), and own calculations

Real Consumption

Polasek studied the period from 1965 to 1982 on a quarterly basis in order to estimate the causal relationship between the FRG's and Austria's real GNP and real consumption.[3] He calculated Geweke causality measures (a causality measure in the sense of Granger), and investigated the effect of stationarity transformations for the quarterly series.[4]

Causality measures indicate statistically how significantly a forecast of Austrian variables such as GNP or consumption can be improved not only by using their own history but also by including the history of FRG variables. If the statistical inclusion of the FRG data improves the forecast of Austrian

---

ment rate only rose from 1.6 percent (1973) to 2.0 percent (1975).

2. Between 1971 and 1982, the West German and Danish economies both grew by 27 percent, the Belgian economy by 30 percent, whereas Austria managed an increase of 38 percent (all in real terms).

3. Wolfgang Polasek, "Time Series Relationships between Germany and Austria for GNP and Consumption," unpublished paper (1987).

4. For practical purposes, stationarity means that the sample data have a constant mean (no trend) and a constant variance.

variables, then it can be said that the FRG variable "causes" the Austrian variable.[5]

For the fourth differential of real GNP and real consumption, which eliminates seasonal patterns within a year in the quarterly data, Polasek found that about 60 percent (of a possible 100 percent) of Austria's GNP and consumption is "caused" (in the sense of Granger) by the FRG's GNP and consumption. Only 20 percent can be attributed to feedback and to instantaneous causality. In the same study, he concluded that Austria's real consumption was more quickly influenced by West German GNP than by Austrian GNP. The correlation analysis presented in Tables 8.1 and 8.2, as well as Polasek's study, indicate that at the level of real aggregates the Austrian economy is highly influenced by the West German economy.

The Statistical Record, the Monetary Sector

A way to determine how Austrian monetary data correlate with West German data is to compare their respective inflation rates. Because only domestic sources of inflationary pressures are of interest here, the gross domestic product (GDP) deflator and not the consumer price index will be studied. The GDP deflators of Belgium and Denmark are again used for comparative purposes. Because the exchange rate system of the Bretton Woods system collapsed in March 1973, that year is used as the benchmark.

Table 8.3 clearly reveals the strengthened monetary cooperation between European central banks after 1973: The correlation coefficients of each of the three small countries increased significantly.[6] Again Austria is leading in each period.

---

5. As is well known, such causality tests require much data to be robust. Otherwise a few outliners, that is, observations strikingly far from some central value like a mean, may easily reverse the causality structure. Because at the level of real aggregates the samples are usually small – Polasek's sample consists of 72 observations only – Polasek's causality results must be interpreted with caution; see also Wolfgang Polasek and Georg Winckler, "Untersuchungen über den Zusammenhang zwischen Geldmarktsätzen in Österreich und der Bundesrepublik Deutschland," unpublished paper (1986).

6. It is interesting to note that for 1973–1985 the correlation coefficients of Belgium with Austria and Denmark are even higher than those with the FRG: For Austria and Belgium the correlation coefficient equals +0.69; for Denmark and Belgium it equals +0.77. This indicates that small open economies neighboring the same big economy and orienting their exchange rate to that economy's cur-

TABLE 8.3

Correlation Coefficients Between Inflation Rates (GDP Deflator) of Austria, Belgium, Denmark, and the FRG

| | Germany | | |
	1955–1972	1973–1985	1955–1985
Austria	+0.56	+0.85	+0.66
Belgium	+0.35	+0.63	+0.47
Denmark	+0.53	+0.79	+0.58

Source: International Monetary Fund, *International Financial Statistics,* monthly publication (various issues)

A study of the correlation between interest rates yields similar results. In this area it is difficult to set the benchmark year, however, because the interest rate linkages between European economies increased only gradually in the late 1970s. A policy of constant nominal interest rates was pursued for Austria until 1979 with the result that Austrian nominal rates fluctuated significantly less than West German rates, though probably with destabilizing effects on the Austrian business cycle.[7]

Given Austria's policy of fixing the Austrian schilling (AS)/FRG deutsche Mark (DM) exchange rate at a nearly constant level, one would expect a close interest rate linkage between the two countries' financial markets, especially between the money market rates, at least after 1979. Causality tests using daily data of the West German and the Austrian money market rates, however, turned out to have negative results: The forecasts of neither variable could be improved by using past data of the other variable.[8]

---

rency have identical problems in controlling inflation. In all three small states the inflation rate was higher than in the FRG. The correlation coefficient for Austria and Denmark equals +0.78.

7. See Georg Winckler, "Probleme der Zinspolitik in Österreich," *Wirtschaft und Gesellschaft* 5, no. 1 (1979), p. 78. The theoretical basis for the proposition of adverse effects is given by William Poole, "Optimal Choice of Monetary Policy in a Simple Stochastic Macro Model," *Quarterly Journal of Economics* 84 (May 1970), pp. 197–216 (here p. 197).

8. Wolfgang Polasek and Georg Winckler, "Untersuchungen über den Zusammenhang."

What Makes the Austrian Economy Move Along the FRG Path?

The main thesis advanced here is that the direct economic linkages between the FRG and Austria play a less significant role in moving the Austrian macroeconomy along the West German path than do the policy decisions of the Austrian government or of the social partners. Austrian economic policy, in a pragmatic way, follows West German policy decisions. Those political decisions transmit the impact of the economy of the FRG to the Austrian economy. The justification of this policy is usually need for preserving Austria's competitive position in West German markets.

This thesis is difficult to prove. Nevertheless, there are several plausible arguments. First, neither the Austrian exports to the FRG nor West German property in Austria are important enough to explain the parallel courses of the West German and Austrian macroeconomy. Second, a study of the Austrian trade unions' wage policy and of the so-called hard-currency policy of the Central Bank will demonstrate how closely Austria conforms to policy decisions of the FRG.

The Importance of Austrian Exports to the FRG

As was noted above, in 1973 when the trade-creating effects of Austria's free trade arrangements with the EEC and the ECSC came into effect (Austria's exports to FRG have since risen disproportionately[9]), the correlation between the two countries' growth rates decreased. This already indicates that Austria's export performance can hardly explain the comovements between West German and Austrian real aggregates.

The share of GDP exported to the FRG from Austria, Belgium, and Denmark is reported in Table 8.4. Belgium's share is the highest. Hence, one would expect that Belgium's real GDP exhibits a high correlation with the West German GDP. Yet its correlation coefficients are below Austria's. The Austrian share of tourism revenues in GDP from FRG sources can be esti-

---

9.   The share of exports to the Federal Republic fell from 26.8 percent in 1960 to 21.8 percent in 1973 (trade-diverting effects of the EC) but then rose to 30.8 percent in 1980 (trade-creating effects of the 1972 free trade treaties), it then fell to 30.1 percent in 1985 and again rose to 35.0 percent in 1988. Imports from the FRG remained nearly stable all the time: 1960, 40.0 percent; 1973, 41.7 percent; 1980, 40.8 percent; 1985, 40.9 percent; but they rose to 44.5 percent in 1988.

mated as approximately 4.3 percent in 1960, 6.2 percent in the peak year 1982, 5.8 percent in 1985, and 4.6 percent in 1989.[10] In all cases, the cyclical pattern of exports to the FRG differs from the cyclical pattern of West German and Austrian GDP.

TABLE 8.4

Share of Exports of Goods to Germany (percentage of GDP)

	Austria	Belgium	Denmark
1960	4.8	5.2	4.6
1965	4.8	8.2	3.6
1970	4.6	11.2	2.6
1975	4.4	10.4	3.0
1980	7.1	11.4	4.8
1985	7.8	12.5	4.7

Source: International Monetary Fund, *International Financial Statistics,* monthly publication (various issues)

The Importance of West German Property in Austria

One could perhaps argue that West German ownership of Austrian companies is so important that these companies, experiencing the same growth and cyclical pattern as companies in the FRG, ultimately bring about the high correlations between the West German and Austrian economies at the macroeconomic level.

Though West German ownership is growing in Austria, in general it seems not to be critical. For a demonstration of this point, two types of information will be used:

1. information regarding the *stock* of West German ownership in Austria
2. information regarding the West German share of newly established foreign companies in Austria (*flow* information)

---

10. This share was calculated by weighing the export revenues of tourism (according to the balance of payment statistics) with the ratio of West German tourists to all foreign tourists.

With regard to the stock of foreign capital in Austria, the information provided by the Austrian National Bank is the most important source. Because direct country-by-country figures are difficult to evaluate — many companies invest in foreign countries via third countries for tax purposes[11] — the Austrian National Bank revises the initial information by regrouping direct investment data according to the ultimate location of the investing companies' headquarters. These revised data are presented in Table 8.5.

Summarizing Table 8.5 one can conclude that the West German influence is important in advanced industries (metals, automobiles, electrical equipment, chemistry). Only 7 percent of all employees working in industry and only 1 to 2 percent of all Austrian employees, however, can be considered to be under the control of West German companies.

The flow dimension was analyzed by using various publications of the Chamber of Labor (*Kammer für Arbeiter und Angestellte Wien*), which lists the names and the ownership of equity of newly established foreign companies in Austria. These lists show that the FRG is the leading investor country.[12] They also reveal that West Germans tend to set up many small companies in Austria, many of which operate in the fields of wholesale trade and services (marketing, tourism, data processing). Yet when looking at the overall size of their equity capital, these companies seem too small to be economically important.

Looking at the largest foreign investments in Austria during the last decade, one finds that a U.S. company, General Motors, leads the list. The direct investment project by *Bayrische Motorenwerke* (BMW/FRG) — the implementation of the project started in 1981 and is planned to last until 1990 — only ranks second. Both investments are by far the most important foreign investments in Austria, each amounting to AS 10 billion.

Many West German companies in Austria are not export-oriented but rather tend to exploit the protected Austrian home market, for example in the electrical equipment sector. One cannot therefore combine the two arguments (export-import links and FRG property in Austria) in explaining the parallel economic development in the two countries.

---

11. Many West German companies invest in Austria by using Switzerland or Liechtenstein as an intermediate country for tax purposes.

12. Unfortunately these lists are not published at regular intervals.

TABLE 8.5

Austrian Companies with Foreign Direct Investments, End of 1985 (in million AS)

Industry:	Switzerland Liechtenstein	FRG	USA	Other countries	Austrian share	Total equity of companies with foreign dir. investment	Percentage of share of a) for. companies
Metals, automobiles	738	2,737	950	983	1,960	7,368	14
Electric equipment	331	x	x	x	721	4,408	51
Oil, chemistry	565	1,613	1,060	2,701	545	6,483	34
Paper, wood industry	203	498	x	x	1,073	2,143	11
Textiles, clothing	380	620	x	x	375	1,765	20
Provision-industry	253	340	240	169	593	1,595	18
Building industry ("Steine, Keramik, Bau")	654	576	x	x	600	1,998	17
Other	444	x	x	x	495	1,102	11
Total industry	3,568	7,444	2,765	6,725	6,362	26,862	22

Table 8.5 continued on next page

Table 8.5 (continued)

	Switzerland Liechtenstein	FRG	USA	Other countries	Austrian share	Total equity of companies with foreign dir. investment	Percentage of share of for. companies[a]
Non-industry:							
Energy	89	220	x	x	178	706	2
Transportation, trade	1,225	3,255	1,977	2,659	1,507	10,622	9
Tourism	92	323	175	126	406	1,122	4
Small scale industries (*Gewerbe*)	325	534	161	318	887	2,226	1
Banking sector	752	1,144	746	951	2,885	6,478	14
Insurances	373	735	76	582	560	2,327	
Other	422	263	x	x	324	1,581	1
Total non-industry	3,278	6,474	3,202	5,359	6,747	25,062	4
Sum	6,846	13,918	5,967	12,084	13,109	51,924	9

a) Employees in companies in which the foreign share is more than 50% divided by all Austrian employees working in that sector; not included in the sum are employees in the public sector and farmers.

Source: Mitteilungen des Direktoriums der Oesterreichischen Nationalbank, Heft 5 (1988). (Only companies with equity of more than 1 million AS are included in this survey.)

Austria's Pragmatic Orientation Toward the FRG

Because economic policy deals with a wide range of issues, it is difficult to assess the degree of policy influence of one country on another. Yet, three general points can be advanced: First, Austrian policymakers and the social partners are eager to maintain Austria's competitive position in West German markets, especially Austria's price competitiveness. Wage rates and Austria's exchange rate are set to accomplish this goal.

Second, in other fields of economic policy such as fiscal measures, investment promotion policies, and agricultural policy Austria is more autonomous. Policy-making institutions, however, still aim at keeping Austria's economic performance in line with Western Europe, especially the EC and, to a lesser extent, the FRG. A good example of this kind of medium-term tuning is fiscal policy. Since the early 1970s, Austria has succeeded in achieving lower unemployment rates than other West European countries through a mix of demand- and supply-oriented fiscal measures, for instance, automatic stabilizers, tax incentives for investment, and savings.[13] When in the middle of the 1980s these measures produced fiscal deficits that were relatively high by European and West German standards, fiscal policy became more restrictive.

Third, at the level of the economic programs of Austrian political parties, nearly no West German influence can be discerned. The main reason for this is the parties' emphasis on their own political roots and the intellectual influence of ideas developed outside the FRG, for example the idea of the welfare state.

The Real Effective Exchange Rate

As will be demonstrated below, Austrian economic policy is pragmatically but not programmatically influenced by that of the FRG. In order to understand the pragmatic orientation of the Austrian policy toward the Federal Republic in the field of price competitiveness, one must look at the real effective exchange rate.[14]

---

13. Robert Holzmann and Georg Winckler, "Austrian Economic Policy: Some Theoretical and Critical Remarks on Austro-Keynesianism," *Empirica* 10, no. 2 (1983), pp. 183–203.

14. Effective in this context means only "on average" in an index-theoretic sense.

The real effective exchange rate of a country is defined as the nominal effective exchange rate multiplied by the domestic price level and divided by the foreign price level. Relative changes of the real effective exchange rate, then, equal the sum of the relative change of the nominal effective exchange rate and the domestic rate of inflation, minus the foreign rate of inflation.

The Austrian Central Bank has always kept the mark/schilling exchange rate at a nearly constant level, except for two adjustments in the 1960s (appreciation of the DM in 1961 and 1969) and minor changes since 1970 (see Table 8.6).[15]

TABLE 8.6

Schilling – Mark Ratios (annual averages)

1955	6.19
1960	6.19
1965	6.48
1970	7.09
1975	7.08
1980	7.12
1985	7.03
1989	7.03

Source: Mitteilungen des Direktoriums der Oesterreichischen Nationalbank, monthly publication (various issues)

The correlation between the West German and Austrian inflation rates was much higher in the 1970s and 1980s than it was earlier, and this implies that Austria's real exchange rate vis-à-vis the FRG was more stable after 1970 than before. Especially after 1973, the real exchange rate of the schilling has remained within a stable corridor of 110 to 120 points (1970 = 100).

This relative constancy of the real effective exchange rate indicates that the social partners accept the exchange rate policy (hard-currency policy) of the Central Bank. The social partners allow only price increases comparable to those in the FRG.

The model for wage increases by the social partners can be described best as a productivity-oriented wage policy in which the FRG's (low) inflation rate is used as a basis. This model has not always worked smoothly, however. The

---

15. These "minor" changes, of course, are the object of intensive policy discussions in Austria.

trade unions attempted to achieve "extra" wage increases in 1975. The prices of goods have also followed market pressures. There is voluminous literature in Austria on how the model has worked,[16] what the model has meant for the allocation of resources to the exposed and sheltered sector,[17] how trade unions really have reacted,[18] and which strategic options were promoted.[19] Although there are skeptical voices, most authors agree that the model has performed quite favorably for Austria.

One of the consequences of this pragmatic orientation toward maintaining the price competitiveness with the FRG may explain the correlation between macroeconomic aggregates of the two countries: Both experienced the same fluctuations in their competitive positions in the world markets. Admittedly, a host of structural problems complicates this statement. Again, it remains a puzzle why the 1970s produced a lower correlation between the two countries' aggregates than did the 1960s.

The Lack of Programmatic Coordination

Only a brief account of the results derived from a comparison of the programs of the major political parties can be given here, starting with the conservative parties, the ÖVP for Austria, the CDU for the FRG.

The Austrian ÖVP has gone through different phases since World War II. Until the early 1950s, left-wing Catholicism was very influential. In addition, Skalnik names the French *Mouvement Républicain Populaire* (MRP) as the party toward which the ÖVP oriented itself. As a result of this

---

16. Wolfgang Pollan, "Inflation, Produktivität und Lohnsteigerungen. Ein Vergleich mit der Bundesrepublik Deutschland," in Österreichisches Institut für Wirtschaftsforschung (ed.), *Die internationale Wettbewerbsfähigkeit Österreichs, Österreichische Strukturberichterstattung, Kernbericht 1986*, vol. II, Vienna (1987), pp. 43–75.

17. Helmut Frisch, "Macroeconomic Adjustment in Small Open Economies," in H. Arndt (ed.), *The Political Economy of Austria*, Washington and London (1982), pp. 42–55.

18. Fritz Schebeck, Hannes Suppanz, and Günther Tichy, "Die mittelfristigen Folgen der Wechselkurspolitik für Leistungsbilanz und Inflationsrate," *Empirica* 7, no. 2 (1980), pp. 139–167.

19. Georg Winckler, "Strategische Probleme der Hartwährungspolitik," *Quartalshefte der Girozentrale* 21, no. 3 (1986), pp. 55–69; Georg Winckler and Erwin Amann, "Exchange Rate Policy in the Presence of a Strong Trade Union," *Journal of Economics/Zeitschrift für Nationalökonomie* Suppl. 5 (1986), pp. 259–280.

orientation, policies such as the strengthening of the welfare state in Austria and even the nationalization of industries were endorsed by the ÖVP. After the "French" period, a "German" period lasted until the early 1960s.[20] Its main proponents were Chancellor Julius Raab and Finance Minister Reinhard Kamitz. One of the main ideas of the CDU, the concept of the social market economy, found its way into the ÖVP party programs. This can be seen, for example, in the program *Alles für Österreich* (1952), in which the idea of private property was strongly emphasized. In the 1960s, however, de Gaulle's technocratic conservatism inspired the ÖVP, primarily the group around Finance Minister and Chancellor Josef Klaus. Consequently, the ideas of *competition policy* — a central point in the programs of the CDU and in the theory of the social market economy — were never mentioned in ÖVP programs. In 1972, when the new Salzburg program was adopted (still valid today), reference to the social market economy was only rhetoric because the word competition was used without practical consequences for policy (point 4.4.2 of the Salzburg program). Instead, the program advocated an activist policy for the state, going so far as to propose a *"wirksame Strukturpolitik"* (points 4.4.3, 4.4.4, and 4.4.6 of the Salzburg program).

One finds many Christian social ideas in the CDU's program as well (see especially in the *Grundsatzprogramm* of 1978).[21] These ideas, however, are neither specifically German nor Austrian. They stem from papal encyclicals (*Rerum Novarum, Quadragesimo Anno*, and so on). Many features of technocratic conservatism in Austria can be found in the CDU too, particularly in southern Germany (for example within the CSU). Still, the specific programmatic idea of the CDU, the idea of a social market economy, has never really penetrated Austrian party programs and government declarations.

With regard to the Socialist Party of Austria (SPÖ), no corresponding "German" phase can be discerned as with the ÖVP. It is interesting to note that both the SPÖ and the *Sozialdemokratische Partei Deutschlands* (SPD) of West Germany adopted a new party program in 1958. The program of the SPÖ was still in the Austro-Marxist tradition, whereas the SPD decisively reversed its basic principles that year, taking the line "Soviel Markt wie möglich, soviel Planung wie nötig," (As much free market as possible, as much planning as necessary.) Even the SPÖ's 1978 program, in which Austro-Keynesianism triumphed over Austro-Marxism — "Veränderung der Entscheidungsverhältnisse" (changes in the conditions of decision making) as

---

20. Kurt Skalnik, "Parteien," in Erika Weinzierl and Kurt Skalnik (eds.), *Österreich, Die Zweite Republik*, vol. II, Graz (1972), pp. 197–228.

21. Ulrich Sarcinelli, "Das Grundsatzprogramm der CDU," in Heinz Kaack and Reinhold Roth (eds.), *Handbuch des Deutschen Parteiensystems*, vol. 2, Opladen (1980), pp. 57 ff.

opposed to "Veränderung der Eigentumsverhältnisse" (changes in ownership conditions, point 3.2) – remained very critical toward the political value of the market economy.[22]

Conclusion

Some conclusions concerning the economic impact of the FRG on Austria may be drawn from the information presented in this chapter. There is a striking parallel development of macroeconomic variables in the FRG and in Austria. This parallel can hardly be explained by the export-import link between the two countries or by the value of West German property in Austria. The export-import link demonstrates other cyclical patterns and growth patterns than that of real GDP; West German ownership in Austria is not important.

The parallel is probably the outcome of the pragmatic orientation of Austrian policy institutions toward West German economic policy. The wage and price policies of the social partners, as well as the Central Bank's exchange rate policy, support this thesis. West German political parties do not, however, influence the economic programs of the Austrian parties.

---

22. "Sozialistische Wirtschaftspolitik beschränkt sich nicht darauf, Fehlentwicklungen der Marktwirtschaft jeweils im nachhinein zu korrigieren. Wo Produktions- und Investitionsentscheidungen vor allem am erwarteten Gewinn ausgerichtet sind, werden immer wieder Arbeitslosigkeit, Inflation und Stagnation auftreten." ("Das neue Programm der SPÖ," Wien 1978, point 3.2).

9

Austrian-EC Trade Relations:
Evolution Toward Integration*

D. Mark Schultz

With its application on 17 July 1989 for membership in the three European Communities, Austria has moved through an important transitional phase in its integration policy. Since the late 1950s, Austria has struggled to resolve the dilemma of how to balance its close economic integration with the EC with the political autonomy that its status as a permanently neutral country requires. By applying for membership in the EC, Austria has reversed the strategy embodied in the 1972 FTAs with the EEC and the ECSC, which attempted to combine a close economic relationship with political distance. Austria is now opting for a strategy that brings the political relationship up to the level of economic integration. This chapter discusses that shift, focusing on the considerations that led the Austrian government to the conclusion that advanced economic integration required full membership. The analysis shows that the EC's initiative to establish a genuine single market — the "1992" program — threatened to disrupt Austria's existing and future participation in the West European economy. In response, Austria concluded that if it was to secure its economic position vis-à-vis the EC, and exert any control over the future development of this position, it would have to exercise its influence from within the EC. Austria's situation suggests,

*   The author gratefully acknowledges financial support from the Social Sciences and Humanities Research Council of Canada, the Austrian Federal Ministry for Science and Research, and Nuffield College during the research for this chapter. Portions of this chapter have been incorporated into the author's doctoral thesis which was submitted to the University of Oxford in July 1989.

therefore, that trade liberalization and economic integration produce pressures for closer political ties.

Austria had apparently resolved the challenge of achieving economic integration with the EC without compromising its political autonomy when it concluded its FTAs with the EC.[1] The FTAs provided for the reduction of tariffs on manufactured goods to zero on 1 July 1977, with the exception of agricultural products and certain "sensitive" goods that the Community insisted had to be placed on an extended tariff-reduction schedule. These sensitive products included specialty steels and special metals, as well as wood and paper products.

The FTAs established a free trade zone, with minimal political content, in order not to infringe on Austria's neutrality obligations. The Community did not insist that Austria harmonize its tariffs with the EC's Common External Tariff so that Austria could retain control of its trade policies vis-à-vis third countries. Instead, the agreements established a system of origin rules and safeguards — including competition regulations and controls on government subsidies — to ensure that neither party's industries would be disadvantaged by policy differences. In addition, Austria was exempted from Community trade actions against third parties if these were politically motivated; a special regime was negotiated to govern the development, production, and trade of arms (Article 21); the Mixed Committee (*Gemischter Ausschuß*) established to oversee the agreement was based on parity and unanimity as the decision-making rule; and the FTAs could be suspended if the international situation warranted or could be terminated with twelve months' notice (Article 34).[2]

As Table 9.1 shows, the FTAs provided the framework for the reintegration of Austria's exports into Community markets. From the late 1950s to the early 1970s, the EC's share of Austria's total exports had declined — from 49.6 percent in 1958 to 38.7 percent in 1972 — a decline that could be attrib-

---

1. Austria concluded four agreements: an Interim Agreement and a Comprehensive Agreement with both the EEC and the ECSC. The texts of the agreements are to be found in the *Official Journal of the European Communities*, 1972 L300/2 and 1973 L350/3. References in this chapter are to the Comprehensive Agreement with the EEC.

2. For brief descriptions of the FTAs and commentaries, see Manfred Scheich, "The European Neutrals After Enlargement of the Communities: The Austrian Perspective," *Journal of Common Market Studies* 12 (1973), pp. 235–247; and Hellmuth Straßer, *Der Weg Österreichs zu den Verträgen mit Brüssel*, Vienna (1972). For detailed analysis of the economic aspects of the FTAs, see Jan Stankovsky, "Die österreichischen Integrationsverträge mit den Europäischen Gemeinschaften," *Monatsberichte des österreichischen Institutes für Wirtschaftsforschung* (hereafter cited as *Monatsberichte*) 47, no. 2 (1974), pp. 74–94.

TABLE 9.1

Austria's Exports and Imports by Area (as a percentage of total Austrian exports and imports [commodities])

	EC^a		FRG		$EFTA^b$	
	Exp.	Imp.	Exp.	Imp.	Exp.	Imp.
1955	51.1	52.5	25.1	35.4	12.1	12.0
1958	49.6	54.3	25.1	38.9	10.9	11.4
1961	49.5	59.5	27.5	42.9	15.1	12.8
1964	47.5	58.8	27.9	41.7	19.2	14.6
1967	40.7	58.5	22.2	41.7	22.5	18.2
1970	39.4	56.0	23.4	41.2	26.6	19.6
1972	38.7	57.9	22.4	41.9	29.0	18.8
					19.1^c	11.4^c
1973	49.2	64.5	21.8	41.7	18.2	12.0
	39.0^d	58.2^d				
1974	44.3	61.5	19.7	40.1	17.4	10.9
1975	44.2	62.3	21.9	40.0	15.3	10.6
1976	46.6	63.4	23.4	41.1	14.4	9.7
1977	49.5	65.3	26.6	42.2	13.4	9.3
1978	52.4	65.4	29.1	43.3	12.8	9.0
1979	53.5	64.8	30.3	42.3	12.2	8.4
1980	55.2	62.4	30.8	40.8	12.4	7.9
1981	52.8	58.9	29.1	38.9	12.1	7.6
1982	53.1	61.2	29.3	40.6	11.7	7.7
1983	53.7	62.7	30.8	41.5	10.7	7.8
1984	53.3	60.4	29.6	39.9	10.8	7.9
1985	54.2	61.1	30.1	40.9	10.8	8.0

a   EC: to 1973, EC 6; to 1981, EC 9
b   EFTA: from 1972, minus Great Britain and Denmark; includes Finland
c   EFTA minus Great Britain and Denmark
d   EC 6 (assuming no new members)

Source: Österreichisches Statistisches Zentralamt (ÖStZ), *Statistisches Handbuch für die Republik Österreich (Handbuch),* various years; author's calculations.

uted to the rise of trade barriers between Austria and its major markets in West Germany and Italy after the formation of the EC and to weaknesses in Austria's trade structure that these barriers exacerbated, such as Austria's heavy reliance on exports of price sensitive raw materials.[3] By 1978, over half of Austria's total exports were again sold in the Community. There was a corresponding steady increase in the percentage of Austria's GDP involved in trade with the Community (Table 9.2). Although these developments are consistent with expectations based on integration theory,[4] the EC's expansion from six to twelve members also increased the proportion of Austria's total trade going to the Community.

The commodity composition of Austria's exports to the Community has also improved, with the percentage of manufactured products (Standard International Trade Classification — SITC — 5–9) in total exports increasing steadily and going increasingly to the Community (Tables 9.3 and 9.4). The expansion of both exports and imports of manufactured goods is also consistent with expectations for increased intra-industry trade and specialization as a result of trade liberalization.

Against these positive developments, however, the fact that Austria continues to play its traditional role in the West European division of labor must be balanced. The trade deficit with the EC persists (Table 9.5), though it has recovered from the mid-1970s highs. Export composition problems are more persistent. Austria continues to rely heavily on exports of resources and basic manufactured goods in exchange for imports of higher-value finished goods from the EC. The distribution of Austria's trade balance with the Community by commodity classification given in Table 9.6 shows this exchange pattern clearly, with Austria running large deficits in machines and vehicles (SITC 7) and "other" finished goods, in other words, consumer goods[5]

3. Michael Fitz, "Verlangsamung des österreichischen Exportwachstums," *Monatsberichte* 37, no. 8 (1964), pp. 302–311; "Strukturelle Schwächen des österreichischen Exportes," *Monatsberichte* 33, no. 11 (1960), pp. 460–469.

4. For tests of integration theory using Austria's FTAs, see Fritz Breuss and Jan Stankovsky, "Westeuropäische Integration und österreichischer Außenhandel," in Hanspeter Hanreich and Gerhard Stadler (eds.), *Österreich-Europäische Integration*, Baden-Baden (1979), pp. 1–73; and Fritz Breuss, *Österreichs Außenwirtschaft 1945–1982*, Vienna (1983), pp. 91–123.

5. An article by Jan Stankovsky, trade expert at the *Österreichisches Institut für Wirtschaftsforschung*, suggests that these structural problems are becoming more acute: With few exceptions, Austria's exports are growing in the industries with low-value products and declining demand and in the wrong (low-income) markets. See "Die Stellung der österreichischen Exportwirtschaft in der internationalen Arbeitsteilung," *Monatsberichte* 58, no. 9 (1985), pp. 573–582. See also Fritz Breuss, "Außenwirtschaft," in Hanns Abele et al. (eds.), *Handbuch der österreichischen Wirtschaftspolitik*, Vienna, 1st ed. (1982), pp. 345–359; and Jiri

TABLE 9.2

Austria's Exports as a Percentage of GDP
(by export market [commodities])

	Total	EC^a	FRG	$EFTA^b$
1955	16.93	8.66	4.25	2.98
1958	17.40	8.63	4.36	1.89
1961	17.30	8.57	4.75	2.61
1964	16.58	7.88	4.62	3.18
1967	16.47	6.70	3.66	3.70
1970	19.76	7.79	4.62	3.18
1972	18.72	7.24	4.20	5.43
1973	18.76	9.23	4.08	3.41
		7.32^c		
1974	21.56	9.56	4.24	3.76
1975	19.95	8.81	4.36	3.04
1976	20.99	9.79	4.91	3.03
1977	20.32	10.06	5.40	2.73
1978	20.91	10.96	6.09	2.67
1979	22.45	12.02	6.80	2.74
1980	22.74	12.54	7.01	2.82
1981	23.84	12.60	6.94	2.88
1982	23.54	12.50	6.90	2.75
1983	23.05	12.38	7.10	2.48
1984	24.47	13.05	7.25	2.64
1985	25.90	14.05	7.81	2.79

a   EC: to 1973, EC 6; to 1981, EC 9
b   EFTA: from 1972, minus Great Britain and Denmark; includes Finland
c   EC 6 (assuming no new members)

Source: ÖStZ, *Statistisches Handbuch für die Republik Österreich (Handbuch),* various years; author's calculations.

(SITC 8). These exchange patterns reflect a deeper industrial structural problem, which plays an important role in the development of Austria's integration policy.

Skolka, "Außenhandelsverflechtung der österreichischen Wirtschaft. Ein Input-Output Vergleich zwischen 1964 and 1976," *Monatsbericht* 54, no. 10 (1981), pp. 594–603.

TABLE 9.3

Austria's Commodity Exports and Imports by Commodity Classification (SITC)
(as a percentage of total exports/imports to/from the specified area)

EXPORTS

Year	Trading Partner	(0)	(1)	(2)	(3)	(4)	(5)	(6)	(7)	(8)	(9)	(0+1+4)	(2+3)	(5–9)
1960	Total	4.36	0.16	18.68	2.43	0.03	3.91	47.09	16.32	7.07	0.09	4.55	21.11	74.34
	EC	7.29	0.27	29.47	4.51	0.04	1.65	41.24	9.17	6.19	0.17	7.60	33.98	58.42
	FRG	4.80	0.4	19.77	8.27	0.03	1.73	47.26	10.86	6.87	–	5.24	28.04	66.72
1965	Total	5.08	0.18	13.09	3.27	0.04	4.77	40.37	20.37	12.83	0.06	5.30	16.36	78.34
	EC	8.14	0.27	20.77	5.52	0.07	2.16	36.68	14.65	11.72	0.02	8.49	26.29	65.22
	FRG	3.0	0.3	14.1	8.9	0.07	2.3	44.3	14.8	9.6	0.03	3.4	23.0	73.6
1970	Total	4.38	0.19	10.03	2.53	0.04	5.63	39.40	24.08	13.69	0.03	4.61	12.56	82.83
	EC	6.87	0.31	18.07	5.46	0.08	2.62	35.90	18.80	11.85	0.03	7.27	23.53	69.20
	FRG	2.7	0.43	10.1	8.8	0.05	2.6	42.3	20.7	12.2	0.05	3.2	18.9	77.9
1975	Total	3.60	0.40	7.09	2.06	0.07	8.32	37.47	27.35	13.57	0.05	4.07	9.15	86.78
	EC	4.47	0.60	10.95	3.34	0.13	5.01	37.00	22.76	15.68	0.06	5.20	14.29	80.51
	FRG	2.7	1.1	5.7	6.6	0.14	5.5	37.1	24.5	16.6	0.1	3.9	12.2	83.8

EXPORTS

Year	Trading Partner	(0)	(1)	(2)	(3)	(4)	(5)	(6)	(7)	(8)	(9)	(0+1+4)	(2+3)	(5-9)
1980	Total	3.51	0.55	8.82	1.59	0.07	8.81	35.55	27.68	13.25	0.17	4.13	10.41	85.46
	EC	3.18	0.56	11.44	2.36	0.11	7.46	33.85	25.92	14.86	0.26	4.79	13.81	82.35
	FRG	1.5	0.8	5.6	3.7	0.15	7.5	32.7	29.8	17.8	0.4	2.4	9.3	87.9
1985	Total	3.81	0.35	5.45	2.07	0.09	9.14	33.84	31.30	13.76	0.17	4.26	7.52	88.22
	EC	3.36	0.34	7.13	2.32	0.12	8.54	33.03	31.13	13.95	0.08	3.83	9.45	86.73
	FRG	1.9	0.5	3.7	4.0	0.22	8.0	31.8	34.0	15.8	0.1	2.6	7.7	89.6
1986	Total	3.53	0.27	5.28	1.25	0.05	8.65	32.86	33.21	14.81	0.08	3.85	6.53	89.62
	EC	2.94	0.20	6.70	1.50	0.06	7.64	32.7	34.0	14.22	0.06	3.21	8.21	88.59
	FRG	1.65	0.23	3.30	2.65	0.09	7.49	31.77	36.64	16.08	0.09	1.98	5.94	92.08

Table 9.3 continued on next page

TABLE 9.3 (continued)

							IMPORTS							
Year	Trading Partner	(0)	(1)	(2)	(3)	(4)	(5)	(6)	(7)	(8)	(9)	(0+1+4)	(2+3)	(5-9)
1960	Total	13.25	0.99	13.02	9.45	1.48	7.91	20.03	28.66	5.23	0.03	15.72	22.47	61.01
	EC	5.83	0.76	6.08	7.25	1.12	9.66	24.04	37.95	7.29	0.02	7.70	13.34	78.96
	FRG	1.8	0.3	4.4	6.5	0.6	9.8	24.1	43.7	8.6	0.03	2.6	10.9	86.4
1965	Total	12.57	1.16	9.59	7.35	1.27	8.72	21.07	30.63	7.83	0.01	14.99	16.94	68.07
	EC	7.29	0.71	4.67	5.00	0.58	9.82	22.52	39.99	9.41	0.01	8.58	9.67	81.75
	FRG	2.3	0.6	3.8	4.7	0.6	9.9	22.7	45.1	10.4	0.01	3.4	8.5	88.2
1970	Total	7.64	0.86	9.17	8.27	0.87	9.83	22.51	31.18	9.68	0.01	9.37	17.44	73.19
	EC	4.07	0.54	4.28	5.91	0.52	11.27	22.97	39.86	10.56	0.02	5.13	10.19	84.68
	FRG	2.1	0.4	3.4	5.6	0.4	11.6	23.4	41.8	11.1	0.02	2.9	9.0	88.0
1975	Total	6.51	0.81	6.97	12.63	0.82	9.48	20.20	29.70	12.85	0.02	8.14	19.60	72.26
	EC	4.29	0.59	3.06	4.10	0.71	11.28	22.44	38.25	15.27	0.01	5.60	7.15	87.24
	FRG	2.9	0.4	2.4	3.9	0.8	11.6	22.4	40.3	15.1	0.02	4.1	6.4	89.5

IMPORTS

Year	Trading Partner	(0)	(1)	(2)	(3)	(4)	(5)	(6)	(7)	(8)	(9)	(0+1+4)	(2+3)	(5-9)
1980	Total	5.54	0.42	6.66	15.50	0.42	9.26	19.31	28.61	14.13	0.16	6.39	22.16	71.46
	EC	3.76	0.40	3.57	4.34	0.35	11.44	22.76	35.78	17.41	0.18	4.51	7.91	87.58
	FRG	2.8	0.3	2.7	3.8	0.4	11.8	22.4	39.4	16.2	0.2	3.6	6.6	90.0
1985	Total	5.44	0.39	6.30	14.87	0.47	9.99	18.17	29.84	14.38	0.15	6.31	21.17	72.52
	EC	4.09	0.33	3.71	3.83	0.37	11.78	21.91	35.81	18.11	0.07	4.79	7.54	87.67
	FRG	2.8	0.2	3.2	4.2	0.4	11.2	21.6	39.6	16.8	0.09	3.3	7.4	89.3
1986	Total	5.71	0.39	5.46	8.67	0.31	10.09	19.22	33.80	16.16	0.20	6.41	14.13	79.46
	EC	3.89	0.35	3.24	2.20	0.24	11.49	21.74	37.85	18.94	0.07	4.48	5.43	90.09
	FRG	2.6	0.2	2.8	2.3	0.2	11.0	21.5	41.9	17.4	0.10	3.1	5.1	92.8

(0) Food
(1) Beverages and Tobacco
(2) Raw Materials
(3) Mineral Fuels

(4) Fats and Oils
(5) Chemicals
(6) Semi-Manufactured Goods
(7) Machines and Transport

(8) Finished Products
(9) Miscellaneous
(0+1+4) Agricultural Products
(2+3) Resources
(5-9) Manufactures

Source: Total trade from 1960 to 1980, from Fritz Breuss, *Österreichs Außenwirtschaft 1945-1982,* Vienna (1983), Tables 90 and 92, pp. 383, 386; remaining figures for 1960 from ÖStZ, *Statistik des Außenhandels Österreichs 1960,* Teil B; and other years from ÖStZ, *Der Außenhandel Österreichs, Serie 2,* various years; author's calculations.

TABLE 9.4

Distribution of Austria's Commodity Exports by Commodity Classification (SITC) and Export Market (percentage of total Austrian exports of that commodity)

Year	Trading Partner	(0)	(1)	(2)	(3)	(4)	(5)	(6)	(7)	(8)	(9)	(0+1+4)	(2+3)	(5-9)
1960	Total	84.1	82.9	79.3	94.5	72.0	21.1	44.0	28.2	44.1	93.8	84.0	81.1	39.4
	EC	29.6	65.7	27.9	92.5	30.4	11.9	26.9	17.8	26.1	2.1	30.9	35.7	24.0
	FRG	9.7	7.1	5.4	4.8	19.0	12.1	15.3	11.6	18.8	2.9	9.7	5.4	14.6
1965	Total	74.1	71.3	74.2	78.8	78.9	21.1	42.4	33.6	42.6	20.9	74.7	75.1	38.8
	EC	16.8	50.7	30.9	78.1	46.2	13.9	31.4	20.73	27.1	17.0	18.2	40.3	26.9
	FRG	16.8	13.9	7.2	2.7	2.9	14.1	19.7	15.0	30.6	18.7	16.6	6.3	19.9
1970	Total	61.9	63.4	71.0	85.2	83.0	18.3	35.9	30.3	34.1	43.6	62.2	73.9	32.9
	EC	14.3	51.9	23.4	81.8	28.8	11.0	25.1	20.1	20.9	38.1	16.0	35.2	22.0
	FRG	17.8	15.0	8.5	0.3	4.8	18.4	29.0	24.6	38.2	31.6	17.6	6.9	28.5
1975	Total	54.8	66.7	68.2	71.6	81.7	26.6	43.6	36.7	51.0	46.1	56.4	69.0	41.0
	EC	16.6	58.5	17.5	69.8	44.2	14.4	21.6	19.6	26.7	42.4	21.2	29.2	21.1
	FRG	12.1	12.1	5.6	2.5	0.9	10.2	16.4	14.9	24.0	5.3	11.9	4.9	16.5

Year	Trading Partner	(0)	(1)	(2)	(3)	(4)	(5)	(6)	(7)	(8)	(9)	(0+1+4)	(2+3)	(5-9)
1980	Total	49.1	55.6	70.6	80.7	79.6	45.9	51.8	50.9	61.1	83.4	50.5	72.1	52.4
	EC	13.0	43.8	19.5	72.1	66.5	26.2	28.4	33.3	41.5	74.4	18.0	27.6	31.9
	FRG	10.8	8.8	5.1	2.3	1.6	9.6	14.4	10.5	19.7	14.5	10.4	4.6	13.5
1985	Total	49.4	53.7	73.4	62.7	76.1	52.4	54.7	55.8	56.8	27.0	50.4	70.4	55.1
	EC	15.4	39.5	20.2	58.6	69.2	26.3	28.3	32.7	34.6	19.0	18.6	30.8	30.6
	FRG	8.0	21.8	6.4	3.6	1.2	8.8	10.9	8.4	18.2	39.1	9.0	5.6	11.0
1986	Total	50.0	45.5	76.3	72.5	74.1	53.1	59.8	61.4	57.7	48.2	50.0	75.5	59.4
	EC	15.3	28.0	20.4	69.6	62.9	28.4	31.7	36.1	35.6	34.3	16.8	29.8	33.6
	FRG	10.2	28.7	6.5	2.7	0.5	9.5	12.1	8.9	21.4	28.7	11.3	5.8	12.2

(0)	Food
(1)	Beverages and Tobacco
(2)	Raw Materials
(3)	Mineral Fuels
(4)	Fats and Oils
(5)	Chemicals
(6)	Semi-Manufactured Goods
(7)	Machines and Transport
(8)	Finished Products
(9)	Miscellaneous
(0+1+4)	Agricultural Products
(2+3)	Resources
(5-9)	Manufactures

Source: Total trade from 1960 to 1980, from Fritz Breuss, Österreichs Außenwirtschaft 1945-1982, Vienna (1983), Tables 90 and 92, pp. 383, 386; remaining figures for 1960 from ÖStZ, Statistik des Außenhandels Österreichs 1960, Teil B; and other years from ÖStZ, Der Außenhandel Österreichs, Serie 2, various years; author's calculations.

TABLE 9.5

Austria's Commodity Trade Balance as a Percentage of GDP (by area)

Year	Total	EC^a	FRG	$EFTA^b$
1955	-4.57	-2.64	-3.37	0.41
1958	-2.95	-2.35	-3.56	-0.43
1961	-4.06	-4.14	-4.41	-0.13
1964	-4.78	-4.68	-4.29	0.07
1967	-4.56	-5.61	-5.10	-0.14
1970	-4.79	-6.02	-5.51	0.45
1972	-6.43	-7.32	-6.33	0.70
1973	-6.60	-7.44	-6.49	0.36
		-7.15^c		
1974	-5.65	-7.17	-6.67	0.80
1975	-4.95	-6.70	-5.60	0.40
1976	-7.45	-8.23	-6.77	0.26
1977	-9.18	-9.21	-7.06	-0.01
1978	-6.62	-7.04	-5.84	0.18
1979	-6.93	-7.00	-5.63	0.28
1980	-9.02	-7.28	-5.95	0.32
1981	-8.49	-6.07	-5.37	0.48
1982	-5.80	-5.45	-5.00	0.50
1983	-5.92	-5.79	-4.93	0.21
1984	-6.04	-5.38	-4.93	0.23
1985	-5.63	-5.21	-5.10	0.28

a   EC: to 1973, EC 6; to 1981, EC 9
b   EFTA: from 1972, minus Great Britain and Denmark; includes Finland
c   EC 6 (assuming no new members)

Source: ÖStZ, *Statistisches Handbuch für die Republik Österreich*, various years; author's calculations.

TABLE 9.6

Austria's Commodity Trade Balance with the EC by Commodity Classification (nominal value and percentage of total deficit)[a]

Year	Total Deficit (in mill. AS)	(0)	(1)	(2)	(3)	(4)	(5)	(6)	(7)	(8)	(9)	(0+1+4)	(2+3)	(5-9)
1960	-6.161	-0.144	-0.119	+3.046	-0.848	-0.226	-1.767	+1.034	-6.549	-0.610	+0.021	-0.489	+2.198	-7.871
		(2.3)	(1.9)	n.a.[b]	(13.8)	(3.7)	(28.7)	n.a.	(106.3)	(9.9)	n.a.	(7.9)	n.a.	(127.7)
1965	-12.914	-0.776	-0.178	+2.521	-0.545	-0.173	-2.754	-0.161	-10.083	-0.766	-	-1.127	+1.976	-13.764
		(6.0)	(1.4)	n.a.	(4.2)	(1.3)	(21.3)	(1.3)	(78.1)	(5.9)		(8.7)	n.a.	(106.6)
1970	-22.463	-0.094	-0.187	+3.076	-1.459	-0.244	-5.066	-1.376	-15.118	-1.994	+0.001	-0.525	+1.617	-23.553
		(0.4)	(0.8)	n.a.	(6.5)	(1.1)	(22.6)	(6.1)	(67.3)	(8.9)	n.a.	(2.3)	n.a.	(104.9)
1975	-43.964	-1.786	-0.256	+3.218	-2.242	-0.653	-8.578	-1.449	-25.766	-6.47	+0.019	-2.695	+0.976	-42.244
		(4.1)	(0.6)	n.a.	(5.1)	(1.5)	(19.5)	(3.3)	(58.6)	(14.7)	n.a.	(6.1)	n.a.	(96.1)
1980	-73.571	-3.487	-0.096	+7.066	-5.627	-0.561	-13.322	-3.106	-38.447	-15.956	-0.033	-4.144	+1.439	-70.864
		(4.7)	(0.1)	n.a.	(7.7)	(0.8)	(18.1)	(4.2)	(52.3)	(21.7)	(0.04)	(5.63)	n.a.	(96.32)

Table 9.6 continued on next page

TABLE 9.6 (continued)

Year	Total Deficit (in mill. AS)	(0)	(1)	(2)	(3)	(4)	(5)	(6)	(7)	(8)	(9)	(0+1+4)	(2+3)	(5-9)
1985	-69.202	-4.287	-0.207	+4.223	-5.641	-0.744	-14.585	+6.902	-34.059	-20.794	-0.010	-5.238	-1.418	-62.546
		(6.2)	(0.3)	n.a.	(8.2)	(1.1)	(21.1)	n.a.	(49.2)	(30.1)	(0.01)	(7.6)	(2.1)	(90.4)
1986	-67.094	-4.554	-0.546	+4.964	-2.900	-0.524	-15.622	+7.980	-33.408	-22.419	-0.065	-5.624	+2.064	-63.534
		(6.8)	(0.8)	n.a.	(4.3)	(0.8)	(23.3)	n.a.	(49.8)	(33.4)	(0.1)	(8.4)	n.a.	(94.7)

a   EC 6 (assuming no new members)
b   not applicable

(0)	Food	(4)	Fats and Oils
(1)	Beverages and Tobacco	(5)	Chemicals
(2)	Raw Materials	(6)	Semi-Manufactured Goods
(3)	Mineral Fuels	(7)	Machines and Transport
		(8)	Finished Products
		(9)	Miscellaneous
		(0+1+4)	Agricultural Products
		(2+3)	Resources
		(5-9)	Manufactures

Source: ÖStZ, *Statistisches Handbuch für die Republik Österreich*, various years; author's calculations.

Austria's Integration Policy and "1992"

To the mid-1980s, the Austrian government was generally satisfied, above all, with the comprehensive FTA with the EEC and with its functioning. Though evolution in the relationship was anticipated in the agreement (Preamble and Article 32), the government focused its efforts on managing specific irritants within the FTA framework. By working with the Community and the member states and in conjunction with Austria's partners in EFTA, Austria worked to resolve three particular problems: (1) the deterioration of Austria's trade balance with the EC in agricultural products; (2) the trade administration system (especially the complex and costly rules for documenting trade and the country-of-origin rules); and (3) transport policy, which was outside the FTA.[6] Fundamental change in Austria's relationship with the Community was not on the agenda, and, indeed, after 1972 the government's attention moved to other issues, such as developing export markets in Eastern Europe and the Middle East.

In the mid-1980s, this general satisfaction was replaced by renewed, fundamental debate over the future of the relationship with the EC — a debate that was reminiscent of the pre-1972 discussions in both tone and vocabulary. Personnel changes in government — particularly the rise of the SPÖ conservative wing under Chancellor Franz Vranitzky and the return to government of the conservative ÖVP in coalition with the SPÖ after the 1986 election — played an important role in the development of Austria's integration policy. Without a doubt, however, the most significant factor accounting for the new debate in Austria was the EC's move toward completing its internal integration. As the scope and thrust of the Community's agenda became apparent, Austria, as well as the other EFTA states,[7] perceived that "1992" threatened to disrupt the relationship that had developed on the basis of the 1972 FTAs unless Austria took steps to secure its access to the EC market.

---

6. See Thomas Beuss, "Perspektiven für eine engere Zusammenarbeit zwischen der Europäischen Gemeinschaft und den EFTA-Mitgliedstaaten," *Außenwirtschaft* 40, no. 4 (1985), pp. 341–387; H.E. Brunner, "Die Ursprungsregeln im europäischen Freihandelsraum," *Außenwirtschaft* 32, no. 1 (1977), pp. 58–60; "Agrarisches Handelsbilanzdefizit steigt," *Wiener Zeitung* (hereafter *WZ*), January 25, 1981; Horst Braun, "Tirol: Herz der Alpen vor dem Infarkt," *Wirtschaft und Umwelt*, no. 2 (1977), pp. 10–12.

7. See "Swiss get the shivers about being in the cold," *The Guardian*, 7 April 1987; and Steven Greenhouse, "The Growing Fear of Fortress Europe," *The New York Times*, 23 October 1988.

To understand the scope of the challenge Austria faced, it is useful to review briefly the Community's plans. The "1992" initiative began in December 1982, when the Community's summit conference requested a plan from the Commission to complete the EC's internal integration.[8] The Commission produced its recommendations in the White Book (Doc. Com. [85] 310), which proposed the complete liberalization of trade in the Community and went beyond this by proposing the free movement of persons, services, and capital to support free trade in goods. According to the Commission, this program would create a truly integrated market, to allow economies of scale; a flexible market, to facilitate the optimum utilization of inputs; and the conditions for the market's dynamic development.[9]

The principal recommendations in the White Book were:

1. the elimination of remaining quantitative restrictions on traded goods
2. the elimination of border controls on goods and persons
3. the elimination of technical trade barriers through the harmonization of industrial norms and product standards so that a good could move freely inside the EC once it qualified for sale in one member's market
4. the liberalization of government procurement
5. the elimination of barriers to labor, service, and capital mobility
6. the harmonization of value-added and consumption taxes
7. the extension of research and development (R&D) cooperation

The White Book provided the basis for the Single European Act, which after ratification by all EC member states entered into force in 1987. The Act affirmed the goal of developing the EC into a single market "without internal frontiers, in which the free movement of goods, persons, services, and capital is ensured."[10] To achieve this, the Act extended the Community's authority by adding sections to the Treaty of Rome covering monetary policy, social (primarily labor) policy, regional development, R&D, and environmental protection. It also placed EC cooperation in foreign policy (EPC) on a legally binding foundation. To ensure that progress is actually made, the Act also extended qualified majority decision making to two-thirds of the approximately three hundred changes that would be necessary to realize the

---

8. For general discussions of the *White Book* see Jérôme Lugon, "Das Europa von morgen. Die Antwort des Weißbuches," *EFTA-Bulletin* 27, no. 1 (1986), pp. 5–7; and Paul Luif, "Neutrale und europäische Integration. Neue Aspekte einer alten Problematik," *Österreichische Zeitschrift für Politikwissenschaft* (hereafter *ÖZP*) 16, no. 2 (1987), pp. 117–121.

9. Lugon, "Das Europa von morgen," p. 5.

10. European Communities Commission, *Single European Act*, reprinted in *Bulletin of the European Communities*, Supplement 2/86, (1986), Article 13.

single market. Although the White Book began by recommending free trade at the national borders, it went well beyond this to reach policies that had previously been within the jurisdiction of the members.

Given the existing links between Austria and the EC, any improvement in the Community's economic performance would have benefits for Austria by increasing demand for Austria's products, by allowing Austrian producers to achieve economies of scale in exports for the EC market, or by cutting down on administration costs and on the time goods spend on borders inside the EC waiting to clear customs.[11] Despite these potential advantages, Austria viewed the Community's proposals less as a business opportunity than as a cause for anxiety because of the likelihood that the development of the single market would have as a corollary increased discrimination against third countries, which would jeopardize Austria's current and future integration with the EC.

To a degree, increased discrimination against Austrian producers as a result of the 1992 initiative would be unavoidable. In general, the 1972 FTAs put Austria's companies on equal terms with Community-based firms in the EC market: All had tariff-free access to the market, and all were disadvantaged by the fragmentation of this market by nontariff trade barriers (NTBs) and by discriminatory public policies. The 1992 initiative threatened this equality by increasing the advantages of producing inside the Community. These advantages would arise, for example, when Community members recognized the other members' industrial norms and standards, licensing and regulatory policies in service industries, or professional qualifications automatically, whereas Austrian-based companies would have to clear these regulatory hurdles in each EC state. Likewise, Community-based producers would be able to participate in the EC's R&D programs automatically, but non-EC companies could have to negotiate their participation on a case-by-case basis. The single market could mean, then, that Austria-based companies would face administrative impediments that their competitors inside the Community would not. Although it would be possible to circumvent these barriers, it would be uncertain, difficult, time-consuming, and therefore costly.

A second threat that was less explicitly expressed in Austria — but potentially more significant than the relatively benign administrative discrimination — was the question of the Community's trade policy post-1992. Since its inception, the Community had been a condominium of two orientations to trade: a liberal tendency, generally identified with West Germany, Great Britain, the Netherlands, and Denmark, and a more protectionist tendency

---

11. Walter Ertl, "Österreich und die Vollendung des Binnenmarktes," *Wirtschaftspolitische Blätter* 34, no. 3 (1987), p. 313.

usually supported by France and Italy. The EC could permit these divergent orientations by allowing members to retain some control over their trade policies — for example, the administration of contingency protection laws and the negotiation of voluntary export-restraint agreements with third countries — but the price the Community paid for this was the fragmentation of its internal market by border controls, necessary to ensure that exports from third countries could not enter a more protectionist member state by moving first through a more liberal member. If the Community were to dismantle its internal controls on the flow of goods, it would have to articulate a genuine Community trade policy so that controls on trade with third countries could be moved from the members' borders to the Community's borders with the rest of the world.[12]

The potential threat to Austria in the development of an EC trade policy is that this would be more consistent with France's or Italy's relatively protectionist approach to trade and would disrupt Austria's access to its major market in West Germany. As well, if the EC turned more protectionist in the future, as part of a general breakdown of the international trade system, for example, Austria would be an outsider, but more vulnerable than most because of its high dependence on the Community market.

The magnitude of these potential threats cannot be quantified with any precision because much of the discrimination would be hidden — foregone economies of scale, or lost dynamism as a result of not participating in the Community's R&D programs, or the displacement of investment from Austria to the EC as firms moved to secure their access to the Community. Clearly gross measures of Austria's export dependence on the EC favored in journalists' commentaries exaggerated the threat to Austria because not all exports would be jeopardized. It is likely, though, that since the EC's agenda focuses on establishing the conditions for developing new industries, the 1992 initiative would strike exactly at those industries that the Austrian government would be relying on to play a leading role in Austria's economic restructuring.

As well as the myriad economic considerations affecting Austria's response to 1992, there is an important psychological dimension. In Austria, there was widespread apprehension that the Community's further integration would leave Austrians standing outside a new European social and cultural community. Austrians feared, for example, that the liberalization of the movement of people within the Community would mean that they would become second-class Europeans, subject to immigration and passport con-

---

12. Hans-Eckhart Scharrer, "EG-Protektionismus als Preis für die Verwirklichung des europäischen Binnenmarktes?" *Wirtschaftsdienst* 66, no. 12 (1986), pp. 619–624.

trols placed at the EC's borders to administer a common immigration and security policy. Austrians had several provocative illustrations of how standing outside the Community could affect them personally: the Bavarian proposals for AIDS tests for workers from non-EC states; the French visa requirements for non-EC citizens; proposals for a "European" passport for EC nationals only; and work permit problems.[13]

Not all of the factors contributing to the new discussion of the integration policy in Austria were negative. Just as manufacturers who had adjusted to free trade with the EC after 1972 had the most to lose from the creation of new barriers through 1992, they also saw the potential to gain from a barrier-free continental market. Many industrialists also anticipated liberalization in the service industries, which they felt were uncompetitive in Austria and which placed industry as a whole at a competitive disadvantage. Accordingly, the two major business associations — the Federal Chamber of Commerce (*Bundeskammer der gewerblichen Wirtschaft*) and the Austrian Industrialists' Association (*Vereinigung Österreichischer Industrieller* — VÖI) — were vocal supporters of closer integration.[14] Likewise, the Austrian labor movement was generally supportive of further integration. This reflected both its traditional position, that competitiveness was best served by liberal trade policies, as well as the view that workers' interests as consumers are not served by protecting Austrian industry.[15]

Austria's "Global Approach" and the Membership Option

The Austrian government quickly realized that, in addition to the potential economic costs that 1992 could impose on Austria, the Community's ini-

13. See Engelbert Washietl, "Aufmarsch der Österreicher," *Die Presse* (hereafter *Presse*), 16–17 March 1985; Andreas Unterberger, "Der noble Exclusivklub zu Brüssel," *Presse*, 14 March 1987; and Christian S. Ortner, "Besuchen Sie Europa, solange es noch geht," *profil*, 17 November 1986.

14. See the article by the President of the Vienna VÖI, Manfred Mautner Markhof, "Ein Baustein für Europa," *Presse, Eco-Journal*, 22 January 1988; and comments by the president of the Federal Chamber of Commerce, Rudolf Sallinger, "EG-Appell Sallingers an Koalition: Parteiinteressen zurückstellen," *Presse*, 7–8 December 1988.

15. See the outline of Labor's position in *Zwischenbericht zur aktuellen Integrationsdebatte aus der Sicht des ÖAKT* (= *Österreichischer Arbeiterkammertag*), Vienna (1987).

tiative presented a *political* challenge. The government saw that if Austria maintained a detached position vis-à-vis the EC, Austrian businesses and consumers would adjust to the new regime that the 1992 initiative was establishing in Europe according to the resulting market incentives. Austrian companies, for example, would be under strong pressure to avoid losing export opportunities by gearing their production to conform to the norms and standards that the Community would establish or by locating production facilities in the EC to circumvent trade barriers. A passive stance outside the Community would imply that Austria was abdicating decision-making power to the EC in important areas of industrial and trade policy and was relying on good fortune or the EC's goodwill to protect Austrian interests. Accordingly, the SPÖ-ÖVP coalition government referred to the "great challenge" of integration policy, and affirmed that it

> will ensure, through consistent efforts towards integration and internationalization, that Austrian business will be able to participate in the dynamic of the large European market and the technology programmes of the EC, and that existing or threatened discrimination will be dismantled or averted.[16]

The concern for participation in the development of EC policy signaled a significant shift in the terms of Austria's integration policy debate from the 1960s to the 1980s. Whereas, in the 1960s, the arguments for an FTA focused on the economic justifications for minimizing discrimination against Austria's exports, the discussion in the 1980s was more political. Proponents of a closer political relationship argued that by remaining outside the Community Austria could not detach itself from developments inside the EC, but would be forced to react to policies that it could not influence. This, it was argued, would result in the "satellization" of Austria. The most important aspect of this line of argument was that it placed neutrality in a new light, with the argument that neutrality would be jeopardized more by staying outside the Community than it would be by joining the EC and thereby gaining some influence over its development.[17]

---

16. Eine neue Partnerschaft für Österreich, (The government program [*Regierungserklärung*]), 28 January 1987, reprinted in *Pd-Aktuell* 21, no. 1 (1987), n. p.

17. See comments by Andreas Khol, ÖVP foreign policy expert and member of Parliament, "Österreich und die Europäische Gemeinschaft," *Europa-Archiv* 41, no. 24 (1986), pp. 699–708; Peter Jankowitsch, former foreign minister and SPÖ foreign policy expert, in Andreas Unterberger, "Wien: Neue Debatte um Beitritt zur EG," *Presse*, 16 November 1985; and Manfred Scheich, former ambassador to the EC and chairperson of the Austrian Working Group on European Integration, in "Wiens Neutralität spezifisch; EG-Beitritt kann Souveränität stärken," *Presse*, 12–13 November 1988.

It is interesting that although the potential satellization of Austria as a result of close economic integration with the Community only became a central theme in Austria's EC debate in the 1980s, the problem was anticipated from the beginning. In 1962, for example, an early and influential formulation of the Community's position vis-à-vis EFTA cautioned that association with the Community (albeit in the form of a customs union) "would probably have the result for the countries in question that they would be bound in many different areas by the Community's decisions without having, for their part, a right to a say in the matter in the Community's institutions."[18]

Some critics of the 1972 FTAs had also argued that the agreements left out large areas of policy-making in which the EC was active, or would be active, and suggested that Austria would find itself bound to EC policies without having a voice in formulating these policies with the result that, over the long term, Austria's authority would be progressively "hollowed-out."[19]

In the 1970s, the government was not concerned with the lack of input into Community decision making. For example, Foreign Minister Bielka spoke of the EC as a "core" striving toward "as dense and comprehensive an integration as possible," and around this core "in a somewhat looser form, those member states who are able to participate in the integration process, but who for good reasons are not — or not yet — in a position to accept an

---

18. Political Committee, European Parliament, "Die politischen und institutionellen Aspekte des Beitritts zur Gemeinschaft oder Assoziierung mit ihr," doc. 122 (the *Birkelbach Report*), 15 January 1962, para. 105, reprinted in *Auszüge aus dem Birkelbach-Bericht, Österreichische Zeitschrift für Außenpolitik* (hereafter *ÖZAP*) 2, no. 3 (1962), p. 166.

19. This image was used by Gerfried Mutz, "Die rechtlichen Probleme der EG-Abkommen," in Bundeskammer der gewerblichen Wirtschaft (ed.), *Probleme der Abkommen zwischen Österreich und der Europäischen Gemeinschaft*, Vienna (1973), p. 51. See also comments in the parliamentary debate on the FTAs at Sten. Prot. des NR, XXIII. GP., 39. Sitz., 25 July 1972 by Alois Mock, pp. 3512, 3514–3515; and Otto Scrinzi (FPÖ), pp. 3493 and 3509. See also comments by other legal commentators, e.g., Theo Öhlinger, "Institutionelle Grundlagen der österreichischen Integrationspolitik im rechtlichen Sinn," and Gustav Kucera, "Langfristige Aspekte der österreichischen Integrationspolitik," both in *Institutionelle Aspekte der österreichischen Integrationspolitik*, Vienna (1976/1977), pp. 96 f. and pp. 306–308, respectively; and Fried Esterbauer, "Die Stellung Österreichs im Europäischen Integrationsprozeß und die Möglichkeit einer EG-Mitgliedschaft," in Fried Esterbauer and Reinhold Hinterleitner (eds.), *Die Europäische Gemeinschaft und Österreich*, Vienna (1977), p. 124.

all-embracing integration into the future Europe."[20] This indifferent approach was now being abandoned.

The Austrian government's initial response to 1992 was a multitrack strategy designed to minimize the divergence of Austrian policies from those of the Community, to reduce or abolish trade barriers, and to lay the foundation for future integration. The "global approach," as it became known, was developed by Andreas Khol, an ÖVP member of Parliament and an influential party foreign policy expert. Khol suggested that closer integration with the Community could be realized in stages by first concluding several individual agreements with the EC and then by winding these together into a comprehensive treaty that would give Austria a voice in Community decision making.[21] In keeping with this strategy, Austria affirmed its willingness to cooperate in most of the areas on the White Book agenda, going beyond trade to include agriculture, R&D, transportation, monetary and economic policies, and even foreign policy in areas such as South Africa and development assistance when neutrality was not an issue.[22]

To pursue its goals, the government used bilateral (Austrian-EC), multilateral (EFTA-EC), and unilateral (autonomous policy-harmonization) action. The guiding principle was pragmatism, so the government initially declined to describe its goal in institutional terms. Chancellor Vranitzky spoke cryptically of "quasi-membership" in the EC but also suggested that membership might be possible in "a second phase in the 1990s."[23] Likewise, Alois Mock, ÖVP vice-chancellor and foreign minister, asserted that in the new environment Austria's old ad hoc approach to the Community was inadequate,[24] but he too insisted that, for political reasons, the question of membership was "not relevant."[25]

20. From a speech delivered on 5 April 1975, quoted in Hans Mayrzedt and Waldemar Hummer, *20 Jahre österreichische Neutralitäts- und Europapolitik (1955–1975)*, vol. 1, Vienna (1976), pp. 496 f.

21. Khol, "Österreich und die Europäische Gemeinschaft."

22. See Vranitzky's comments in an interview with Carl Ströhm, "Wir wollen näher an die EG heran; die Neutralität ist kein Hemmschuh," *Die Welt*, 30 March 1987; and Andreas Unterberger, "Europäische Umarmung," *Presse*, 7 August 1986.

23. In Andreas Unterberger, "Neue EG-Diskussion in Österreich: Wird Beitritt Wiens unumgänglich?" *Presse*, 27 December 1986; and in interview: "Wir wollen näher an die EG heran," *Die Welt*, 30 March 1987.

24. Alois Mock, "EG-Länder wollen vorerst noch unter sich bleiben," *Neues Volksblatt*, 28 March 1987.

25. Alois Mock, "EG froh über Verhalten Wiens. Staatspolitik gegen Vollbeitritt," *Presse*, 24 March 1987.

Several considerations recommended the global approach. By avoiding formal negotiations, the Austrian government could proceed faster because the framework already existed in the 1972 FTAs and in EFTA.[26] The government also deprived domestic interests of a focal point for their claims for preferential treatment, which formal negotiations would surely provide.[27] This last consideration was important because it was necessary to preserve a comprehensive agreement both to capture the benefits of integration as well as to avoid accusations from the Community that Austria was attempting to "pick the raisins from the cake" by selecting only the advantages of integration.[28]

Perhaps most important was the calculation that the global approach was consistent with the EC's position, which was not sympathetic to membership applications. Though EC spokespersons consistently affirmed that the Community would be willing to consider Austria's membership application at any time, there were other signals that the Community was preoccupied with completing the 1992 initiative and the integration of Spain and Portugal into the EC, and would not consider new members until these projects had been completed.[29]

Another consideration was the EC's reluctance to confront the difficulties that Austria's neutrality presented. Some in the Community feared that the addition of another neutral member might impede the Community's closer cooperation in foreign policy and military areas.[30] Austrians did little to allay these concerns when, to answer their own neutrality problem, they insisted that a member can always exempt itself from Community measures by

---

26. Andreas Unterberger, "Mock skizziert seine Außenpolitik. Verzicht auf neuen EG-Vertrag," *Presse,* 2 February 1987; and interview with Alois Mock, "Keine Bittsteller!" *Die Furche,* 13 February 1987.

27. The author thanks Georg Winckler, Institute for Economics, University of Vienna, for emphasizing this calculation. See also Andreas Unterberger, "Viele Worte um wenig Europa," *Presse,* 7 March 1987.

28. This phrase and the original reproach is from the *Birkelbach Report,* para. 90. See note 18. Austrians react vehemently against this charge. See, e.g., Vranitzky's comments, "Wir wollen näher an die EG heran," *Die Welt,* March 30, 1987.

29. See e.g., comments by Willy de Clercq, former EC Commissioner for External Relations, "12 Zwerge hinter sieben Bergen," *Presse,* 25 March 1987.

30. See comments by Belgium's Foreign Minister Leo Tindemans quoted in "Tindemans skeptisch über Aufnahme Neutraler in EG," *Arbeiter-Zeitung,* 6 May 1987; and by Spain's Foreign Minister Francisco Ordonez, "Österreich ist Europa," *Presse,* 9 December 1988.

invoking the 1966 Luxembourg Compromise[31] and by declaring the issue in question to be a matter of vital national importance and thus outside the Community's jurisdiction.

A related concern is the fear that an application by a neutral state would force the EC to define its own long-term goals regarding cooperation in foreign policy and military affairs even before negotiations could begin. This would mean that the Community would have to work out a common position on this question, and there is still fundamental division regarding how far Community cooperation in these areas should go.[32] It is possible, of course, that recent developments in Eastern Europe will resolve this problem for Austria, if changes should go so far as to reduce the significance of Austria's neutrality and to give Austria greater latitude in participating in a common Community foreign policy. Likewise, developments could reduce the Community's incentives for formulating a defense policy that would be inconsistent with Austria's neutrality.

Much of Austria's efforts under the global approach was concentrated on using EFTA as an avenue for closer integration with the EC following the opportunity opened by the 1984 EFTA-EC Luxembourg Declaration. The declaration marked an important change in the Community's often dismissive attitude toward EFTA because it affirmed the importance of the EFTA-EC relationship and committed the two sides to cooperation to extend the Community's single market into a "(West) European Economic Space" that would include EFTA.[33] The Luxembourg Declaration echoed the White Book's agenda, providing for cooperation to achieve the

1. harmonization of industrial norms and standards
2. elimination of technical trade barriers
3. simplification of trade administration and origin regulations
4. elimination of unfair trade practices, government subsidies inconsist-

31. For the text of the Luxembourg Compromise, see *Bulletin of the European Communities*, no. 3 (1966), p. 8.

32. See the discussion in Georg Possanner, "SPD gegen 'Fußnotenmitglied' in EG; Kohl: weiterer Neutraler kein Problem," *Presse*, 24 June 1988; Georg Possanner, "Nato positiv zu Wiens EG-Ambitionen. Gute Chancen auch für Abrüstungskonferenz," *Presse*, 30 April-1 May 1988; Andreas Unterberger, "EG-Außenminister über Wiens Kurs skeptisch," *Presse*, 16 October 1987; and Otmar Lahodynsky, "Mock sondiert in Brüssel bei EG-Politikern; Willy De Clercq: Wien soll sich nicht beirren lassen," *Presse*, 22-23 October 1988.

33. "Gemeinsame Erklärung des Ministertreffens der Europäischen Gemeinschaften und ihrer Mitgliedstaaten mit den Staaten der Europäischen Freihandelszone in Luxemburg am 9. April 1984," *Europa-Archiv* 39, no. 12 (1984), pp. D339 f.

ent with the 1972 FTAs, and liberalization of government procurement

5. R&D cooperation
6. more intensive consultations in transport, agriculture, fisheries, and energy policy
7. economic and monetary policy cooperation
8. coordination of labor, cultural, consumer protection, environmental protection, tourism, and intellectual property policies

Austria was able to achieve some important goals through the global approach.[34] EC-EFTA committees were formed to coordinate developments in a range of areas, with emphasis on trade liberalization, R&D, procurement, and environmental protection. Since January 1985, the two groups have been working with the European committees *Comité Européen de Normalisation* (CEN) and *Comité Européen de Normalisation Electrotechnique* (CENELEC) to develop European standards, particularly for telecommunications equipment. Beginning in January 1986, a simplified system of origin rules was adopted for trade in machines. Since autumn 1986, a contact group has been meeting to discuss capital movements, services, and subsidies.

Bilaterally, in 1986 Austria and the EC established a committee to allow Austria to voice its opinions on Community policy initiatives before decisions were finalized. In 1987, Austria and the EC ratified a framework agreement to govern Austria's participation in Community R&D programs, and the first of regular ministerial meetings between Austria and the EC took place in Vienna. In 1988, the Community established a permanent mission in Vienna — the first in any EFTA country — and the two organizations adopted a single document for trade, based on the Community's new administration system.

Austria also undertook unilateral steps to keep pace with developments in the Community. Austria examined 150 recommendations from the EC Commission for the realization of the single market with the goal of reducing inconsistencies between Austrian regulations and Community policy if possible.[35] In addition, following Switzerland's example, since 1987 all legislation

---

34. European Community Commission, "Die Gemeinschaft und die EFTA-Länder: Durchführung der Gemeinsamen Erklärung von Luxemburg vom 9. April 1984," *Mitteilung der Kommission an den Rat,* KOM (85) 206, 13 May 1985; Martin Judge, "Die EFTA-EG-Beziehungen zwei Jahre nach Luxemburg," *EFTA-Bulletin* 27, no. 2 (1986), pp. 6 f.; Leopold Gratz, "Kontakte mit EG vorbereitet; Regelmäßige 'Konsultationen' fixiert," *Presse,* 15 March 1986.

35. "Beratungen zur EG-Politik," *Wiener Zeitung,* 18 March 1987.

proposed in Austria must be reviewed with regard to its conformity with EC regulations in order to minimize incompatibilities.[36] One concrete effect of this policy was the product liability law that Austria developed in 1987, which was based on EC guidelines for the new Community law.[37]

Although the global approach was able to solve some of the problems of discrimination or of uncoupling that the 1992 initiative posed for Austria, over time the limitations of this strategy became apparent. Unilateral measures proved inadequate for several reasons. First, of course, they were not reciprocal. In addition, harmonization could not produce a barrier-free trade relationship no matter how far this was taken because Austrian companies would still face administrative discrimination when they produced outside the Community. Harmonization was also necessarily reactive, which, besides not giving Austrians any influence over developments, also put them at a competitive disadvantage if producers in the Community had access to information regarding future developments (and could prepare their business plans accordingly) before Austrian companies.[38]

Likewise, although EFTA-EC cooperation had benefits, progress had been slow and limited. Given EFTA members' diverse interests and goals vis-à-vis the Community, EFTA could not adequately play its role as an avenue for contact with the Community. This limitation was compounded because EFTA lacked centralized decision-making and executive institutions, which complicated negotiations with the Community. On the other side of the relationship, the EC was ambivalent to close links with EFTA. Despite the Community's desire to cooperate with EFTA — affirmed in the Luxembourg Declaration, and again by EC Commission President Jacques Delors in a speech to the European Parliament on 17 January 1989[39] — the Community's approach made meaningful cooperation difficult. The EC insisted, as it had since 1958, that cooperation with EFTA could not prejudice the Community's integrity, in other words, its autonomous decision-making ability or its further integration.[40] The EC also resents the suggestion that it

---

36. "Intensive Diskussion über EG-Frage; 'Europaprüfung' für alle Gesetze," *Presse,* 9 October 1987.

37. See Willibald Posch, "Produkthaftungsgesetz," *Österreichisches Recht der Wirtschaft* 6, no. 26 (special volume, February 1988), pp. 65–76.

38. "Der österreichische Integrationsbericht", *Presse,* 24 June 1988, selections from Government of Austria, *Der Bericht der Arbeitsgruppe für Europäische Integration.*

39. Text of Delors' speech reprinted in *Bulletin of the European Communities,* supplement 1/89.

40. See European Community Commission, "Die Gemeinschaft," sect. 1, para. 5. See also the *Birkelbach Report* (above, note 18), paras. 89, 90, 92, and 94; and

should extend the benefits of access to the single market to outsiders who are not willing to pay the price by accepting the obligations of full membership.[41] This attitude places clear limits on cooperation with EFTA because participation or cooperation without decision-making rights becomes, in effect, an invitation to outsiders to harmonize their policies with the Community's.

As the limitations on the global approach became apparent, the arguments in Austria favoring full membership with all the rights and obligations that are entailed became more widely accepted. In June 1988, these considerations were wound together in the report submitted by the Government's Working Group for European Integration. The report concluded:

> The question that Austria now faces is, therefore, if consultation and decision-making rights inside a broad – and as a result also pluralistic – amalgamation of states such as the EC does not afford more creative possibilities in the sense of scope for negotiations and options than does remaining outside while being bound to developments by compulsion and harmonization.[42]

This comment acknowledged the need for a closer political association in order to manage economic integration, thereby clearing the way for a membership application. The group's report was significant not just because of the analysis but also because of who was speaking. The group was composed of representatives from the important government ministries, the Social Partners,[43] the VÖI, and the National Bank. The report thus could be interpreted as the consensus on which the government would proceed, and, indeed, a series of reports from the political parties and interest groups involved appeared through the last half of 1988 and the first half of 1989 reaffirming this analysis.[44] The momentum culminated in the membership application

---

European Community Commission, "Stellungnahme der Kommission an den Rat zu den Beziehungen der erweiterten Gemeinschaft mit den nicht beitrittswilligen Mitgliedstaaten der EFTA und dem mit der EFTA assoziierten Staat (16 June 1971)," *Bulletin der Europäischen Gemeinschaften* 4, no. 6 (1971), Beilage 3/71; and the "First Memorandum of the Commission of the European Economic Community to the Council of Ministers of the Community," 26 February 1959, para. 9, quoted in Willy Zeller, "Die bisherige Haltung der EWG gegenüber den Neutralen," in Hans Mayrzedt and Hans Christoph Binswanger (eds.), *Die Neutralen in der Europäischen Integration*, Vienna (1970), p. 204.

41. See Willy de Clercq's comments quoted in "EG-Außenminister: Keine Ausnahmen für Österreich," *Presse*, 9–10 April 1988.

42. See the report quoted in footnote 38.

43. The Social Partners are: the Federal Chamber of Commerce, the Chambers of Agriculture, the Chamber of Labor, and the Austrian Federation of Unions.

44. For a review of these reports, see Manfred Rotter, "Mitgliedschaft, Assoziation, EFTA-Verbund. Die Optionen der österreichischen EG-Politik," *ÖZP*, no. 3

itself. As regards the neutrality issue, Austrian international lawyers argued, above all, that the EEC Treaty itself contained provisions (Articles 223 and 224) that allow for nonparticipation in EC measures incompatible with Austria's obligations as a permanently neutral state.[45] Whether the Community accepts this Austrian position remains to be seen.

Conclusion

In the first stages of its relationship with the EC, the Austrian government believed that it could make close economic integration with the Community compatible with political autonomy by opting for a loose relationship with the EC — free trade. As the Community again became a dynamic institution with the 1992 program, this position became untenable. The 1992 initiative posed three challenges to Austria. Given the existing close links, pressures developed to ensure that the domestic business environment and arrangements with the EC were constructed so that barriers would not arise between Austria and the Community market. Because Austria was a small trade partner and non-EC member, Austria had limited influence on Community policy and therefore bore the responsibility for adjusting its policies to conform to the Community's. This was also a dynamic problem because Austria had to track Community developments and not simply undertake one-shot harmonization, which made the issue of where decision-making power and control resided a recurring problem. After informal arrangements failed to give Austria the role it wanted inside the Community's institutions, the government concluded that only membership in the Community fulfilled the EC's terms for full participation in the single market, and only full participation satisfied the requirements of Austria's economic integration with the EC.

(1989), pp. 197–208.

45. See the chapter by Hanspeter Neuhold in this volume and the literature quoted there.

10

The Saskatchewan Potash Industry and the 1987 U.S. Antidumping Action*

Bruce W. Wilkinson

In recent years the United States has used its antidumping and counter-vailing duty laws and regulations not just to create a "level playing field" but to protect declining industries. Recent studies[1] have, inter alia, documented the protectionist nature of the U.S. actions with regard to the levying of countervailing duties on Atlantic groundfish and softwood lumber. This chapter initially examines this protectionist hypothesis with regard to the 1987 U.S. antidumping action against Canadian potash.[2] It commences with a very short historical sketch of previous U.S. antidumping actions in support of the potash industry. Then it considers in some detail the U.S. laws and

---

* This is a slightly altered version of an article previously published in *Canadian Public Policy/Analyse de Politiques* XV, no. 2 (1989).

1. A.M. Rugman and A. Anderson, "A Fishy Business: The Abuse of American Trade Law in The Atlantic Groundfish Case of 1985–1986," *Canadian Public Policy/Analyse de Politiques* 13, no. 2 (1987), pp. 152–164; F.J. Anderson and R.D. Cairns, "The Softwood Lumber Agreement and Resource Politics," *Canadian Public Policy/Analyse de Politiques* 14, no. 2 (1988), pp. 186–196.

2. Muriate of potash is the product generally referred to in discussions and trade statistics. It is often considered to be the same as potassium chloride (KCl) but is actually only 96.5 percent KCl. Other statistics may use the K_2O equivalent; that is the amount of the potassium oxide in the potash. To arrive at the K_2O equivalent, the product metric tons of potash must be multiplied by 61. In trade contracts for potash, 60 percent K_2O content is normally guaranteed. (Pure KCl is called Sylvite and contains 63.177 percent K_2O.)

198 BRUCE W. WILKINSON

regulations and their application to the potash investigation, as well as the Saskatchewan response, and concludes that once again the United States has gone much beyond the provision of a level playing field. The next section argues that neither the current, new Canadian-U.S. trade agreement nor the negotiations scheduled over the next five to seven years after the conclusion of the FTA with regard to antidumping and countervailing duty definitions and procedures are likely to prevent this type of determination against Canada in the future. The final section briefly considers the monopolistic power possessed by the Canadian producers in this industry, and why it seemed to take a U.S. antidumping allegation for it to be exercised.

A Brief Historical Perspective

In an attempt to protect its domestic potash industry against imports, the United States instituted two previous sets of antidumping actions against foreign exporters. The first was in the autumn of 1967 in response to the growing competition from the then incipient Canadian potash industry. (The action at that time was against France and West Germany as well.) Antidumping duties were never levied, however, because the Saskatchewan government in 1969 instituted production quotas, marketing controls, and a floor price in order to limit production, bring world supply into better balance with demand, and raise world prices. The consequence was that both world and U.S. prices increased, and for about the next decade U.S. production stabilized (see Figure 10.1).[3]

As U.S. production began to diminish more noticeably in the 1980s, the United States charged four other foreign countries — Israel, the GDR, Spain, and the USSR — with both dumping potash in the U.S. and subsidizing their production. These nations together accounted for only 8 percent of U.S. imports and 6.7 percent of the domestic U.S. market. The initial determinations by the U.S. authorities produced dumping margins ranging from 44 percent to 187 percent for the countries involved. But the final determination (see the next section for how U.S. initial and final determinations operate) resulted in no dumping duties (or countervailing duties) being levied,

---

3. For detailed studies of this from a variety of perspectives see J.G. Richards and L.R. Pratt, *Prairie Capitalism: Power and Influence in the New West,* Toronto (1979); D.L. Anderson, "The Saskatchewan Potash Industry: Alternative Strategies for Future Development," *Discussion Paper* 264, Economic Council of Canada, Ottawa (1987).

although the entire process was lengthy and created considerable inconvenience and cost for the accused parties.[4]

The 1987 case we are about to examine is therefore not an isolated event in the potash industry. It is simply a recent example of U.S. action to protect a declining industry.

FIGURE 10.1

Potassium Chloride: U.S. Imports and Production

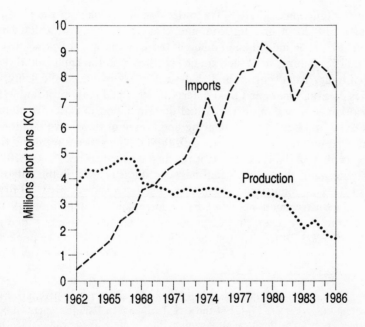

Source: "Potassium Chloride from Canada: Determination of the Commission of Investigation No. 731-TA-374 (Preliminary) under the Tariff Act of 1930, together with Information Contained in the Investigation", U.S. International Trade Commission, Washington, D.C., March 1987, figures 3 and 4, pp. A-15 and A-35.

4. Additional information on these actions may be found in G.S. Barry, "Potash," *Canadian Minerals Yearbook: Review and Outlook,* Minister of Supply and Services, Ottawa (1986; 1987).

U.S. Antidumping Rules and Procedures

On 10 February 1987, two New Mexico companies submitted to the U.S. International Trade Administration of the Department of Commerce (USITA) and to the independent agency, the U.S. International Trade Commission (USITC), allegations of dumping by Canadian potash producers. This submission put the U.S. regulatory wheels in motion.

For dumping to be determined, three things must be present:

1. sales in the U.S. at below fair value
2. material injury or threat of material injury to the industry concerned[5]
3. evidence that the less than fair value sales are causing the injury[6]

It is the function of the USITA to decide initially whether the allegations warrant a full-blown investigation, and, if so, to proceed with determining whether sales have indeed been made in the U.S. market at below fair value. The USITC, in turn, must determine whether material injury or threat of material injury has occurred and that such injury is due to the sales. Both agencies do preliminary and final determinations, and both must find in favor of the original allegation in their final determination in order for dumping duties to be imposed. The sequencing and timing of these investigations are summarized in Table 10.1. As indicated therein, the process from the time a petition is filed until a final verdict is reached normally takes 280 to 310 days.

Three general characteristics of the procedures help to tilt the outcome in favor of the U.S. industry involved. Consider these in turn. First, all firms in the U.S. industry need not support endorsement of a petition. A single "manufacturer, producer, or wholesaler in the United States of a like product" (Section 771 [9] [c]) can file the petition.[7] In this potash case, one of the two petitioning firms — the New Mexico Potash Corporation — was newly

---

5. Material injury means damage that is not "inconsequential, immaterial, or unimportant" (Section 771 [7] [7] of the U.S. Tariff Act of 1930 [as amended by subsequent bills up to the present, including the Omnibus Trade Bill of 1988]). Subsequent section references are to this act as amended.

6. Under the GATT Anti-Dumping Code (to which the United States has agreed), Article 5 paragraph 1, requires that any petition for an antidumping investigation must contain "a causal link between the dumped imports and the alleged injury." This has not been made a specific part of the U.S. legislation, although the U.S. law (Section 731 [2]) does say that the material injury is supposed to be "by reason of imports of that merchandise."

7. Under Section 732 (a) the U.S. Department of Commerce, the USITA can commence an antidumping investigation itself, without having received a petition, if it decides that such an investigation is warranted.

established to operate a mine being disposed of by Kerr-McGee Corporation. The other company was Lundberg Industries Inc., which bought a Carlsbad mine from a major potash producer, the Potash Company of America (which has substantial production in Canada) for a fraction of what it would cost to open a new mine.[8] In other words, the petition was made by companies that had taken over two mines disposed of by long-established potash producers, which apparently did not rate the mines as worth retaining (even though they accounted for 41 percent of U.S. capacity).

Second, a petition is supposed to contain such "information as is reasonably available" (Sec. 732 [b] [1]) to the petitioners that supports the allegations of both sales at less than fair value and material injury. However, the petition may *not* contain all the elements required that can be reasonably expected to be available to the petitioners (such as information on actual or potential declines in market shares, prices, profits, employment, and the like), and the petition will still be acted on by the two agencies. This anomaly occurs because, on the one hand, the USITC's position is that it is essentially the USITA's job and not its own to determine whether the petition contains all the data necessary to justify an investigation (see Table 10.1, line 1.). Yet, strangely enough, the USITC generally does not wait for the USITA decide if the facts warrant a formal inquiry before it commences its own study of whether potential or actual material injury has occurred. In this potash case, the USITC initiated its own investigation of injury the day after the petition was presented to it and the USITA, that is on 11 February 1987. On the other hand, the USITA's position is that it is the USITC's responsibility to decide on whether material injury is involved. Thus its decision to proceed with an investigation does not require evidence of material injury.[9] The effect of this curious evasion of responsibility by the two authorities charged to examine allegations of dumping is that there is a high probability that any petition will be acted on, even if poorly documented by the petitioner(s). Accordingly, uncertainty for and disruption of foreign goods entering the United States may exist for about the next ten months. Even if the final determinations of the USITA and USITC do not support the allegations, the uncertainty and costs could spell the end of export efforts for some foreign producers, particularly small and/or less well-financed ones.

---

8. For about Cdn$ 7 million. A new mine costs well over Cdn$ 100 million. Lundberg Industries has since gone into receivership.

9. N.D. Palmeter, "Injury Determinations in Antidumping and Countervailing Duty Cases: A Commentary on U.S. Practice," *Journal of World Trade Law* 21, no. 1 (1987), pp. 7–45.

TABLE 10.1

The sequence and normal timing for determination of sales at less than fair market value and material injury by the US International Trade Administration (USITA) and the US International Trade Commission (USITC)

Section of *US Tariff Act* of 1930

Line (as amended)	Agency	Time period in days
		20 40 60 80 100 120 140 160 180 200 220 240 260 280 300 320
1. 732(c)	USITA	--- |20 Determines if an investigation is warranted.
2. 733(a)	USITC	----- |45 Preliminary determination of *material injury* (If negative, ITA does not proceed. The case is closed.)
3. 733(b)	USITA	------- |160 Preliminary determination of *sale price less than fair value*[1] (Could be negative or affirmative, but investigation continues).
4. 735(a)	USITA	|235 Final determination of *sale price less than fair value* (75 days after preliminary determination).[2]
5a. 735(b)	USITC	|280 Final determination *of material injury* when ITA's *preliminary* determination of sales less than fair value was *affirmative*.[3]
b.		|310 Final determination of *material injury* when ITA's preliminary determination of sales less than fair value was *negative* but final determination was *affirmative*. (75 days after ITA's *affirmative* final determination).

1 This could be extended to 210 days after the initial petition in 'extraordinarily complicated cases'.
2 This could be extended to 135 days under some circumstances.
3 This could be measured as 120 days after the ITA's preliminary determination or 45 days after ITA's final determination.

Source: Derived from *US Tariff Act* of 1930 as amended.

Third, material injury is defined *only* in terms of producer interests; that is, from the perspective of the petitioners. In U.S. antidumping law there is no provision for the interests of consumers of a product to be taken into account when calculating whether dumping is injurious to the economy. Consequently, although in the past the Antitrust Division of the U.S. Department of Justice has submitted briefs to the USITA and USITC on particular antidumping cases, and the U.S. Federal Trade Commission has done the same with particular emphasis on the overall costs and benefits of antidumping actions, the USITC is under no legal obligation to take such submissions into account when deciding whether material injury to the United States has occurred.[10] In the USITC's preliminary determination of injury in regard to potash, the interests of and effects on the agricultural community, which absorbs 93 percent of all potash used in the United States, were not even discussed.

This lacuna is an interesting contrast to the Canadian law (the Special Import Measures Act) that specifically provides that the public interest, rather than just the narrow interest of competing producers, may be taken into account when determining whether antidumping duties should be levied. It is also in contrast to the EEC law that provides that Community interests should be taken into account, such as those of "consumers, import-using industries, and exporting industries."[11]

The Determination of Material Injury with Respect to Potash by the USITC

The preliminary finding of the USITC was that the U.S. potash industry was materially injured because of imports from Canada of potassium chloride. The members of the USITC based this conclusion

> on the poor performance of the domestic industry, the substantial and increasing market penetration of Canadian imports, and the apparent adverse impact of imports on prices for the domestic product during the period of investigation.[12]

---

10. K. Stegmann, "Anti-Dumping Policy and the Consumer," *Journal of World Trade Law* 19, no. 5 (1985), pp. 466–484.

11. Ibidem, p. 473.

12. "Potassium Chloride from Canada: Determination of the Commission in Investigation No. 731-TA-374 (Preliminary) Under the Tariff Act of 1930, Together With the Information Obtained in the Investigation," USITC, Washington, D.C., (March 1987), p. 3.

Consider these three claims. Difficulties in the U.S. potash industry are not a new phenomenon. Since 1966–1967 when the United States was still the world's largest producer of potash (accounting for 19 percent of world production), U.S. production has declined fairly steadily. By 1986, the United States accounted for only 4.2 percent of world production, 3.5 percent of world capacity, and 1 percent of world reserves (Table 10.2). U.S. reserves and production are expected to continue declining. Imports have exceeded U.S. domestic production since 1968, as Figure 10.1 portrays, and in 1986 accounted for over 90 percent of U.S. consumption. Canada, with the largest and most economically mined potash reserves in the world — 48 percent of the world reserves — supplied 93.4 percent of those imports in 1986.

TABLE 10.2

World Potash Reserves, Capacity, and Production (1986)

Country	Percentage of Reserves	Percentage of Capacity	Percentage of Production
Canada	48.1	31.6	24.7
USSR	32.8	33.5	34.0
GDR	8.7	9.2	12.2
FRG	5.5	8.0	7.7
United States	1.0	3.5	4.2
France	0.3	4.8	5.7
Israel	*	3.4	4.4
Spain	0.3	2.3	2.5
Other	3.3	3.7	4.6
Total	100.0	100.0	100.0

* Not available

Sources: For percentages of reserves and capacity, USITC, *Potassium Chloride from Canada: Determination of the Commission in Investigation No. 731-TA-374 (Preliminary) Under the Tariff Act of 1930, Together With the Information Obtained in the Investigation,* Washington, D.C. (1987), Table 3, p. A-9. For percentages of production, U.S. Department of Interior, "Metals & Minerals," in *Minerals Yearbook,* vol. 1, Washington (1988), p. 766.

The USITC noted these facts in their preliminary report and observed that "the condition of the domestic industry during the investigatory period (1984–1986) reflected the overall decline the domestic industry has been experiencing over the past decade."[13]

Yet they still concluded that imports from Canada were the key source of material injury even though only two of seven U.S. producers (presumably the two petitioning firms, although no names were revealed) reported lost sales due to imports from Canada. The commission focused on the fact that the Canadian share of total U.S. consumption rose to an all time high in 1986 of 84.3 percent. As for the other factors regarding the long-run decline of the industry, the commission's members contented themselves by saying, "In any final investigation, these factors will be further examined."[14]

It was undoubtedly easier for them to take this rather cavalier attitude to these issues because the U.S. legislation does *not* contain Article 3, paragraph 4, of the GATT Anti-Dumping Code on injury determination (to which the United States is a party). This article makes it very clear that dumped imports must be shown to be the *cause* of the injury and that "injuries caused by other factors must not be attributed to the dumped imports." Some of the other factors mentioned include "contraction in demand ... competition between the foreign and domestic producers ... developments in technology ... and the productivity of the domestic industry" — the very factors relevant to this particular case.[15]

With regard to the effect of Canadian imports on prices, the USITC analysis was even less convincing. The commission's own surveys revealed that U.S. potash producers' *net* (free on board – f.o.b.) prices on sales in the United States actually fell *faster* than did those of Canadian exporters during the period under review.[16] Even though the U.S. legislation says the commission is to look for evidence of "significant price *undercutting* by the imported

---

13. Ibidem, p. 7.

14. Ibidem, p. 10.

15. There have also been other instances in which the USITC has ignored the U.S. commitments under the GATT Anti-Dumping Code, in particular Article 3, paragraph 4, of that code; see N.D. Palmeter, "Dumping Margins and Material Injury: The USITC is Free to Choose," *Journal of World Trade Law* 21, no. 4 (1987), pp. 173–175.

16. U.S. domestic sales prices for coarse potash diminished from an index of 100 to 81.5 from the beginning of 1985 until the end of 1986, whereas the Canadian index for sales into the United States dropped only from 100 to 86.5 over the same period. For granular potash, the U.S. index declined to 77.5, whereas the Canadian fell only to 98; USITC, "Potassium Chloride from Canada: Determination of the Commission," p. A-40, Table 18.

merchandise"[17] (italics mine) it did not let this initial price information stop them in their endeavor to find material injury.

They went on to note that transportation costs averaged around 40 percent of *delivered* price and that Canadian producers typically had substantially lower transport costs than did U.S. producers — for several reasons. They frequently sold in larger volumes than did the U.S. mines and were thus able to ship both by barge (the cheapest form of transportation) and by unit trains (the next cheapest) rather than by single rail cars or trucks. The Canadian firms were also observed to have negotiated very favorable freight rates with both Canadian and U.S. railways. In addition, for the large upper Midwest U.S. market, Saskatchewan producers generally were closer than were producers in New Mexico. Thus, once transportation costs were introduced, it is not surprising that the USITC found that Canadian *delivered* prices were frequently (although not always) below U.S. prices in the same markets.[18] It is surprising, however, to see such price differences, based as they primarily are on transportation cost differences, used as evidence that the U.S. industry was being "materially injured by reason of allegedly lower than fair value imports from Canada."[19] This is particularly so, given that it is not even the commission's responsibility to be calculating the price differences (it is the USITA's duty to do this), and more important, given that Sections 772 and 773 of the U.S. Tariff Act of 1930 (as amended) make it clear that the foreign price to be used in comparing with U.S. prices is the price at the producer's gate, that is, excluding transportation costs![20]

---

17. Section 771 (7) (C) of the U.S. Tariff Act of 1930 (as amended). This provision is also in the GATT Anti-Dumping Code, Article 3 paragraph 2.

18. In thirty-five weekly observations for the U.S. Midwest (Illinois, Indiana, Iowa, Missouri, and Ohio), upper Midwest (Michigan, Minnesota, and Wisconsin), and Tennessee, thirty-one observations showed Canadian delivered prices to be below U.S. prices. For deliveries to Texas, Oklahoma, and Georgia, however, Canadian prices were all above U.S. prices; see USITC, "Potassium Chloride from Canada: Determination of the Commission," pp. A-43 f.; Tables 19 and 20. On average, these crude survey numbers suggested that Canadian delivered prices were about 10 percent below U.S. delivered prices.

19. USITC, "Potassium Chloride from Canada: Determination of the Commission," p. 12.

20. Section 772 (d) (2) (A) of the U.S. Tariff Act of 1930 (as amended) says that the exporter's price on sales in the United States should be reduced by "any additional costs, charges, and expenses, and United States import duties, incident to bringing the merchandise from the place of shipment in the country of exportation to the place of delivery in the United States."

In arriving at its determination of material injury (by a 5 to 0 vote), the commission also used some confused and inaccurate economic analysis to dismiss the significance of the 9 percent decline in the value of the Canadian dollar in terms of the U.S. dollar as a reason for the greater competitiveness of the Canadian product.[21] As well, it chose to minimize the importance of its own surveys, which revealed that fast deliveries by Canadian suppliers, because they had warehouses close to the main U.S. markets (which U.S. suppliers did not have), was another reason why U.S. buyers purchased Canadian rather than U.S. potash. The commission also assigned no importance to their own data, which revealed that U.S. potash exports actually increased from 1984 to 1986 and were at an all-time high in this latter year. They argued that this was simply because New Mexico producers had a transportation cost advantage over Canadian producers in South American markets — even though, as we have just seen, they used the cheaper transportation costs on Canadian sales to the U.S. market as part of their evidence of dumping by Canadian producers. They ignored too that even in 1984 the unit value of their exports was 18.6 percent below the unit value of their domestic shipments and that this margin widened to 36.2 percent by 1986.[22]

The chairman of the commission wrote a separate judgement on the case. This judgement, inter alia, simply accepted the dumping margin alleged by the petitioners of 42.86 percent as evidence of dumping. It also concluded that, because third country foreign producers were already operating at capacity, the elasticity of supply from these sources was very low. Therefore, Canada had greater power to damage the U.S. market by cutting prices. This line of reasoning supposedly provided support for the idea that material injury was being inflicted by reason of imports from Canada. No thought was given to the possibility (to which we shall return in the final section) that

---

21. They argued that since *aggregate* producer, or wholesale, prices had fallen in the United States by 3.5 percent over the period, while the Canadian *aggregate* producer price index had risen by 4.3 percent, this change should have wiped out 7.8 percentage points of the 9 percent exchange rate change favoring Canadian potash producers; USITC, "Potassium Chloride from Canada: Determination of the Commission," pp. A-45 f.). Their argument in essence was that potash prices should have followed precisely the aggregate price indexes for producer goods in both countries so that over 7 percentage points of the advantage to Canadian producers of the 9 percent decline in the Canadian dollar would be removed. This is clearly an inappropriate use of price index information.

22. USITC, "Potassium Chloride from Canada: Determination of the Commission," p. A-17. One could argue that the U.S. industry was itself dumping abroad. This, apparently, is quite an acceptable type of behavior — as long as it is the United States that is doing it.

market power by one set of suppliers plus barriers to entry by other potential external suppliers (in this case due to their lack of additional capacity) are usually not associated with price cuts — unless there is considerable competition among them. Finally, in a statement similar to that of the majority USITC determination, the chairman observed "that most of the facts presented are also consistent with a U.S. industry experiencing a decline in its resource base," but preferred to delay considering this argument until the case went to a final determination.[23] The message seems to be clear: The USITC is geared to give the domestic petitioners every benefit of the doubt and to minimize the significance of those factors that might otherwise halt the investigation.

The Determination of Sales at Less Than Fair Value by the USITA

To determine if the foreign producers' sales in the United States are at less than fair value, the USITA compares the price at which the goods are sold in the United States with the price at which they are sold in the foreigner's market, that is, with the "foreign market value."[24] The estimation of these prices is complicated. The methodology is designed so as to establish what these prices are at the producer's gate.[25]

To calculate the U.S. price in this potash case, charges such as for inland freight in Canada, water freight, U.S. inland freight, insurance, handling charges, and brokerage were all subtracted "where appropriate"[26] from the price payed by buyers in the United States. For the Canadian firms that had affiliates in the United States handling their sales *after* the potash had been shipped to the United States, additional deductions were made by the USITA for items such as advertising, warranty, commissions, and credit charges.

---

23. USITC, "Potassium Chloride from Canada: Determination of the Commission," p. 23, note 18.

24. In the USITA revised regulations on Anti-Dumping Duties as a result of the Trade and Tariff Act of 1984, Washington, D.C. (19 CFR, Part 353), "foreign market value" is distinguished from "fair value" but is normally meant to be an indicator of fair value as well.

25. See the U.S. Tariff Act of 1930 (as amended), Section 772 and 773.

26. This is the USITA's phrasing; USITA, "Potassium Chloride from Canada: Preliminary Determination of Sales at Less than Fair Value," Washington, D.C. (1987), p. 7.

Foreign market value may be established by the USITA in one of three ways. The first is the selling price of the product in the exporter's domestic market. For this method to be used the firm's domestic sales must be at least 5 percent of sales to third countries, and at least 10 percent of all these sales must be above production costs as calculated by the USITA. The second alternative is to use the sale price in a single third country whose selection is based on a number of criteria such as whether that market is deemed to be similar to the U.S. market. The third approach is to *construct* a foreign market value. This method entails estimating the producer's production costs and adding on 10 percent or more for general expenses and a minimum of 8 percent for profit.[27]

In this potash case, the U.S. petitioning companies submitted that "home market and third country prices were made at less than the cost of production and that constructed value should be used to compute foreign market value."[28] But the USITA used all three methods, according to whether, in their judgement, their rules were satisfied. One firm did not have sufficient sales within Canada and so sale prices by Canoptext (the marketing corporation for all offshore sales by Saskatchewan producers) in Japan were employed. Two others had insufficient sales in Canada deemed to be above what the USITA had calculated to be their costs of production, so constructed costs were used. Two other firms had some sales in Canada that satisfied the USITA's criteria and some that did not. Thus for five of the eight firms, *constructed* (not actual) foreign market values were used for all or at least some of the comparisons with the calculated sale prices in the United States.

In their computations the USITA estimated costs of production based on the submissions by the individual producing firms and then adjusted those reports where, in its judgement, the amount stated by the firms "did not fully reflect the costs incurred by the company."[29] Once the basis costs were estimated, including general expenses (which turned out to be, after adjust-

---

27. The original GATT text, Article 6, paragraph 1, as well as the Anti-Dumping Code agreed to in the Tokyo Round of the GATT negotiations, Article 2, paragraph 3 and paragraph 4, also allow for these three methods, although details are not spelled out. For example, according to Article 2, paragraph 4, of the Anti-Dumping Code says there can be an allowance of "a reasonable amount for administrative, selling, and any other costs, and for profits. As a general rule, the addition for profit shall not exceed the profit normally realized on sales of products of the same general category in the domestic market of the country of origin."

28. USITA, "Potassium Chloride from Canada: Preliminary Determination," p. 7.

29. Ibidem, p. 8.

ments, greater than the minimum 10 percent), 8 percent for profit was added on because actual profit recorded by the firms "was less than the statutory minimum."[30]

Consider what is involved here. Firms are not allowed, according to this methodology, to operate at less than 8 percent profit, let alone with losses.[31] It is like saying that, by law, weaknesses in demand for a product are not allowed to exist. Nor are firms allowed to lower their prices when demand is weak. Yet we know that it may be necessary, and certainly very appropriate, for firms to operate at a loss in the short run when the plant and the equipment are already in place.[32] If the price that a firm believes it can achieve for its product (precise demand curves are not easily or accurately estimated) is less than what will cover average total costs, it is still worthwhile for the firm to operate as long as the price is greater than variable costs so as to cover at least a portion of fixed costs. With potash mines it is very important to keep them operating because to attempt to start them up again after a lengthy shutdown is difficult and may be more expensive than to keep them running. At this time, the Saskatchewan potash industry was operating at only about two-thirds of capacity. Competition among firms for a share of the U.S. market was intense. One would therefore expect prices to be below average total cost and for losses to be experienced — as indeed they were.

Another characteristic of the U.S. methodology may also bias the facts so that sales at less than fair value are observed. Although it may not have influenced the results in this case (the details were not available), the approach is worth mentioning, for it highlights the protectionist nature of the U.S. procedures. When comparing U.S. price with foreign market value (however that value is determined)

> if an individual comparison yields a negative number because United States price exceeds foreign market value, the comparison is not included in the averaging and, therefore, cannot offset sales with dutiable margins. *This technique guarantees that any instance of dumping, however isolated, cannot be easily negated by fair trade practices* (italics added).[33]

---

30. Ibidem, p. 10.

31. It should be noted, however, that in this regard the Canadian law is not better. It has followed the U.S. example and established an 8 percent profit rate (Regulations Respecting Special Import Measures 11 [B] [v]).

32. It is certainly short-run analysis that is appropriate here, for the USITA looked only at sales into the United States for the six months between 1 September 1986 and 28 February 1987.

33. S.A. Coffield, "U.S. Canada Natural Resources Trade: Sources of Conflict/Prospects for Agreement," in Owen J. Saunders (ed.), *Trading Canada's*

The resulting dutiable margins that the USITA established in their preliminary determination of 20 August 1987 for the individual Saskatchewan suppliers of potash were as follows:[34]

Potash Corporation of Saskatchewan	51.90 percent
International Minerals and Chemical Corporation	9.14 percent
PPG/Kalium	26.67 percent
Central Canada Potash	85.20 percent
Potash Company of America	77.44 percent
All Others	36.63 percent

These were calculated as the difference between the USITA's estimates of foreign market values and the prices on sales in the United States. Responses from the industry suggest that the percentages bore little relationship to the actual differences in prices charged by these firms on their sales in the United States compared with their production costs, sale prices in Canada, or prices on sales to third countries. Valid or not, the above producers were ordered to make cash deposits or to post bonds equal to the above margins on all new sales or deliveries after 21 August 1987.[35]

An interesting point arises with respect to the exceptionally high antidumping margin calculated for Central Canada Potash (CCP). For this firm, the foreign market value was determined by employing Canpotex's prices on sales to Japan. What is strongly suggested by the USITA's numbers is that Canpotex, apparently because it spoke with a single voice for all Saskatchewan producers in offshore sales (so that there was no price competition among them), was able to exact a much higher price from Japan than CCP was exacting on sales in the United States. Canpotex is not permitted to handle sales to the United States for one reason: Some of the firms that are shareholders in it are U.S.-owned. To avoid any charges being laid against them under U.S. antitrust laws, they must refrain from being party to any monopoly marketing agency selling into the United States.[36] Thus we have

Natural Resources, Toronto (1987), p. 129. My examination of Canadian rules did not suggest that this type of procedure is followed in Canada.

34. USITA, "Potassium Chloride from Canada: Preliminary Determination," pp. 13 f.

35. Even as the USITA established these margins, it noted that the Canadian share of U.S. consumption had actually *decreased* from 84 percent in 1986 to 74 percent in the first five months in 1987; USITC, "Potassium Chloride from Canada: Determination of the Commission," p. 12.

36. A lawyer from a Washington legal firm even sits at Canpotex shareholders meetings (the shareholders being all the potash-producing companies in Saskatchewan) to assist the members in avoiding statements or actions that might trans-

the fascinating spectacle of one branch of the U.S. government (the USITA) finding fault with a corporation's competitive pricing behavior in the United States, which probably would not have occurred if it were not for the fact that another branch of the U.S. government (the Antitrust Division of the Department of Justice) was entrusted with ensuring that pricing in the United States was competitive! In other words, if Canpotex had been permitted to handle sales to the United States, CCP's price in the United States (and that of other Saskatchewan producers) would likely not have been as low.

The next stage in the U.S. antidumping procedures would have involved the USITA making a final determination of sales prices less than fair value by 3 November 1987, seventy-five days after its initial determination. Then, forty-five days after that, on 18 December the USITC would have had to make its final determination of material injury. Before these determinations occurred, however, the initial findings of the USITC and the USITA, plus the financial losses being experienced by the Saskatchewan potash industry, produced responses by the Saskatchewan government and the Saskatchewan producers, which caused the U.S. investigation to be suspended.

The Saskatchewan Response

On 1 September 1987, the government of Saskatchewan introduced legislation empowering it to regulate all potash production in the province. This legislation did three main things:

1. made the cabinet responsible for approving any expansion of productive capacity
2. gave the cabinet the authority to set the total quantity of potash to be produced in any set period
3. established a Potash Resources Board with the responsibility of "allocating the total allowable provincial production between the mines to achieve a fair balance between producer and crown interest"[37]

This legislation is within the constitutional power of the province because Section 92A of the new Canadian Constitution Act, passed in December

gress U.S. antitrust legislation. Incidentally, Canpotex does not sell in Canada either.

37. Government of Saskatchewan, Department of Energy and Mines, "Saskatchewan Moves to Protect Potash Industry," *News Release,* Regina, 1 September 1987, p. 2.

1981, expressly gives the provinces the right to make such laws with respect to their natural resources.[38] Essentially, the government was saying to the industry that if it could not discipline itself with regard to new investment and production, the government would do it for it.

Even before the legislation was announced, however, the government-owned, and largest, potash producer – the Potash Corporation of Saskatchewan (PCS) – accounting for nearly 50 percent of production, had begun taking steps to reduce the huge losses it had experienced in 1986 and early 1987.[39] Senior management was changed, employees were laid off, production was severely cut, and price discounting was reduced in an attempt "to get pricing back into the hands of the producer."[40] Within four days after the Saskatchewan legislation was introduced, PCS raised its price on sales to the United States by 60 percent (US$ 46 per metric ton), which was in excess of the 51.9 percent dumping margin calculated on its U.S. sales by the USITA. (This increase was to be refundable if the USITA did not assess a dumping margin in its final determination.) The other Saskatchewan producers quickly followed with similar price increases.

The changing attitudes of the Saskatchewan government and the potash industry were noted in the offshore markets. Even before the Saskatchewan legislation, the premier's suggestion that the province was about to take action that would take the excess capacity there off the world market raised the price for which Canpotex was able to sell potash in Asia by US$ 10 per metric ton.[41]

The United States was quick to react also. Three weeks after the Saskatchewan government's legislation was announced, the USITA reported that it was going to delay its final determination as to whether Canadian potash was being sold in the United States at less than fair value from 3 November until early January. This meant that there would be time for negotiations with the Saskatchewan industry.

On 7 January, an agreement between the USITA and the Saskatchewan industry was announced.[42] It was not, however, a "negotiated" agreement in

---

38. The Saskatchewan government carefully stayed away from setting a floor price for exports – an action that in 1970 had resulted in a constitutional challenge.

39. Losses in 1986 were Cdn$ 103 million, and in the first quarter of 1987 losses were Cdn$ 23 million.

40. C. Childers, quoted in "Trimmer Potash Corp. Bouncing Back," *Financial Post*, 31 December 1988–2 January 1989.

41. From discussions with a Canpotex official.

42. Actually the agreement was reached on 9 December 1987, but then thirty days was allowed for submissions by interested parties.

the true sense of that word, in which some give and take was involved. The condition agreed to by the Saskatchewan exporters was taken verbatim out of the U.S. Tariff Act of 1930 (as amended), Section 734 [c] [1] (B). It required that Canadian exporters to the United States henceforth price their potash so that the

> *amount by which the estimated foreign market value exceeds the United States price will not exceed 15 percent of the weighted average amount by which the estimated foreign market value exceeded the United States price for all less than fair value entries* by [the] producer/exporter that were examined during the Department's investigation. (The part in italics is the part taken directly from the Tariff Act of 1930, as amended).[43]

An interesting aspect of the U.S. law is that Section 734 [c] [1] also says that the agreement with foreign exporters must "eliminate completely the injurious effect of exports to the United States ... [and ensure that] the suppression or undercutting of price levels of domestic products by imports of that merchandise will be prevented."

That is, the U.S. law apparently assumes that by exporters raising their original prices sufficiently to cover 85 percent of the dumping margin calculated by the USITA, the price difference between foreign and domestic products and their injury to U.S. producers will be removed! The implication is that the U.S. law assumes the dumping margins calculated by the designated procedures will exaggerate the dumping margins by 15 percent.

In any event, the evidence is clear that the U.S. system is designed not just to ensure "fair trade" or "a level playing field," but also to protect U.S. industries such as potash, which, because of the depletion of low-cost reserves, cannot compete with low-priced imports from abroad. The idea that trade should be based on comparative advantage, due in turn to differing relative factor endowments, seems to have been lost to the U.S. authorities.

The type of biased analysis by the USITC and USITA in this potash case is similar in principle to what we know was done with regard to Atlantic groundfish[44] and softwood lumber.[45] In these latter two cases, the U.S. system was employed not just to counter the advantage enjoyed by Canada

---

43. Potassium chloride from Canada with 0.5 percent or less of sodium chloride is excluded from the agreement because one U.S. buyer testified that the domestic industry could not meet its requirements for low sodium potash; USITA, "Suspension of Antidumping Investigation: Potassium Chloride from Canada," Washington, D.C. (January 8, 1988), pp. 2 f.).

44. Rugman and Anderson, "A Fishy Business," pp. 152–164.

45. M.B. Percy and C. Yoder, *The Softwood Lumber Dispute & Canada-U.S. Trade in Natural Resources,* Halifax (1987); Anderson and Cairns, "The Softwood Lumber Agreement."

because of relatively abundant resource endowments, but also due to differences in resource management policies and greater productivity. Protectionism was the underlying motive in each case. This conclusion is consistent with the fact that, at a 1987 conference, James A. Baker III, then secretary of the treasury in the Reagan administration, proudly stated that the administration had taken care of the nation's interests effectively by giving it more new protection from imports than any previous administration in the past half-century![46]

Some Implications for the Future

The potash investigation, coming as it did during the final stages of negotiations of the incipient comprehensive bilateral FTA between Canada and the United States, raises an important question for the future. Will the FTA change anything? That is, will Canada now be in any better position to avoid such biased, protectionist charges in the future? It was argued forcibly by Rugman and Anderson and others such as Macdonald that the FTA was needed to do just this.[47] Although this is not the place for a full-scale analysis of the Canadian-U.S. agreement, a few comments can be made that indicate that little progress has actually been made to reduce Canadian vulnerability to similar future U.S. actions.

First, existing U.S. antidumping (or countervailing duty) laws and regulations remain untouched by the FTA. In fact, as a consequence of the 1988 U.S. Omnibus Trade Bill, which takes precedence over the FTA,[48] some of the antidumping provisions are actually strengthened and/or made more specific. These include provisions to give the U.S. agencies new authority to estimate foreign input costs in construction of their estimates of foreign market values (Section 1318), to monitor products downstream from the one on which the antidumping or countervailing duty is levied (Section 1320), to

46. J.J. Schott, "The Free Trade Agreement: A U.S. Assessment," in J.J. Schott and M.G. Smit (eds.), *The Canada-United States Free Trade Agreement: The Global Impact,* Halifax (1988), p. 11.

47. See Rugman and Anderson, "A Fishy Business," and others such as D.S. Macdonald, "Canada-United States Trade Liberalization: Implications for Canada's Natural Resource Industries," in J. Owen Saunders (ed.), *Trading Canada's Natural Resources,* Toronto (1987), pp. 69–79.

48. One of the reasons originally given by supporters of the FTA was that it would give Canada an exemption from the U.S. Omnibus Trade Bill – a hope that was not realized.

police the antidumping or countervailing duty orders (Section 1321), and a number of other amendments having to do with steel products (Section 1322), short life cycle merchandise (Section 1323), processed agricultural products (Section 1326), and material injury (Section 1329). .

The FTA does provide for a binational panel review of final antidumping (and countervailing duty) determinations. (There is no provision for panel review after the preliminary determinations, which was when the potash case was settled.) But even here a panel can only decide whether the determinations were in accord with the existing U.S. law — which is defined as consisting of "the relevant statutes, legislative history, regulations, administrative practice, and judicial precedents" (Article 1904 [2]).

A good case could be made that, quite apart from the protectionist statutes and regulations whose implications we have noted in reviewing the potash situation, there are enough administrative practices and judicial precedents available from other cases that it will be extremely difficult for any binational panel to overthrow final determinations. If the U.S. authorities expressly take into consideration all the factors that their rules require, weigh them, and conclude that the evidence supports a determination of dumping, then it is highly doubtful that any bilateral panel will have any basis for reversing a determination. The panel may quibble that a different set of weights should have been used, such as in deciding whether material injury has really occurred and the cause of this injury, but this is not likely to provide a firm basis for rejecting a U.S. decision. The only merit in a binational panel procedure may be that it could take less time (only 315 days from the date a request is made for a panel to be established) than a case taken to the U.S. courts (although, as I have argued elsewhere, it may sometimes not be as quick as an appeal to the GATT).[49]

Canadian officials emphasize the negotiations that are to ensue during the next five to seven years after the conclusion of the FTA whereby new roles governing dumping and subsidization are to be developed so as to "obviate the need for border remedies."[50] Some observers were optimistic enough to argue that during the initial negotiations the definition of dumping could be limited to include only predatory behavior. (This is behavior in which a domestic industry is forced to close down due to cheap imports, and then foreign firms can raise their prices once again without much fear of new competition arising.) Antidumping rules could then, supposedly, have been

49. Bruce W. Wilkinson, "The Canada-United States Economic Integration Agreement and the GATT," in M. Gold and D. Leyton-Brown (eds.), *Tradeoffs on Free Trade: The Canada-U.S. Free Trade Agreement*, Toronto (1988), pp. 55–64.

50. Canada Department of External Affairs, *The Canada-U.S. Free Trade Agreement*, Ottawa (1987), p. 268.

eliminated and predatory behavior could have been dealt with using competition laws.[51] The reason given in Canada as to why these matters were not satisfactorily dealt with in the negotiations is that "the two sides recognized that developing a new regime was a complex task and would require more time."[52]

However, the United States never really took seriously the Canadian attempts to develop new rules. It waited until just two or three weeks before the deadline for the negotiations to be concluded before presenting its proposal regarding subsidies — a proposal that was unacceptable to Canada because of its extremely one-sided nature.[53] Moreover, the U.S. system will not be readily altered because of the many bureaucratic groups and lobbies which have extensive vested interests in its continuation. The United States may once again not give the matter serious attention until the deadline for negotiations is nearly up.[54] In doing this, the United States would gain great leverage to get its own way, and it would retain the existing plethora of trade remedies. If there is a failure to reach bilateral approval of the rules to govern dumping and subsidies, the U.S. legislation passed to enact the trade agreement requires the President to *justify to the Congress why the entire agreement should even be continued* (Section 410 [a]). By the end of seven years, Canadian integration with the United States would be so extensive that there would be much pressure on Canadian officials to do whatever was necessary to preserve the FTA at that time.

In conclusion, it is not all clear that the recent Canadian-U.S. trade package will produce, now or in the future, much improvement in the way the United States administers its "fair trade" laws with regard to dumping. Certainly no one should expect that the removal of tariffs as a consequence of the trade deal will remove the possibility of antidumping actions. Potash has been tariff-free in the United States since 1930.

Saskatchewan Monopolistic Power

One final aspect of this potash case deserves mention. The U.S. action, although biased to protect the U.S. potash sector, did stimulate price

51. MacDonald, "Canada-United States Trade Liberalization."

52. Canada Department of External Affairs, *The Canada-U.S. Free Trade*, p. 268.

53. G. Ritchie, quoted in "Business Subsidies," *Financial Post*, 18 November 1988. Gordon Ritchie was the deputy trade negotiator for the Canadian-U.S. deal.

54. G. Ritchie, quoted in "Faceoff on Subsidies Still Poses Challenge," *Financial Post*, 31 December 1988.

increases for the Saskatchewan potash industry, both in the United States and in world markets. The situation resulted in price increases for potash in world markets that would otherwise have taken the markets themselves three or four years to produce.[55] Nor were prices raised only on sales to the United States. In offshore markets, the price increase that was made possible on Canpotex sales during August 1987 of US$ 10 to US$ 71 per metric ton, was followed by additional price hikes of US$ 10 per metric ton in January 1988 after the Saskatchewan firms complied with U.S. law, and a further US$ 10 increase to US$ 91 per metric ton in August 1988. By January 1989, the offshore price was US$ 101 per metric ton.[56] Although these offshore increases have not produced returns at the minehead as high as the higher prices in the United States,[57] they, along with some expansion of world potash demand, nevertheless enabled the industry to improve its performance in 1987 and 1988.[58]

The question that arises from this information, which we will pursue briefly here, is: Why did the Saskatchewan industry (government and producers) wait for the U.S. antidumping action against it before it began to take steps to restrict action and to raise prices? The question becomes of

---

55. J. Douglas, quoted in "Potash Bill Sends World Prices Soaring," *Globe and Mail*, 17 September 1987.

56. This was for standard muriate of potash (KCl) with a 61 percent K_2O content, shipped f.o.b. from Vancouver. To arrive at the price received by producers at their mines in Saskatchewan, between Cdn$ 30 and Cdn$ 38 (or about US$ 27) must be substracted for transportation costs. From Green Markets, "Fertilizer Market Intelligence Weekly" (various issues), and a discussion with a senior Canpotex official.

57. To illustrate, the January 1988 U.S. price was about US$ 100 per metric ton of standard muriate at the Saskatchewan minehead compared to US$ 81 for offshore potash sales f.o.b. Vancouver, from which the transportation costs back to Saskatchewan have to be substracted. Even in January 1989, by which time prices in the United States were reported to have decreased to about US$ 85 compared with US$ 100 a year earlier (while offshore prices had risen to about US$ 101, f.o.b. Vancouver, after transport costs back to the mine were deducted), the return on sales to the United States was still greater. It is next to impossible to make detailed comparisons of returns to individual producers at the minehead because accurate transportation costs to the various U.S. markets are a closely guarded secret.

58. Saskatchewan Energy and Mines reported that 1987 prices for the industry were on average 15 percent higher than in the previous year. The improved performance is also in part due to countries such as China and India buying potash again after a few years absence from world markets and to more acreage being sown in the United States.

even greater interest when we note four other facts. First, the *only* place in the world in which there was significant excess capacity (outside the United States) was Saskatchewan.[59] For some years the offshore potash industry had been functioning at full capacity (95 percent or above).

Saskatchewan's position with regard to potash was thus akin to that of Saudi Arabia with respect to oil, only more favorable. It had nearly 50 percent of world reserves, 30 percent of world potash capacity, and nearly 50 percent of world trade in potash. And because its competitors had little, if any, excess capacity, at least in the shorter run of three to five years (unlike Saudi Arabia whose competitors have substantial excess capacity), Saskatchewan was in a stronger position than Saudi Arabia to restrict production and to put upward pressure on prices, without fear of having its huge U.S. market completely or largely usurped by imports from offshore.

Second, as noted earlier, two decades before, when the United States perceived its potash industry as severely threatened by the surge of cheaper potash from Saskatchewan, antidumping charges were instituted against Saskatchewan (as well as French and West German) imports. These charges were deflected, and world prices increased primarily because of restrictions on production being imposed in that province. One would think that the lesson from that time would not have been forgotten — or ignored — namely, that Saskatchewan could favorably influence world potash prices.

Third, the remaining four significant producers of potash — the USSR, the GDR, Israel, and Spain — were charged by the United States with dumping and subsidization in the mid-1980s. Although the final determinations did not support the initial allegations, these producers had clearly been given a message that low prices on their sales in the United States that would hasten the diminution of the U.S. industry were not acceptable. Thus, all the noteworthy potash-producing nations had received signals that the United States was prepared to take such action as was necessary to protect its potash industry from lower prices abroad.

Fourth, the Saskatchewan industry was facing financial difficulties from the excess capacity and from existing low potash prices. The incentive therefore existed to adopt measures that might improve the industry's profitability.

No single, straightforward answer can be given to the question of why action was not taken by the industry well before the U.S. dumping allegations. It is easy enough to suggest that fear of U.S. antitrust laws or of other legal action was what deterred the government and/or industry from some sort of joint measures. After all, following Saskatchewan's legislation to institute production quotas and raise prices in 1969–1970, a variety of U.S.

59. See Table 10.2, which indicates that Canada was the only nation whose share of world production was substantially below its share of world capacity.

lawsuits were instituted against those U.S. firms in Saskatchewan that were party to the new measures. Again, subsequent to Canadian uranium producers joining with other third-country producers in a cartel to control supply and price of uranium outside the United States (after the United States itself had initiated measures to prevent imports of uranium for its domestic utilities), charges were laid by U.S. consumers against uranium firms for having formed this cartel.[60]

Fear of U.S. legal action, however, cannot be the whole story. Once the initial determination was made in the United States of Canadian potash sales there at less than fair value, it took the Saskatchewan government only ten days to produce legislation to control output and to thus indirectly stimulate price increases in the United States, which did not produce any court challenges by U.S. interests. Note also that there has not been any governmental challenge made to the price leadership that the dominant firm, PCS, exercised in the autumn of 1987 and in January 1988 and that was followed by the other producers.[61]

Another possible explanation for the failure of the Saskatchewan industry to capitalize on its own monopolistic position can be derived from the work of Richards.[62] One of his conclusions in studying the effectiveness of provincial rent collection from the Saskatchewan potash industry was that the

---

60. D.G. Haglund, "Protectionism and National Security: The Case of Canadian Uranium Exports to the United States," *Canadian Public Policy/Analyse de Politiques* 12, no. 3 (1986), p. 459–472.

61. The theoretical analysis of the Saskatchewan potash industry by F. Flatters and N. Olewiler, "Dominant Government Firms in an Oligopolistic Industry: The Case of Saskatchewan Potash," *Working Paper* 29, Centre for Resource Studies, Kingston (1984), suggested that there would be good reason for the dominant firm (PCS) to choose the output that would maximize its own profits, if the remaining firms were to accept that output as given when establishing their own outputs (a Stackelberg equilibrium). Their work also suggested, however, that there would be little incentive for a government-owned firm (like PCS) and for private-sector firms to form a cartel. In reaching this conclusion, however, they only compared the cartel possibility with a stable Nash-Cournot or Nash (noncooperative) equilibrium in which each firm was setting its output on the presumption that the other producers' outputs were set and would not be altered. But the situation of extensive competition that existed among producers for sales in the U.S. market prior to the second half of 1987 could hardly be characterized as a stable Nash-Cournot equilibrium. Both prices and quantities were being altered in the struggle for U.S. sales.

62. J.G. Richards, "The Saskatchewan Potash Industry: An Exercise in What Could Have Been," in Thomas Gunton and John Richards (eds.), *Resource Rents and Public Policy in Western Canada*, Halifax (1987), pp. 119–146.

government, in owning about one-half of the industry via PCS, faced the dilemma of trying to act in a way that would legitimize it in the eyes of the private producers while simultaneously attempting to maximize rent extraction. He concluded that it did not accomplish either objective very well.

Pushing his argument further, one might thus question whether the PC "free enterprise" government that came into power in 1982 was simply more reluctant than earlier NDP governments to interfere in market processes by either dictating what policies PCS should follow or by establishing production quotas for it and the remaining firms in the industry when excess capacity existed.[63] This possibility, plus a failure to recognize — or at least to act on the knowledge — that existing excess capacity was in Saskatchewan, not in the world industry generally, and that new additions to capacity elsewhere would take several years to occur (by which time it was expected that demand would be greatly increased), may account for the lack of Saskatchewan action to exploit its monopolistic power.[64]

It is clear, however, that the Saskatchewan government eventually concluded that the management of PCS was as much at fault during this time too. A shakeup in management was instituted in March 1987 with the removal of nine top managers of the firm. Several new staff members, including the president, were brought in from outside the firm.

Whatever the reason for the failure of Saskatchewan to capitalize on its monopolistic position until the United States took measures to protect its own industry, it seems clear that the U.S. antidumping allegations helped to encourage such action.

Another question that we can only mention briefly here is if U.S. antidumping actions are taken in the future against other Canadian industries, will the overall results be as palatable for Canadian producers? A full answer to this would require a much more detailed analysis of Canadian industries

---

63. The previous NDP government's policy prior to 1973 had been one which, through its prorationing, was essentially to limit individual producers' outputs so as to allow joint profit maximization "subject to the political constraint of full capacity American production" (Richards, "Saskatchewan Potash Industry," p. 130). After 1973, the government's policy was one of having PCS as a residual monopolist, again producing subject to the political constraint of permitting the U.S. industry to operate at close to capacity, while also allowing private Saskatchewan producers the right to maintain "historical production levels" (ibidem).

64. See Barry, "Potash." There was, however, one major new mine in the USSR that came into production in late 1987 with a phase one capacity of about 625,000 metric tons K_2O. (Originally, this mine was reported to have had severe water problems.) But even so, with the increased Soviet emphasis on improving domestic agriculture, the expansion of demand for fertilizer was expected to exceed expansion in production. (Ibidem).

than is possible in this chapter. Casual empiricism suggests that the only other sector that might be in the position of the potash industry would be the uranium industry, which has abundant, very high-quality reserves in Saskatchewan. There is a clause in the Canadian-U.S. trade deal prohibiting restrictions on energy goods, except to "respond to direct threats of disruption in the supply of nuclear materials for defense purposes" (Article 907 [d]), however that may be interpreted. But whether antidumping charges are a possibility and what the results might be for the uranium industry — or for any other industry — will be left for other investigators to consider.

PART FIVE

Cultural and Media Relations

11

Postwar Austrian Writers: The Problem of Publishing and Recognition

Adolf Haslinger

The Problem of Defining Austrian Literature

Before German reunification, there were four different countries in which authors wrote their works in German: the FRG, the GDR, Switzerland, and Austria. German is the official and the dominant language in these countries, even though there also exist minorities who speak other languages and who have their own literature, for example, the Slovene minority in Carinthia in the southern part of Austria next to Yugoslavia.

The last few years have shown that some authors have been able to make an important contribution to the literature of their countries even, or especially, by their works written in another language. It was an astonishing experience for many Austrians to learn recently that there is a literature written in Austria that they do not know and that they cannot read and understand at all. As examples, I should mention Florijan Lipuš' novel *Der Zögling Tjaz* (1980) and Gustav Janus' poems (1983), both translated into German by the Austrian writer Peter Handke, who was born in Carinthia and who spent his childhood there. It is interesting to note that Lipuš' novel was published in Austria, Janus' poems in Germany.

The complex and complicated problem of formulating an apt definition of "Austrian literature" is not to be solved simply. No one has found a magic prescription to determine, on the basis of a German text alone, whether a particular work has been written by an author who was brought up in Switzerland, the FRG, the GDR, or Austria. Numerous books exist on that topic, but the conclusions are relatively poor. There are several characteristic features that join to mark a work of Austrian literature: It contains literary references to New Austria or Old Austria; the author lives in New Austria or has lived in Old Austria, or was born in either country; the author writes in a German language with typical Austrian idioms or expressions.

In a special way, Austrian literature is able to show that literature is not only an outcome of a special geography or of a certain language. Even though the same language is used, Austrian literary history is no longer expected to imitate or parallel the development of German literary history, as was very often the case in the past. Differences do exist, and different interpretations of German or Austrian scholars attest to that fact.

Before illustrating this phenomenon, I want to turn to a question of terminology. In the well-known weekly, *Die Zeit* (published in Hamburg), some time ago I read the sentence: "Heinrich Böll, Günter Grass, Thomas Bernhard und Peter Handke sind die vier größten deutschen Schriftsteller" (... are the four greatest German writers). The adjective *"deutsch"* in this sentence is a semantic mistake, a major and misleading one. It does not mean *"deutsch,"* but *"deutschsprachig"* (German-speaking), referring to authors who write in German. This semantic incongruence is often used by German scholars and critics. In *Kindlers Literaturgeschichte der Bundesrepublik Deutschland,* which has four volumes, including one on Austrian literature, one can find articles and broad treatments of the following twentieth-century Austrian authors: Ingeborg Bachmann, Richard Billinger, Max Brod, Hermann Broch, Elias Canetti, Max Hölzer, Ödön von Horváth, Robert Musil, Johannes Mario Simmel, Franz Werfel, and others. The writers of this *Literaturgeschichte* put all these writers in one German pot.

The political and literary interpretation by Austrians of the importance of the year 1945 has differed from its respective treatment in the Federal Republic. Norbert Leser characterizes the Austrian political point of view as follows:

> Yesterday's victors and vanquished were thrown together in the prisons and concentration camps of the Third *Reich,* at the front or in the air-raid shelters at home. Thanks to this unsought opportunity they were able to enlarge their intellectual horizons and acquire the broader political awareness for which the conditions did not exist in the First Republic. It took first-hand experience of the lessons of National Socialism to bring these old rivals to their senses and to bring home to them that Austria's independence and self-sufficiency was something to be treasured. Like democracy, it was not until they no longer enjoyed it that they appreciated how much they had lost. The terrible detour of National Socialist

oppression was perhaps necessary in order to create the psychological basis on which Austria's future after 1945 could be built.[1]

Hans Wolfschütz notes on the same theme:

This newly-found unity was reflected in the composition and policies of the first provisional government formed in April 1945 immediately after the surrender of Vienna to the Soviet forces. It was made up of Socialists, Catholics, and Communists and was led by Dr. Karl Renner, who ironically enough had been the first Chancellor of the First Republic in 1918. The coalition government then had been purely provisional and had broken up in 1920 as a result of ideological differences; now, in 1945, it considered itself to be more than an executive instrument for political decision imposed from outside; it saw itself above all else as the standard-bearer of the universal Austrian desire to gain national independence and to reconstruct the country from the considerable debris of the War.[2]

Like Germany, Austria was divided into four occupation zones, and its capital was placed under Four Power control. Unlike Germany, however, it was subsequently *not* divided into two Austrias. This means that Austrians of very different political opinions, who in 1934 had been bitter enemies, decided to make common efforts to build a new country. The situation in the FRG was quite different from that.

1945: Continuity or New Beginning?

As to the literary interpretation of the year 1945, German scholars, on the one hand, have tended to describe it by using slogans like *Nullpunkt* (zero hour), *Kahlschlag* (complete deforestation), *Trümmerliteratur* (literature of ruins), and *Neubeginn* (new beginning). All of these terms convey the idea of a total destruction and the beginning of something fundamentally new that eradicates the past. Austrian scholars, on the other hand, did not use such expressions. They preferred to show the continuity of the Austrian development. There were several efforts to bridge the gap from 1938 to 1945. One of these efforts, for example, was by Otto Basil, author, poet, scholar, and editor of a literary journal, *Plan*, that existed between 1945 and 1948. Therein he gathered almost all the names of young writers who are now famous in Aus-

1. Norbert Leser, "Das Österreich der Ersten und Zweiten Republik," in Norbert Leser and Richard Berczeller (eds.), *Als Zaungäste der Politik*, Vienna and Munich (1977), p. 128.

2. Hans Wolfschütz, "The Emergence and Development of the Second Republic," in Alan Best and Hans Wolfschütz (eds.), *Modern Austrian Writing: Literature and Society After 1945*, London and Totowa, N.J. (1980), p. 6.

trian literature: Ingeborg Bachmann, Elfriede Mayröcker, Ernst Jandl, Herbert Eisenreich, and others. Beside the conservative journal, *Turm,* Otto Basil's *Plan* was the most important instrument for Austrian authors to get acquainted with the international works of Ernest Hemingway, James Joyce, Virginia Woolf, John Steinbeck, and others.

But the 1945 *Plan* was not the first one Otto Basil edited. He had already published three issues of the journal *Plan* in 1938. The last one had been confiscated by the police in March 1938. Its main topic had been *surréalisme.* This represents a form of continuity in Austrian literature, for *surréalisme* turned out to be the central issue (*Gretchenfrage*) in Austrian literature after 1945. It divided the generations of writers in Austria more than it ever did in Germany. Traditional writers refused every form of *surréalisme* and every form of innovation in literature, but young progressive writers praised it and imitated its techniques. Mainly Austrian writers, such as Ilse Aichinger, Ingeborg Bachmann, and Paul Celan, transformed surrealistic techniques into a modern way of writing poetry and prose. The same writers read their works for the first time in 1952 at a meeting of the *Gruppe 47* in Niendorf on the Baltic Sea. Walter Jens praised this meeting as the birth of a new German literature.

The Literary Market in Austria and in the FRG

After World War II more publishing houses were eliminated and destroyed in Germany than in Austria because the damages of the war were heavier in the former country. The Austrians, therefore, expected Vienna to become the center of publishing and book production of all of the German-speaking countries in Europe.

In 1947 sixty-one publishing houses existed in Austria that produced works of prose and poetry. This was approximately one-quarter of all Austrian publishing firms. But subsequent developments in the industry were negative and did not justify the high hopes of the early period. During the 1960s, only one-third of the literary publishers were left. It should not be a surprise that this decline was mainly influenced by what happened in the publishing field in the FRG.

During the first years after World War II the borders between Austria and Germany were more or less closed, and there was no trade involving books, journals, and newspapers. This situation can be illustrated by a letter written in 1947 by the famous Austrian author Hermann Broch and sent from Princeton to Vienna. In it he asked his friend, the less famous Austrian author George Saiko (1892–1962), to buy some interesting books in Germany. Broch did not realize that Saiko could not buy any books in Germany at that time because, as an Austrian citizen, Saiko was not allowed to import German books into Austria.

The first complicated treaties that set a fixed ceiling on exports of books and journals were concluded in 1948. There were two further treaties in 1949 and in 1951, but they were soon cancelled. Finally, in July 1953, eight years after the end of the war, the total liberalization of the bilateral trade of books and journals between Austria and the FRG opened the borders and influenced developments in the commercial publishing field.

A book written in German must be sold in Austria *and* in the FRG in order to become a literary and commercial success. Before 1938, 70 percent of total Austrian book production was exported to different countries, and 80 percent of that was exported to Germany. (Currently the situation is almost identical.) These figures demonstrate in a very persuasive manner that Austrian book publishing after World War II could not exist without the ability to export to Germany.

Such dependence on exports has not been without problems, however. After the currency reform in 1947, the difficulties of selling books increased in general. The closed German border had the effect of compelling Austrian companies to reduce their publishing programs and the number of editions. By lowering the number of copies printed, costs increased. This situation, moreover, was much more complicated. The main reason for that was the so-called "second currency reform" in 1947. It was very important from a commercial point of view to reduce the number of banknotes in Austria and to avoid price speculation. This was the first step in the *Wiederaufbau* (reconstruction). The book market, however, fell into a sales crisis. Complications in the production of paper were one of the reasons for this.

Conclusion

Relations in the literary sphere between Austria and the Federal Republic are distinctly different from that of economic and political relations. As can be widely observed in asymmetrical relations, knowledge of the state of literature in the superordinate country is high among informed readers and intellectuals of the subordinate country, but the reverse is not true. For an Austrian intellectual it is not only normal but even necessary to read *Die Zeit* and *Der Spiegel,* as Frederick Engelmann notes in Chapter two in this volume. (That Austrian intellectual is also expected to read the *Neue Zürcher Zeitung* at least every Friday.)

Knowledge of the literature of the superordinate country is a necessity for Austrian writers, but the challenge is greater than that. It is the aim of nearly every Austrian writer, and a significant step to overall success, to play an active role as an author in the superordinate country. In creative cultural fields such as literature, art, theater, journalism, and architecture, it is possible for Austrians to be actively successful in the superordinate country. A comparable career in the economic and political life of the superordinate country would be more complicated and more difficult to achieve.

It is necessary for a successful Austrian author to publish and sell his or her books with a West-German publishing house. Murray Hall calls this phenomenon the export of authors from Austria to Germany and the import of literature from Germany to Austria.[3] In the literary field, both countries are linked in a complicated pattern. It would be a mistake to assume that the export of authors and the import of literature is a recent development. Actually, it has been an established pattern in the literary history of both countries. A quotation of the *Deutsche Börsenblatt* from 1919 may illustrate this: "Even a perfunctory observation shows that the German book publishing trade makes its living to a substantial degree from the works of Austrian authors."

3. Murray G. Hall, "Österreichische Verlagsgeschichte: Autorenexport – Literaturimport," *Lesezirkel. Literaturmagazin* 14 (1985), pp. 3–6.

12

Decolonizing Canadian Literature: The Deconstructive Paradigm

Stanley Fogel

> "The moment anything acquires the status of a cultural idol ... it ceases to be interesting."
>
> E. Said

Traditionally, literature is a solid edifice, a club with fixed and selective membership; traditionally, literary criticism is hagiography, the passing of a hallowed tradition, a clean, well-lighted place. Grooming and maintaining a national literature are redolent of such a framing. The creation and inflation of cultural idols, the entitlement to a place in the literary firmament, the development and enshrining of a well-defined national identity, as well as literature — these are the staples and the raison d'être of "Canlit."

Canlit, of course, is by no means the only nationalistic mixing of literature and literary criticism. Many countries, both nascent and powerful, seek to appropriate their artists' works to augment their images. Also, there is a compelling reason for the stridency of "Canlit": proximity to the United States. That proximity, many Canadians fear, promises not merely dissolution of a cultural identity, but the nonrecognition that any identity exists. Nonetheless, at this point in time, Canada's literary situation is hardly a threatened one. Canadian literature courses and programs are featured prominently at all levels of schooling. Journals such as *Canadian Literature* and *Essays on Canadian Writing* have produced a good many numbers and volumes. Ph.D.s on all aspects of Canadian literature and culture have been awarded in Canada in percentages probably greater than those of other national literatures. Margaret Atwood and Robertson Davies have become exceedingly famous internationally: Translated into many languages, their works are reviewed in *The New York Times Book Review* and *The New York Review of Books*.

Canlit critics, nonetheless, still see their mission as one of constructing rather than deconstructing. "Searching for the national identity is a kind of congenital art form in Canada, which has provided both the theme for many poets and novelists and the substance of much critical observation and expectation."[1] Certainly if *Canadian Literature in the 1970s* is any indication, that predilection among critics and novelists for writing about a Canadian identity works deleteriously on Canadian literature. Of all of Davies' works it is "The Canada of Myth and Reality," a clichéd and jingoistic essay on nationalism, that was chosen by editors Edwards and Denham. The strain of creating an identity dominates the tone of Davies' hortatory piece:

> it is in poetry and fiction that the questers repose their greatest hopes. A Canadian literature, recognizable as such at home and abroad, is what they want. But the creation of a national literature is almost as slow as the building of a coral atoll; toil as we may, the recognizable island will not rise above the waves in a very great hurry. But we are working at it, and we have made rather more progress than some of our more anxious Canadian watchers seem to understand.[2]

The Canadian critics' fixation on nationalism is understandable given the Social Sciences and Humanities Research Council guidelines (which, after all, promise remuneration for patriotic forays into criticism). Understandable, too, is the Canadian fiction writers' preoccupation with the theme, although the reasons for this preoccupation are more paradoxical. In a short essay in *Books in Canada*,[3] Roch Carrier provides a witty insight into the fate of the writers whose separatist visions have become ensconced, institutionalized, in the Parti Québecois' (PQ) assumption of power. They have, he tells us, become peripheral to the ideological thrusting of an inchoate but compelling national identity. Carrier mentions that one writer, who clamored for the implementation of PQ programs, can be found "buying the blue shirts his Cabinet minister will wear on television." The majority of the preempted but comfortably co-opted writer-prophets can also be found "in one of the fashionable restaurants: they've all put on weight since the PQ came to power." Those whose perspectives don't exactly coincide with PQ positions are also silenced, "stifled by guilt, or they choose to put off the act of writing till later,

---

1. W.H. New, *Among Worlds: An Introduction to Modern Commonwealth and South African Fiction*, Erin, Ontario (1975), p. 101.

2. Robertson Davies, "The Canada of Myth and Reality," in P. Denhan and M.J. Edwards (eds.), *Canadian Literature in the 1970s*, Toronto (1980), p. 9.

3. "The Party is the Pen," February 1979.

telling themselves they must do nothing against the PQ before it's been given a chance." Carrier, in short, taunts his confrères with the knowledge that, as his title indicates, the party is the pen, that the party stamps its ideological configurations on the province, and that beside this monolith the writer is insignificant.

National identities are inflated constructs, products of advertising and politics. The uproar that Davies writes about in "The Canada of Myth and Reality" ("at present the uproar is for a Canadian identity") is one that is not primarily of the artist's making. That he or she succumbs to an obsession with it consigns him or her, as Carrier discerns in the Québecois writer's situation, to irrelevance; it dispossesses him because there are agencies with far greater powers than writers of fiction have to package and label the identity. Carrier's essay, "The Party is the Pen", consigns the construction of a public and viable identity to more willing, if much less trustworthy and imaginative, creators; his artist is too idiosyncratic, too subversive for such a function.

Most English Canadian writers, it should be noted, do not subscribe to the programmatic growth of an identifiably Canadian literature, except insofar as that literature is a diverse body of work identifiable as Canadian only by virtue of the fact that it was written by those who were born in and/or live in Canada. Nonetheless, there is on the part of Davies and Atwood, to name the best known, the occasional hagiographic attempt to nurture their country in their literature. Moreover, their purpose is not merely disinterested uplift; it is the making of a tradition in the image of other national literatures. Finding a distinctive voice, freeing itself from colonial fetters, enshrining its greats and proclaiming their greatness — these are the stereotyped dimensions of empire-building, literary variety. If, as seemingly every Canadian critic contends, the Canadian identity and Canadian image are too meagerly conceived by those at home and abroad, then the enunciation of a Canadianization program has surely become an important genre. Diagnoses and prescriptions, assessments and manifestos abound. Northorp Frye's *The Bush Garden: Essays on the Canadian Imagination,* Atwood's *Survival: A Thematic Guide to Canadian Literature,* Ronald Sutherland's *Second Image: Comparative Studies in Quebec/Canadian Literature,* and the collection entitled *Read Canadian: A Book about Canadian Books* edited by Robert Fulford, David Godfrey, and Abraham Rotstein are only some of the major statements that attempt to develop a sense of the country via its primarily literary products. The writers of these books share the presupposition that yoking Canadian nationalism and the Canadian literary enterprise is a salutary, even a valuable, activity.

When Davies writes in "The Canada of Myth and Reality" that "one of the tasks of the Canadian writer is to show Canada to itself,"[4] he does not mean the revelation of a repugnant image, some monstrous reified entity such as Americans Robert Coover and William Gass present. On the contrary, he and the other practitioners of the genre refer to an as yet uncreated but nascent identity that has a significant and important role to play, namely the fostering of a cohesive and identifiable sense of place. Although, Atwood maintains in an interview with Graeme Gibson,[5] that she is no politician and therefore eschews propagandistic prose, she, too, accepts Davies' premise that to sustain and to nurture her country are far from nugatory or jingoistic purposes. Certainly it is true that she has pursued such ends primarily in her nonfiction, most notably in *Survival*, in the interviews she has given, and in the occasional pieces she has been called upon to write. Despite the fact that only the occasional diatribe intrudes and obtrudes in her novels, most prominently in *Surfacing*, her concerns with individuals' identities and their tenuous hold on those identities, as well as her handling of the form of fiction indirectly and metaphorically, yield a sense that she is committed to establishing a national place as well as an individual person.

Clearly what the works by Frye, Sutherland, Atwood, Fulford, and other nationalistic critics are redolent of is an urgency to establish the significance and congruence of the Canadian experience, to give it the intellectual and cultural testaments that will demarcate place with the specificity and, more important, the unanimity with which Walt Whitman's *Leaves of Grass* and Abraham Lincoln's *Gettysburg Address* demarcate American history, American progress. "Fifteen Useful Books," an appendix of sorts to *Survival*, "The Ten Best Canadian Books" in *Read Canadian*, and Frye's "Preface to an Uncollected Anthology" (of English Canadian poetry) in *The Bush Garden* attempt emphatically to reveal to the reader, who it is assumed is bereft of an indigenous tradition, that core texts aspiring to the status of Canadian classics have been written, do exist, and need only a broad currency and consensus to provide that solid definition to Canadian culture that concomitantly would reduce the notion that this is an ill-defined country devoid of such points of fixity and communion as the Statue of Liberty, Daniel Boone, and *Moby Dick*.

The germ for *Read Canadian*, Fulford explains, was just such a situation as the above in which a lack of knowledge of Canadian texts by Canadians is displayed. In what is now perhaps a stock anecdote, Fulford tells of a high school English teacher who wanted to engage Canadian literature but who

---

4.	Davies, "Myth and Reality," p. 10.

5.	See Graeme Gibson, *Eleven Canadian Novelists*, Toronto (1973), p. 8.

had received no preparation for such a venture in her Canadian university career. Atwood asserts in *Survival* that "the tendency in Canada, at least in high school and university teaching, has been to emphasize the personal and universal but to skip the national or cultural."[6] Davies, too, reminisces about the Canadian cultural void in which he grew up: "My parents were great consumers of periodicals and printed matter [that] crowded into our house from England and the United States every month."[7] Common motifs and experiences such as those noted above link the overtly nationalistic books. By reiterating the anorectic condition of Canada, the writers of such texts hope to rectify if not eradicate that malaise, to extirpate the sense of void or importation that they feel so dominates the cultural life of their country.

To read Canadian, it is hypothesized, will be to think Canadian, with a distinctive voice that Davies in a surprisingly diffident piece has called an unassuming one. Assessing this country as one that is "so wanting in the rich sense of the past — of an individual self-made past — that is the prized possession of other nations," Davies encourages Canadians to regard themselves as possessors of a voice, albeit one that is not forceful and self-centered. On the contrary, the voice is that of a "secondary character, the hero's friend, the confidant; but the opportunity and heart ... is that of one who may be a hero, and a new kind of a hero, a hero of conscience and spirit, in the great drama of modern man."[8] Regardless of the modesty with which the Canadian character is supposed to be formed, there is here an encouraging sense of place and character. One of the ways to nurture that vision, it is maintained, is to read Canadian literature as an extension of Canadian nationalism. Davies writes that "so many Canadians who are eager to bring forth a new spirit seem to think that we have no past or that it is unworthy of consideration." To rectify that situation he draws attention to Douglas LePan's 1948 poem, "Coureurs de bois", which yields the image of a "Wild Hamlet with the features of Horatio,"[9] the supportive friend from whom Davies generalizes about Canadians.

In *The Bush Garden*, Frye offers similar clarification of the sediment of Canadian literature, finding in it the nucleus of a tradition that has been neglected only because it has not been placed in the foreground with the literatures of other countries. He acknowledges the impact of A.J.M. Smith's *Book of Canadian Poetry*, which appeared in 1943, and which, Frye declares, "brought my interest in Canadian poetry into focus and gave it direction.

---

6. Margaret Atwood, *Survival*, Toronto (1972), p. 15.

7. Davies, "Myth and Reality," p. 11.

8. Ibidem, p. 14.

9. Ibidem.

What it did for me it did for a great many others: the Canadian conception of Canadian poetry has been largely formed by Mr. Smith, and in fact it is hardly too much to say that he brought that conception into being."[10] Shoring up the notion of an indigenous literature has as its corollary that indigenous literature's value not intrinsically as literature, but rather extrinsically as a national resource. In his "Conclusion" to the *Literary History of Canada,* Frye contends that Canada has not produced any authors about whom it can be legitimately claimed that they are international in stature, or rather, that they are among the world's major writers. Therefore, "if no Canadian author pulls us away from the Canadian context towards the centre of literary experience itself, then at every point we remain aware of his social and historical setting." For Frye, then, the literature of Canada has a claim on its readers only insofar as that literature divulges a sense of place. He even goes so far as to say that Canadian literature "is more significantly studied as a part of Canadian life than as a part of an autonomous world of literature."[11]

Seen as a matter of survival, Canada's self-image is examined most poignantly, of course, in Atwood's *Survival*. Atwood asserts forcefully that survival is the dominant Canadian motif just as the dominant American motif is the frontier and the dominant British motif the island mentality. Such subsistence self-imaging had led, she postulates, to victimization, to the recurrence of victims as characters in Canadian literature. Canadian authors, though, are seen to be resistant to such passivity. Atwood places them, in her lexicon, in "Position Four: To be a creative non-victim."[12] This relationship to one's society is not the antagonistic, confrontational one that operates for Gass and Coover in the United States; rather, it allows the poet or novelist to act as tutor, as the articulator of goals and ideals that a country might espouse. The enemy for Atwood, Frye, and other Canadian literati is clearly not an active, firmly constituted nation. It is, on the contrary, one that has not been fully formed.

The consignment of the task of empire-building to the literary critic gives him or her control of the discourse as well as a messianic calling (no mere aestheticism or dilettantism involved here). It also permits him or her to canonize those who will take their place as "authors" in a "national" literature. The literary critic then seizes on those "authors" as the country's literary currency. The nationalistic literary critic becomes a professional who authenticates a country's literary experience, validates himself or herself as

---

10. Northrop Frye, *The Bush Garden*, Toronto (1971), p. vii.

11. Ibidem, p. 214.

12. Atwood, *Survival,* p. 38.

the curator of his or her country's literature, and invents and regulates the currency of art (Susan Musgrave's hankies and Hugh MacLennan's baseball cards gaining or losing value according to the whims of the market). The positivistic and acquisitive purpose of such an undertaking is masked as a natural one, the building of a national literature, an unqualified good. Looking into the Lacanian mirror, as it were, produces no ironic glimpses for the Canlit critics. They are sure of their propagandist roles.

In the scheme of the nation-building, contradictory or ironic writers are usually devalued or marginalized. Robert Kroetsch, Audrey Thomas, and Daphne Marlatt, for instance, are fiction writers in Canada who reveal skepticism toward being subsumed in programs of any kind. For them and some others there is a distrust of "place" that is mapped, groomed, known, and fully written. They wish to loosen the relationship of language and place, to make a messier and more anarchic space of both country and text. In this regard they are hostile to the definition of Canlit one can glean from Frye's *The Bush Garden* or Atwood's *Survival*. In this regard, too, they share kinship with the kind of cultural criticism known as deconstructionism. That project, originally an assault on metaphysical consistency, has expanded to include overarching explanations and meanings of all kinds.

Vis-à-vis proper names, for example, J. F. Lyotard differentiates modern and postmodern or deconstructive in terms of the addressee who in the modern frame of reference would be the people. "Postmodern or pagan would be the condition of the literatures and arts that have no assigned addressee and no regulating ideal."[13] Lyotard's anarchistic bent pushes him to champion the avant-garde because it has no fixed address generically or culturally — once it does its force is vitiated. Like Barthes and Foucault for whom the author-function yokes the proper name and the body, restricting the latter in the name of the former, Lyotard in *Just Gaming* celebrates

the awareness that the relation between the proper name and the body is not an immutable one. This bars the way to the very notion of a subject identical to itself through the peripeteia of its history. There is no subject because she or he changes bodies and by changing bodies, she or he, of course, changes passions as well as functions, especially narrative ones. There will be a multiplicity of functions for the same proper name.[14]

In "The Différend, the Referent, and the Proper Names" Lyotard continues to loosen the hold the proper name has on the referent, one seemingly stronger than the one common nouns have on their referents.

---

13. Jean François Lyotard and Jean-Thébaud, *Just Gaming*, Minneapolis (1985), translated by Wlad Godzich, p. 14.

14. Lyotard and Thébaud, *Gaming*, p. 40.

The referent of the name Caesar is not a completely describable essence, even with Caesar dead. Essentialism conceives the referent of the name as if it were the referent of a definition. The referent of a definition is only possible as such. For it to become real, it is necessary to be able to name and show referents that do not falsify the admitted definition. The "object" is thus submitted to the test of reality, which is only negative, and which consists in a series of contradictory attempts to designate cases accessible to the operators of the test through the use of names.[15]

Lyotard is at work here deploying language games to fracture the ontologically solid hold the proper name has on its properties.

Being of no fixed address, undoing nomination, is attractive to postmodernists in diverse ways. For instance, Barthes in *A Lover's Discourse* rapturously describes the state of being "atopos" — without place, stateless, unclassifiable, of a ceaselessly unforeseen originality. (One recalls Barthes' comment that once there are only differences there will be no difference.) The postmodern enterprise has been to scrutinize the taxonomies, catalogs of difference by which we've come to order the world ... and has found them suffused with ideology, rigidity, and stereotype. Thus, Barthes' attempts in *Roland Barthes* to rebut the hegemony of adjectives that usually cluster around proper names and bulk them. Barthes' "reading" of his lover involves dispersion, decentering, the love of being of no fixed address rather than the enumeration and characterization of the loved one (which is why character, linked with causality is rejected by writers of postmodern fiction because of the simplistic, even if it is complex, reading that is produced).

How, though, to write "atopical" pieces about places, to write properly about a place that one does not define, for which every attribution is false. The word, Canada, it has been speculated, carried etymologically the meaning "no place". The problem for a writer with a deconstructionist perspective is how to create fictional or critical places that do not center or colonize this place that is, nonetheless, no place. Fiction writers have a whole array of tricks to forestall teleology or definition. Kroetsch, for example, in *Gone Indian*, reverses myths of vegetation, spring, and fertility; also, his tall tales of Western adventures and settlements reveal their origins in story-telling, not in the discovery of a continent. Thus, instead of celebrating the solidification of a Canadian place in "the wild West", Kroetsch's focus is the constructed quality of the frontier's codification. In *Gone Indian* he is also concerned with those, namely aboriginal peoples, who suffer from the creation of a country, Canada.

---

15. Jean-Francois Lyotard, "The Différend, the Referent, and the Proper Name," *diacritics* 14 (Autumn 1984), pp. 4–14.

"Canlit" and "Cancrit" until *very recently* have been intransigently modern, mapmaking as a way of survival in the bush garden, loving a country that demands its classifications and topology. "Every relationship of hegemony is necessarily a pedagogical relationship," Gramsci wrote, leading nicely into Gallop's comment that "in every act of pedagogy there's an element of pederasty." (Kroetsch: "There's a communal language which one is responsible to. I think the Canadian writer's sense of responsibility to that voice makes him quite different from an American writer quite often. You get a sense almost of submission to that voice in a lot of Canadian writing.")[16] Remember Borges' story about the project of mapping that employed everyone while the country went to ruin (requiring as it did a map commensurate with/ covering the world). And there is Foucault's attraction to visual non sequiturs, what he calls heterotopias:

> heterotopias are disturbing, probably because they secretly undermine language, because they make it impossible to name this and that, because they shatter or tangle common names, because they destroy syntax in advance, and not only the syntax with which we construct sentences but also the less apparent syntax which causes words and things (next to but also opposite one another) to "hang together." [They] dessicate speech, stop words in their tracks, context the very possibility of language at this source; they dissolve our myths and sterilize the lyricism of our sentences. And the proper name, in this context, is merely an artifice: it gives us a finger to point with, in other words, to pass surreptitiously from the space where one speaks to the space where one looks; in other words, to fold one over the other as if they were equivalents.[17]

Thus Foucault's attraction to Magritte as a cartographer of heterotopias, of a painting such as *L'usage de la parole,* the disjunctive, dislocated finger Magritte uses in place of the "i" of "sirene", beside stairs that lead only to a blocked wall, prohibiting, languages verticality. For Foucault, Magritte makes maps that *deny* resemblance or representation, that jam the map-making machinery.

Two projects are evident in cultural Canada of the late twentieth century. The first, the project of discovery and dissemination of an identity and literature, is the one most strongly represented by Canlit. The second, the deconstructive, is gaining adherents. It offers a less sanguine reading of nationalism; it does not offer a hierarchy of writers, Atwood, Davies, and their literary ancestors, that needs to be assimilated as the core of the Canadian cultural experience. Most emerging countries seize the first project as their way of emerging. The deconstructive enterprise is thought to be too effete, too

16. Cited in Peter Thomas, *Robert Kroetsch*, Vancouver (1980), p. 116.

17. Michel Foucault, *The Order of Things*, New York (1970), a translation of *Les Mots et les Choses,* p. 48.

decadent, not affirmative enough. However, a number of Canadian critics, Linda Hutcheon the best known, have begun to reject the hagiographical. In *The Canadian Postmodern,* Hutcheon deliberately produces a messy map, one which confuses Canada's place. It may not be "no place", but it is many places. In those disunited places, the voices of women and aboriginal people are heard; overall, there is perhaps more cacophony than consensus. Better that, the deconstructionist argument goes, than a homogeneous national voice that could become totalitarian. For Hutcheon, literature is whatever literary critics say it is: ungroomed, multiple-sited, it makes for more vital reading than Canlit would have it to be.[18]

18. Parts of this chapter appeared in Stanley Fogel, *A Tale of Two Countries,* Toronto (1984), in a slightly altered form.

13

Media Relations Between Austria and the Federal Republic of Germany*

Hans Heinz Fabris

Historical Background

The history of Austrian-German media relations reaches far back in the history of the two countries. During the nineteenth century, the Habsburg Monarchy, which was then one of the great empires of Europe, became the focus of expanding German economic interests in their move toward southeast Europe. These interests had to be secured by political as well as by journalistic efforts. After World War I, union with Germany was prohibited, but *Anschluß* was pursued by influential groups in both countries.[1]

Long before Hitler seized power, the Weimar Republic had undertaken extensive political and economic efforts to strengthen and expand relations with what had become a small neighboring state. German capital was invested in several newspapers and journals, which clearly revealed their aim to influence public opinion. The largest Viennese advertising agency, *Öster-*

---

* Translation from the German original version by Harald von Riekhoff.

1. See Gerhard Jagschitz, "Die Presse in Österreich von 1918 bis 1945," in Heinz Pürer, Helmut Lang, and Wolfgang Duchkowitsch (eds.), *Die österreichische Tagespresse*, Salzburg (1983), pp. 42–82; Monika Schnürer, "Die filmwirtschaftlichen Beziehungen zwischen Österreich und Deutschland von 1929–1938. Eine Facette nationalsozialistischer Machtübernahme," manuscript, Vienna (1987); Murray Hall, *Österreichische Verlagsgeschichte 1918–1938*, Vienna (1985); Viktor Ergert, *50 Jahre Rundfunk in Österreich*, 3 vols., Vienna (1974, 1975, 1977).

241

reichische Anzeigen GmbH, belonged to Alfred Hugenberg, Germany's newspaper czar and a member of Hitler's first cabinet. A number of journalists, as well as entire editorial staffs, received subsidies from the German Foreign Ministry. The *Anschluß* was not only prepared from the outside by media campaigns but was also promoted by resident German industries by way of direct or indirect subsidies to pro-German publications. Such support was relatively easy insofar as *Anschluß* was the central program of several Austrian political parties, notably the Greater German Party, the Christian Socials, and the Social Democrats.

With the beginning of Nazi rule in Germany, this pressure on Austria via media was increased substantially. The struggle for the political and economic independence of Austria commenced and was also fought in the media realm. At times, the German effort became a regular propaganda war, utilizing radio broadcasts, pamphlets, and other methods. During the aborted coup of the National Socialists in 1934, the Austrian radio station was occupied even before the Federal Chancellery. The Austrian government, which by that time had acquired an authoritarian character, could do little to counteract this pressure. Prohibitions of Nazi propaganda in their own country had little effect as the economic dependence of most sectors of the Austrian media system forced them to orient themselves to the dictates of the stronger Germany. This was particularly true for the traditionally poorly developed book and publishing sectors, which furthermore suffered from the dumping practices of German publishing houses — conducted as part of their overall export offensive.[2]

By the middle of the 1930s the film industry also underwent a de facto economic and political-ideological alignment with the German *Reich* and its massively promoted film industry. Because Austrian films had no chance to be successful without the German market, Jewish actors and camera operators were excluded from film productions in consideration of the Nürnberg racial laws.[3]

Austrian writers, in turn, anticipated large profits from the German market, and the majority of them organized themselves into pro-German associations. Also, in economic branches like the electrical and paper industry, with its close connection with the media sector, there existed a particularly high ratio of German capital during the time of the First Republic.[4]

---

2.   Murray Hall, *Österreichische Verlagsgeschichte*, pp. 146 f.

3.   See Monika Schnürer, "Filmwirtschaftliche Beziehungen."

4.   Norbert Schausberger, *Der Griff nach Österreich*, Vienna and Munich (1978), pp. 60 f.

Thus, when German troops marched into Austria in 1938, this offensive had already been thoroughly prepared by corresponding media policies. The subsequent integration of Austrian media, the incorporation of Austrian radio into the *Reichsrundfunk*, the appointment of commissars to the editorial offices of most newspapers, the closing of several papers, as well as the expulsion and persecution of Jewish journalists, writers, and intellectuals, was achieved with relative speed even if, in the period following, one was to encounter varied forms of internal and external emigration as well as resistance.

After World War II, the Allies tried to restore the functioning of the media in their respective zones of occupation. The Americans were particularly successful in their efforts, and their media and cultural policy was responsible for creating a distinctly Western orientation of Austrian media and journalists.[5] Only after the withdrawal of the Allies in 1955 and the recovery of full national sovereignty was the hegemonical position of the United States gradually replaced by the FRG and its regained influence in the media sector. Media products of the Federal Republic — newspapers, books, films, and records — gradually conquered the Austrian market in the following years. Austrian television, which was started in 1955, soon established close contact with the West German television networks.

In the following sections, an attempt will be made to assess the extent of German influence on the Austrian media system in its diverse sectors and to discuss Austrian interests and efforts as these relate to the West German media market.

Printed Media

Recent developments in the daily newspaper market in Austria are of particular interest. Until recently, dailies were exclusively Austrian-owned. Now media concerns of the Federal Republic have acquired considerable influence over 70 percent of the total publication of daily newspapers. The *Westdeutsche Allgemeine Zeitung* (WAZ), the second largest newspaper concern of the FRG, has acquired a 45 percent interest in the two largest Austrian dailies, the *Neue Kronen Zeitung* and the *Kurier*. In the wake of this engagement, an organizational linkage between both papers was forged by *Mediaprint*, which soon thereafter acquired 74 percent interest in the *Vorwärts* printing company owned by the SPÖ. In this manner, the two Austrian

---

5.   Hans Heinz Fabris and Kurt Luger (eds.), *Medienkultur in Österreich. Film, Fotographie, Fernsehen und Video in der Zweiten Republik,* Vienna (1988).

daily newspapers, which have by far the largest circulation — together 60 percent of the total number printed — and an even higher proportion of advertising, have close economic linkages with one another and with the WAZ (see Table 13.1).

TABLE 13.1

**All Daily Newspapers: Readership and Circulation
(printed copies) 1990**

	Reach	*Percentage*	*Printed Copies*
Neue Kronen Zeitung	2,681,000	42.6	1,075,000
Kurier	941,000	14.9	443,000
Kleine Zeitung	659,000	10.5	268,000
Neue AZ	235,000	3.7	138,000
OÖ. Nachrichten	307,000	4.9	115,000
Tiroler Tageszeitung	262,000	4.2	100,000
Salzburger Nachrichten	217,000	3.4	95,000
Die Presse	210,000	3.3	78,000
Der Standard	242,000	3.8	74,000
Neue Zeit	123,000	2.0	73,000
Vorarlberger Nachrichten	178,000	2.8	71,000
Kärntner Tageszeitung (SPÖ)	103,000	1.6	66,000
Volksstimme (KPÖ)	n.a.	n.a.	47,000
Neue Vorarlberger Tageszeitung	96,000	1.5	37,000
Neues Volksblatt (ÖVP)	69,000	1.1	30,000
Wiener Zeitung	54,000	0.9	27,000
Salzburger Volkszeitung (ÖVP)	25,000	0.4	12,000

Source: Verband Österreichischer Zeitungsherausgeber und Zeitungsverleger (ed.), *Pressehandbuch 1990,* Vienna (1991), p. 14.

This development has greatly intensified the high ownership concentration of Austrian dailies, which had already existed for several years.[6] This development was made possible, inter alia, because Austria has no cartel regulations equivalent to those of the FRG. Small wonder, then, that the papers of political parties have practically disappeared. Moreover, provincial newspapers have also been affected by this trend and have had to search for

---

6. See Institut für Publizistik und Kommunikationswissenschaft der Universität Salzburg (ed.), *Massenmedien in Österreich,* Vienna (1983 and 1986).

new partners. They have sought to strengthen cooperation, for example, by jointly publishing illustrated TV magazines.

The penetration of the WAZ into the Austrian media market has awakened the interest of other FRG media concerns. The largest West German media concern, the Axel Springer AG, now has 50 percent interest in the new daily, *Der Standard*, published by Oscar Bronner, and has 45 percent interest in the *Tiroler Tageszeitung*. In the future, Springer and WAZ may well become engaged in electronic media as well (WAZ and the *Neue Kronen Zeitung* are associated with Radio Luxembourg).

Observers of this development, therefore, speak of a sellout of Austria's domestic media because what its proponents refer to as internationalization has almost exclusively been a one-way street leading to the Federal Republic.[7] As an example of a countertrend, one can refer to the participation of Hans Dichand, the majority owner of the *Neue Kronen Zeitung*, in the *Hamburger Morgenpost* that was established a few years ago. Whether the engagement of West German media concerns in Austria is in response to the latter's ambition to become a full member in the EC, or whether Austria merely plays the role of a test market in the wider global expansion of West German enterprises is as difficult to answer as is the question concerning the impact on other Austrian media, Austrian politics in general, and its policy toward the EC in particular.[8]

In contrast to these considerations, positive effects from FRG involvement are also to be noted, for example, enhanced work opportunities and better professional training for Austrian journalists, improved quality of media products, and associated increased competitiveness stemming from capital inflow and greater journalistic know-how.

Whereas the influence of the FRG on Austrian daily newspapers is a relatively recent phenomenon, West German dominance in publishing firms and in the printing of popular magazines goes back to the 1950s. At that time, German illustrated magazines, imitating the format of U.S. and French magazines, began to replace Austrian illustrated magazines that had reemerged after 1945.[9] Temporarily, the market for illustrated newspapers

7. See for example the acting editor in chief of *Kurier*, Hans Rauscher, in a commentary in *Kurier*, 2 November 1988, p. 1.

8. Hans Heinz Fabris, "Statistenrolle reserviert? EG-Anbindung, Medien- und Telekommunikations-Politik in Europa und Österreich," in Margit Scherb and Inge Morawetz (eds.), *Der un-heimliche Anschluß. Österreich und die EG*, Vienna (1988), pp. 129–149.

9. Kurt Kaindl, "Das Faktische und das Imaginäre. Entwicklung der fotografischen Bildkultur in Österreich seit 1945," in Fabris and Luger (eds.), *Medienkultur in Österreich*, pp. 339–382.

and magazines was almost entirely dominated by publications from the FRG, although some of them appeared with a separate Austrian section, and magazines like *Stern* and *Bunte* had a relatively strong Austrian editorial staff. In turn, numerous Austrian journalists found employment opportunities with West German publishers.

Only in the late 1970s and early 1980s did newly founded Austrian products recover a substantial portion of the domestic market. Most important among them were products like *profil* in the realm of political periodicals, *trend* for economic periodicals, *Rennbahn Express* in the sector of youth magazines, and finally *Zeitgeist*-type journals such as *Wiener, Wienerin,* and *Basta.* The genre of *Zeitgeist* journals even became popular on the West German media market.

Products of the Federal Republic, nevertheless, continued to dominate the Austrian market. Titles such as *Bunte, Hör Zu, Stern, Quick, Neue Revue, Brigitte, Freundin, Für Sie, Neue Frau,* and diverse fashion magazines and special interest products such as *Eltern, Schöner Wohnen, Freizeitrevue,* or *Geo* are all of FRG origin. Numerous titles of quality publications, including academic publications, also belong to this category. This means that foreign trade in newspapers and journals has a distinctively negative balance vis-à-vis the FRG (Table 13.2). Approximately 93 percent of imported journals come from the FRG, and 80 percent of exports go there, which illustrates Austria's extreme degree of dependence on the FRG in this particular sector of the market.

This development is uneven, however, because of the above-mentioned new publications, and, in particular, the success of *Die Ganze Woche,* which was created in 1985 by the Austrian media tycoon Kurt Falk. After the *Österreichischer Rundfunk* (ORF — Austrian Radio and Television) and the *Neue Kronen Zeitung, Die Ganze Woche* has become the third largest mass medium in Austria as measured by the size of its persons reached (Table 13.3).

Electronic Media

German influence on Austrian radio goes back to the founding of the *Radio Verkehrs AG* (RAVAG) in 1924 with active participation by the German electrical industry.[10] On 12 March 1938, the day that Nazi troops marched into Austria, RAVAG was incorporated into the German radio

---

10. See Ergert, *50 Jahre Rundfunk,* vols. 1 and 2.

TABLE 13.2

Austrian Foreign Trade with the FRG in Newspapers and Journals, 1980–1984 (in million schillings)

(1)	(2)	(3) Annual Change	(4)	(5) Annual Change	(6) Foreign Trade Deficit with	(7) Exports as Percentage
Year	Imports	Percentage	Exports	Percentage	the FRG, Total	of Imports
1980	1,265	+9.3	186	+28.3	1,078	14.7
1981	1,350	+6.7	247	+32.9	1,120	18.3
1982	1,445	+7.1	296	+19.9	1,149	20.5
1983	1,620	+12.1	269	-9.3	1,351	16.6
1984	1,662	+2.6	312	+16.0	1,349	18.8

Source: Institut für Publizistik und Kommunikationswissenschaft der Universität Salzburg (ed.), *Massenmedien in Österreich*, Salzburg and Vienna (1986), p. 68.

TABLE 13.3

Austrian Readership of Selected Austrian and FRG Journals and Magazines 1990

	Reach	Percent
profil	491,000	7.8
Wochenpresse	236,000	3.7
Die Ganze Woche	2,168,000	34.4
Bunte	537,000	8.5
trend	620,000	9.8
Gewinn	465,000	7.4
Basta	566,000	9.0
Wiener	579,000	9.5

Source: Verband Österreichischer Zeitungsherausgeber und Zeitungsverleger (ed.), *Pressehandbuch 1990*, p. 17.

broadcasting system. During World War II, the radio stations in Vienna and Graz served as peripheral stations (*ostmärkische Außenstellen*). Radio Salzburg and Radio Innsbruck were integrated into Radio Munich, and the broadcasting station in Vorarlberg became part of Radio Stuttgart. After the liberation in 1945, the Allies reconstructed the radio broadcasting system in their respective occupation zones. The return of the last radio station to Austrian Radio did not take place until 1954.

In 1955, Austria created an independent television system, thereby launching the triumphant victory march of this particular medium. Since then the cooperative relationship of the Austrian and West German networks has become increasingly intensive. It now encompasses technical cooperation and program exchanges — networks in the FRG include several Austrian musical programs, for example, the Salzburg Festival — and it includes close ties, especially with the Second German Television network (*Zweites Deutsches Fernsehen* — ZDF). This cooperation also entails reciprocal purchases of programs and diverse forms of coproduction. The share of independent Austrian television productions shown during prime time, between 8:00 P.M. and 10:00 P.M., has declined to 40 percent.[11] In comparison with the program offerings of other countries, the share of foreign television productions shown on Austrian television, which is approximately 60 percent, appears to be relatively high. The trend toward regional-language television via *3sat*, a satellite program that since 1984 has been jointly produced by the ORF, the ZDF, and the Swiss Radio and Television Company (*Schweizer Radio- und Fernseh-Gesellschaft* — SRG), seems to have reached a peak. The three national networks jointly produce a six-hour program in which they participate in the following proportions: the ZDF 60 percent, the ORF 30 percent, and the SRG 10 percent.[12]

Leo Kirch and his West German media multinational, Beta Taurus, has been a great influence on ORF programming. Since 1984, the ORF together with the ZDF have purchased the rights from Beta Taurus to televise some 1,264 feature films. These films will be shown by the ORF until well into the 1990s. In turn, Leo Kirch has acquired various rights in Austria, including the rights to recordings of performances by Austrian state theaters such as the prestigious Vienna State Opera or the Burgtheater.

Television and radio programs from the Federal Republic were always easy to receive in western Austria. With the spread of cable television, it is now possible to receive them in numerous households in eastern and south-

---

11. Tapio Varis, *Flow of Television Programs in Europe*, Tampere (1984), p. 15.

12. Institut für Publizistik und Kommunikationswissenschaft der Universität Salzburg (ed.), *Massenmedien in Österreich* (1986), p. 95.

eastern Austria. The cable network of Vienna, which has around 250,000 outlets, is regarded as one of the largest in Europe. Cable television disseminates not only German ZDF and *Arbeitsgemeinschaft der öffentlich-rechtlichen Rundfunkanstalten der Bundesrepublik Deutschland* (ARD) and Bavarian television channels but also the new private television channels SAT1 and RTL, plus English ones such as Sky Channel and Super Channel, as well as those from Hungary, Yugoslavia, and Switzerland. West German television programs account for roughly 10 percent of overall viewing time, and virtually all Austrian households will tune in to West German programs at least occasionally.

In the viewing profile of the typical Austrian, the Austrian ORF network will dominate until 8:00 P.M., largely because of the high viewing rates of the evening news, "Zeit im Bild," which is presented on both ORF channels. During later evening hours, however, the viewer frequently shifts to foreign programs. Because the late evening show on the ORF, at least on one of its two channels, is frequently identical to one of the feature programs shown on German television, it is difficult to make a clear distinction between Austrian and German program offerings. It can therefore be understood why series such as the German "Schwarzwaldklinik" or "Derrick", large shows, and quiz programs like "Wetten daß," which attract up to 60 percent of viewers, are pronounced hits with the Austrian general public. One of the consequences of the close collaboration of the ZDF with *3sat* is that guests from the FRG are invited regularly on ORF programs like "Club 2," and occasionally they constitute the majority of performers.

In evaluating the role of the electronic media on relations between Austria and the Federal Republic it is important to bear in mind that Austrian television programs are generally well-received in the FRG, particularly in Bavaria. The close cooperation between the television networks of both countries, furthermore, has created diverse employment opportunities and financial gains for television journalists, scriptwriters, musicians, entertainers, anchormen, and other employees, which would otherwise have barely existed.

As for the future, one may expect that the broadcasting monopoly of the ORF in Austria will not continue throughout the decade of the 1990s. Moreover, if Austrian membership in the EC becomes a reality, one may predict that private stations such as the German SAT1 or RTL will come to occupy an even stronger position in the broadcasting industry. A first step in the direction of deregulation and privatization has already been taken; the ORF and the association of newspaper publishers concluded an agreement on the joint production of radio programs. In the future, one may expect that these stations will develop local programs designed especially for Austrian viewers, which will be produced jointly with newspaper publishers.

The German-Language Book Market

The dependence of Austrian media products on the West German market is particularly pronounced with respect to books. More than half of the books sold in Austria originate in the FRG. The readers' association *Donauland,* which is predominantly owned by Bertelsmann, the world's second largest media concern, dominates the channels of distribution. Every third household in Austria is a member of Donauland.[13] Imports from the FRG account for 84 percent of the total book imports by Austria (Table 13.4). Conversely, only 17 percent of all books imported by the Federal Republic come from Austria. As a result, one speaks today of an all-German-language book market, with the GDR being a special case until 1990.

TABLE 13.4

**Negative Balance Book Trade between Austria and the FRG, 1980–1984
(in million schillings)**

(1)	(2)	(3) Percentage of Total Imports	(4) Imports minus exports	(5) in Percent[a]	(6) Exports	(7) Percentage of Total Exports
Year	Imports					
1980	1,400	83.9	737	111.2	663	83.4
1981	1,398	83.5	671	92.3	727	80.5
1982	1,443	84.7	705	95.6	738	82.2
1983	1,520	83.6	802	111.8	718	78.9
1984	1,644	83.8	972	144.6	672	75.5

a) Column (5) = Column (4) divided by Column (6), then multiplied by 100.

Source: Österreichs Buch und Buchhandel in Zahlen, current years, quoted from Institut für Publizistik und Kommunikationswissenschaft der Universität Salzburg (ed.), *Massenmedien in Österreich,* Vienna (1986), p. 112.

For Austrian authors this meant and still means, on the one hand, that they can find a large market for their works — the share of Austrian authors in West German publications has traditionally been high — and, on the other hand, that they will have to orient themselves toward the perceived interests of the West German readers. Often there remains only a small market niche for specifically Austrian topics, the so-called "Austriaca," which deal with

---

13. See the chapter on books, ibidem.

such themes as the monarchy, the Austrian landscape, and other "exotica." This may provide an explanation as to why Austrian authors did little to partake in the political discourses of their country, which earned Austrian literature the attribute of being apolitical. The Austrian writer Michael Scharang characterized this dilemma in the following manner:

> For me this represented a most unusual situation. In the 1960s I had left a gloomy Austria for the bright West Germany. Now I observed from the vantage of a more liberal Austria a country in which its bourgeois democracy was at war with itself. Nevertheless, even now it was always better to work in West Germany ... Fear of West Germany? May one speak of *Angst* when this is not *en vogue*? Perhaps it already is. What does a foreigner know?[14]

The Motion Picture Industry

In the film industry there also exists a long history of close relations between Austria and Germany.[15] Austrian motion picture production in the 1920s and 1930s was extensively directed toward the German public. Even then only 20 percent of production costs could be recovered on the domestic Austrian market. In film imports, as well, Austria relied on foreign countries, with Germany and the United States traditionally figuring as the two most important sources. Also, many prominent figures from the film world worked in the growing German motion picture industry both before and after the National Socialists' rise to power. After the *Anschluß* of 1938, several film enterprises were destroyed by liquidation or forced sale, and the Austrian industry was incorporated into the *Reich* chamber of films (*Reichsfilmkammer*). At the same time, the "Wien-Film" was created. It produced approximately 50 feature films during the following years of Nazi rule and provided a substantial proportion of the overall motion picture production of the German *Reich*.

This "German heritage" was taken over by the Americans and the Soviets in 1945. Nevertheless, films of the *Wien-Film* or *Heimatfilm* genre continued to be produced well into the 1960s. The Austrians could always count on their appeal to the German market. Until today, Austria's motion picture industry has not yet recovered from the postwar stagnation, despite govern-

---

14. Cited by Hans Heinz Fabris, "Grenzenloser Medienmarkt," *Wiener Zeitung-Extra*, 22 April 1988, p. 1.

15. See, among others, Monika Schnürer, "Filmwirtschaftliche Beziehungen"; Walter Fritz, *Kino in Österreich 1896–1930*, Vienna (1981), and Walter Fritz, *Kino in Österreich 1945–1983*, Vienna (1984).

ment support for the promotion of films and despite repeated successes of Austrian film productions at international festivals. (The film industry of the FRG, too, experienced immense problems during the same period but benefited much earlier from government support.) In Austrian cinemas, films from the Federal Republic continue to rank in second place after U.S. films (Table 13.5).

The Music Market

The record industry has achieved remarkable worldwide growth during recent decades. The internationalization of this industry has progressed extensively. This can be easily recognized by the share of foreign enterprises in Austria (Table 13.6). The greater part of the commercial utilization of the music produced in Austria, the "land of music," with its renowned training institutions, orchestras, and festivals, is handled by foreign firms. In addition, the majority of music played on radio is foreign-produced. Only during the 1970s could one witness some countermovement to this trend of increasing internationalization and foreign domination of Austrian music culture, especially in the field of popular music. This countermovement took the form of *Austro Pop*, whose representatives deliberately used domestic idioms and included Austrian events.

In the music recording industry, one encounters the same structural phenomenon that now appears typical for a wide range of Austrian media products — Austrian performers and composers working under contract with foreign firms. This is the only way to open the international market with its promise of profit and popularity.

Electrical and Electronics Industry

This important economic branch does not belong to the media economy in the narrower sense, but the spheres of production of electronics (television sets, videocassette recorders, radios, stereos, and other electronic systems), and office communications equipment form part of the broader information sector that continues to acquire ever greater importance in the modern information society.

TABLE 13.5

Films Offered in Austrian Cinemas by Country of Origin, 1980–1984

Country of Production	1980	1981	1982	1983	1984	Total	Percentage of Total
United States	107	119	123	113	139	601	36.6
FRG	46	52	56	40	55	249	15.3
France	39	40	43	46	59	227	13.9
Italy	50	36	34	43	35	198	12.1
United Kingdom	11	17	11	11	13	63	3.8
Hong Kong	20	26	21	4	2	73	4.5
Austria	8	11	13	16	17	65	3.9
Japan	1	1	–	–	–	2	0.1
Switzerland	4	6	5	7	5	27	1.7
USSR	–	2	–	2	–	4	0.2
Sweden	–	1	1	3	–	5	0.3
Spain	2	6	2	5	–	15	0.9
Denmark	–	–	1	2	–	3	0.2
Canada	5	5	4	6	3	23	1.4
Greece	–	–	–	–	2	2	0.1
Israel	2	–	–	–	–	2	0.1
Mexico	1	1	–	–	–	2	0.1
Netherlands	1	1	–	–	4	6	0.4
GDR	1	1	2	–	–	4	0.3
Czechoslovakia	2	–	1	–	–	3	0.2
Australia	2	1	7	4	3	17	1.1
Poland	1	1	–	–	–	2	0.1
Hungary	–	1	–	–	–	1	0.1
Brazil	–	–	1	2	–	3	0.2
Ireland	–	1	1	–	2	4	0.2
Jamaica	1	–	–	–	–	1	0.1
Yugoslavia	1	1	1	–	2	5	0.3
Philippines	1	–	1	–	3	5	0.3
Others	–	1	3	10	6	20	1.2
Total	306	331	331	314	350	1,631	100.0

Source: Institut für Publizistik und Kommunikationwissenschaft der Universität Salzburg (ed.), *Massenmedien in Österreich*, Vienna (1986), p. 100.

TABLE 13.6

Market Shares of Recording Companies in Austria, 1981–1985 (percentage)

Companies	1981	1982	1983	1984	1985
PolyGram (with Amadeo)	31.9	28.5	31.1	30.4	29.3
CBS	11.7	14.0	14.3	15.4	12.8
Ariola	17.6	17.0	16.7	14.8	17.4
EMI-Columbia	14.3	15.9	15.4	14.4	13.4
Musica	13.7	14.2	11.6	13.3	13.3
WEA	6.9	5.8	6.5	7.9	10.1
Bellaphon	3.9	4.6	4.4	3.8	3.7

Sources: APA-Medien, 21 February 1986, p. 6.

The Austrian electrical and electronics industry has the highest share of foreign capital — approximately 65 percent — of any sector of its national economy. West German firms and their Austrian subsidiaries have tended to play a special role in this economic sector. In the fields of cable television and telecommunications development for the Austrian postal system, foreign enterprises, headed by the Siemens group and Philips have acquired a position of leadership in developing the infrastructure of the Austrian media and information systems. In the latter field, however, Austrian firms such as Schrack have had a somewhat stronger position. Even though West German electronic firms have invested considerable amounts of money in Austria, this particular component of Austria's foreign trade shows a heavy deficit vis-à-vis the Federal Republic. The largest of these foreign firms are the Siemens group, AEG, and Grundig (see Table 13.7). The manufacture of television sets by a purely domestic Austrian producer has long become a matter of the past.

TABLE 13.7

The Ten Largest Austrian Electronic Firms

Firm	Concentration of Activity	Sales in 1984 (in million schillings)	Employees
Siemens-Gruppe	communication; data technology; energy	14,480	14,376
Philips	entertainment electronics; computers	12,800	9,700
Elin-Union-Konzern	installation	9,524	8,805
IBM	office machines; computers	5,000	2,004
AEG-Telefunken-Gruppe*	installation; construction elements	2,879	2,437
Kapsch	news; data technology; installation	2,300	2,350
Österr. Brown-Boveri	installation; installation technology	2,238	2,177
ITT Austria	news technology; installation	2,095	2,700
Grundig Austria	entertainment electronics	1,935	1,445
Schrack	news technology	1,800	2,450

* Since 1 December 1985 AEG Austria

Source: Institut für Publizistik und Kommunikationswissenschaft der Universität Salzburg (ed.), *Massenmedien in Österreich,* Vienna (1986), p. 173.

Conclusion

The compilation of data on media relations between Austria and the FRG presented in this chapter has touched primarily on the historical and economic aspects of these relations. Further research on Austrian-FRG media relations might be supplemented by the investigation of topics such as cooperation in postal administration, the situation in the paper and printing industry, or data flow in the sector of economic communication.

A comprehensive study on mutual influences in the academic realm would also be of interest given the traditionally close linkage with West German technical sciences, journalism, and communications studies, as well as market and survey research. The influence of the Federal Republic can be deduced from the fact that a sizeable share of the professorships in journalism at the Universities of Vienna and Salzburg has been held by Germans. The literature that is cited in academic publications reveals a distinct dominance of the FRG. The academic publications market is dominated by West German publishers and by FRG specialist periodicals. One can note some counteracting influences, such as individual Austrian scientists who have been appointed to universities in the FRG or who have made an impact on the basis of pertinent publications. But their overall weight has to be seen as relatively minor.

One may conclude that the center-periphery model developed by Johan Galtung and his collaborators can claim validity for the relations between Austria and the FRG for all the spheres that have been discussed, or merely touched on, in this chapter.[16] A historical analysis could demonstrate to what degree these bilateral relations are dependent on external and internal political developments, as well as on economic and cultural policy decisions. This applies to the First Republic, most drastically to the period of Nazi rule from 1938–1945, to the period of occupation by the Allies, as well as to recent years.

Using the examples of the 1970s raises the question: What chance does a small country like Austria have in pursuing independent media, cultural, and economic policies vis-à-vis its big neighbor with whom it shares a common language? In retrospect, it is evident that in the 1970s, when it was definitely on the fast track in Europe, Austria witnessed a strengthening of the domestic market and an enhanced national consciousness that led to numerous innovations in the cultural and media fields. One can point to a number of Austrian success stories. To no small measure they were the result of government assistance and subvention policies, including support of the paper industry, promotion of newspapers, books, publishers, and films, as well as

---

16. See Johan Galtung, "Eine strukturelle Theorie des Imperialismus," in Dieter Senghaas (ed.), *Imperialismus und strukturelle Gewalt*, Frankfurt (1972), pp. 29–104. For the overall problem see Benno Signitzer, *Österreich im internationalen Mediensystem*, university habilitation thesis, Salzburg (1983); as well as Benno Signitzer and Hans Heinz Fabris, "Austria and the International Media System," in Otmar Höll (ed.), *Small States in Europe and Dependence*, Vienna (1983), pp. 220–238.

safeguarding of the position of ORF radio. The founding wave of that period affected the magazine market (e.g., *profil* and *trend*), popular journals, and publishers (e.g., Molden Verlag). It also produced developments that may be labeled "new Austrian literature", "new Austrian film", "Austrian television plays," and "Austro Pop". Austrian productions succeeded in recovering an important share of the domestic market, which had been held previously by West German products. German magazines such as *Spiegel* and *Stern* registered a decline in circulation on the Austrian market, and this led to the closing of their respective editorial offices in Austria. This phase, which was closely identified with the "Journalists' Chancellor" Bruno Kreisky, came to an end in the 1980s. In the period following, one can note a strong expansion of West German media capital in Austria, especially in the newspaper sector.

In order to understand the current situation it is important to realize that traditional bilateral media relations between small nations and their big neighbors, as between Austria and the Federal Republic, which are based on dominance, dependence, and manifold interaction, are increasingly being supplanted by the growing globalization of the media market. The large media multinationals have a decisive influence on this development. They are in a favored position to exploit new marketing, information, and communication techniques. State deregulation policies, which have been carried out in many Western countries, and the integration of hitherto separate data, media, and satellite communication sectors have also aided this internationalization process. The value of information products and the number of employees in the information sector have grown continuously over the past years. One clearly recognizes a change in direction toward an information society, at least when dealing with industrially developed societies.

The positions they come to occupy in the international structure of the media market will be of decisive importance for small countries like Austria: extended assembly lines for large corporations; producers of nonmaterial information products for the economy, culture, and entertainment; suppliers of "handicrafted" cultural productions such as theater and concert performances; or producers of specialized marginal commodities. The outcome will depend on historically developed structures and conditions. Taking the example of the threshold countries or of a small European state like Luxembourg, however, it is evident that the size of a country is no longer the only factor determining development in this process.

One can recognize the above-mentioned process in the relations between the media systems of Austria and the FRG. Experts believe that the strengthened engagement of West German firms in the Austrian newspaper market is not only directed toward capturing the local Austrian market but also regards Austria as a test case for the broader global strategy pursued by these firms.

In Austria itself this process is still beginning. There is little direct investment of U.S., British, French, or Swiss media capital in Austria even though the proportion of these countries' products is quite important in several media sectors. Austria continues to remain under virtually "exclusive" West German influence. The Federal Republic provides almost the entire export market for Austrian media products. Conversely, exports to Austria represent a substantial proportion of West German trade in media products. The balance of trade in these sectors shows a distinct deficit for Austria.

It is more difficult to assess the impact of media relations on politics and culture. This relationship with the FRG has undoubtedly strengthened Austria's cultural integration with the West that was initiated by the United States after 1945. This has also had important implications for the foreign political orientation of Austria and for the political consciousness of both the political leadership and the population as a whole. There is little doubt that many Austrian media sectors, such as film, book publishing, and electronic media, have either directly or indirectly profited from the relationship. In contrast, one could argue that only after the strengthening of the domestic media during the 1970s was there a basis for a serious public discussion on issues of genuine national concern such as the role of Austria during the Nazi period or its national identity.

In evaluating the relationship between Austrian and West German media one would have to undertake a detailed analysis capable of differentiating between cases, media sectors, and distinct historical phases in order to determine whether this relationship has promoted or hindered the development of the Austrian media. In the near future, one should pay particular attention to the consequences of a possible Austrian entry into the EC. Integration into the extended EC internal market, which would also include the media sector, could enhance the general globalization in Austria's media and information orientation, but it could also intensify bilateral relations with the unequal FRG partner.

It is unlikely, however, that this would change anything in the essential quality of Austrian-FRG relations that Engelbert Washietl, a long-time press correspondent in Bonn, once formulated in the following casual manner:

> When Germans meet Austrians the personal chemistry develops as programmatically as in a laboratory: a certain friendliness, holiday nostalgia, benevolence, superficial knowledge and the generosity with which one would treat a partner who quite surprisingly also manages to survive. "Oh you, too, have damaged forests?" or "You have also built a nuclear power station." In both cases the unwritten rank order is preserved: It is taken for granted that the damaged area in the Black Forest must certainly be larger and the rain more acidic than in Austria. ... The "Big-Small" image does not exhaustively treat the relationship between

Austria and Germany but very often the latter is contained within it like the sine curve in a system of coordinates and cannot escape from it.[17]

In many of its sectors, especially films and books, the small Austrian media market could not exist on its own, or it could only exist at a nonprofessional level. It is therefore continuously embraced by the German Big Brother. Depending on changing historical circumstances, this embrace may at times be perceived as helpful but at other times as depressing.

---

17. Engelbert Washietl, *Österreich und die Deutschen,* Vienna (1987), pp. 9 f.

14

Coping with Communications Spillover: Canadian Broadcasting Policy in the 1990s

Frederick J. Fletcher and Martha Fletcher[*]

The history of mass popular culture in Canada has been marked by a concern with the American cultural presence. Just as U.S. governments in the nineteenth century took measures to promote American self-expression in the face of British influence, Canadian governments in this century have tried to contrive policies to foster indigenous culture activity. The cultural dynamism of the United States, a result of its market size and relative affluence among other factors, has threatened repeatedly to swamp development in its much smaller, geographically dispersed neighbor. The dilemmas faced by the producers and distributors of popular culture and by the government have been fundamentally similar since the 1920s. The struggles for survival of Canadian publishing, cinema, radio, and television have a great deal in common. With respect to all of these forms of cultural expression, the evolution of government policy has had certain common features, as the clash of values and interests has been played out against a backdrop of technological changes and market forces.

Our purpose in this chapter is to discuss the fundamental and continuing issues in Canadian broadcasting policy, with primary attention to those resulting from the spillover and importation of American programming. In general, we have chosen to focus on the most difficult case, English-language

---

[*] The views expressed in this chapter by Martha Fletcher are her own and not those of the Government of Ontario.

television, which is accessible to 80 percent of the population. The power of television, coupled with the high cost of program production and distribution, has made it the subject of most concern. Lacking the language barrier, it has been most vulnerable to the effects of spillover. The impact on the French-language broadcasting in Canada has been more like that in other Western countries where the popularity of American programming has also posed a dilemma for cultural policymakers. The objective here is not so much to summarize the evolution of policy as to examine the ways in which the issues have been understood and the policy choices that those understandings have encouraged. We also examine the political forces involved, both domestic and international, and the directions in which policy appears to be evolving as Canadian policymakers look toward the 1990s.

More specifically, we examine the selection of policy objectives, priorities, and governing instruments by the Canadian state as it has tried to cope with the spillover of U.S. broadcast signals. We look, therefore, at the definition of the problem and how it has changed over time, including the extent to which it has been seen as a problem of too much American programming or too little Canadian. In this connection, we examine the focus on the demand side and on the supply side, the degree to which policies have mixed industrial and cultural objectives, the extent to which the objectives have been realistic, and the prescribed roles of public and private broadcasters. Having examined the nature of the problem and the evolution of policy choices, we present two brief case studies that illustrate some of the constraints under which Canadian governments have had to operate. The chapter concludes by suggesting some directions for future policy.

Defining the Policy Problem

In its essence, the problem can be defined either as the dominance of Canadian cultural space by foreign-produced, primarily American, materials or as the lack of Canadian-oriented materials in the Canadian information system. Although these are opposite sides of the same coin, the side on which policymakers focus their attention is significant, as will be seen. For the moment, however, we can ignore that distinction and simply describe the manifestations of the problem. This issue is particularly important in Canada because it is a country based on communications: Its small, regionally dispersed population has depended on state-supported transportation and communication networks for its very existence.

The statistical and economic elements of the problem are generally agreed on and fairly easy to summarize. At each stage of development, the

Canadian media have tended to rely on imported, primarily American, content. The direct spillover of first radio and then television signals from the United States has thus been augmented by their predominance within the Canadian distribution system itself. Recent data show that some three-quarters of all television programs viewed by Canadians are U.S. programs. The figure for drama, the most expensive programming to produce, is 98 percent. More than 95 percent of theatrical films shown in Canada are U.S. imports. About 85 percent of the records and tapes produced in Canada are copied from imported master tapes, and some 75 percent of all books and magazines sold in Canada are of foreign origin, mainly American.[1] Canadian messages predominate only in news and public affairs broadcasting and in newspapers. Even in these areas, much of the feature content and foreign news originates with U.S. syndicates and news services, ensuring that many Canadian outlets present an American view of the world.[2]

Put in terms of market share, domestic products in Canada have about 20 percent of the book market, under 7 percent of the record sales, some 4 percent of television dramas, and less than 2 percent of the cinema market.[3] For television, audience share is significant. The border stations attract about 33 percent of the English-speaking audience, an increase of 9 percent since 1968.[4] This increase can be attributed almost entirely to the spread of cable television, a distribution system that depends for its subscriber base primarily on its capacity to deliver a clear signal from U.S. stations. Imported shows on Canadian outlets account for another 40 percent of audience share. About 30 percent of the television programs available to Canadians originate in Canada, a high proportion of which is news, current affairs, and sports. Less than 12 percent of entertainment-oriented programming is made in Canada.[5] In short, Canadian productions receive less distribution in Canada than do U.S. shows, a continuation of the pattern established for cinema.

The economic consequences of this pattern are fairly clear. The fact that the Canadian communications system relies so heavily on imported content

1. Ross A. Eaman, *The Media Society: Basic Issues and Controversies,* Toronto (1987), p. 171.

2. See J. Scanlon and A. Farrell, "No Matter How It Sounds or Looks, It's Probably Not Canadian." Paper presented at the Conference on Media and Foreign Policy, University of Windsor, 29 October 1983.

3. Rowland Lorimer and Jean McNulty, *Mass Communication in Canada,* Toronto (1987), p. 312.

4. Minister of Supply and Services, Canada, "Report of the Task Force on Broadcasting Policy," Ottawa (1986), p. 90.

5. Lorimer and McNulty, *Mass Communication,* p. 36.

means that Cdn$ 2-3 billion per year leaves the country in fees and other payments. More than 90 percent of the wholesale revenue from the rental of films to theaters and television leaves the country.[6] Canadians suffer from an enormous imbalance of trade in cultural products, largely because of a stunted domestic production section. This imbalance will increase now that cable television companies will be required to pay retransmission fees to U.S. broadcasters for use of their signals. This has been a significant issue of contention between the United States and Canada and was changed as part of the current copyright act revision, in compliance with the Canada-U.S. FTA.

In addition, Canadians seeking careers in popular culture are often forced to move to the United States. In the long run, the strain on Canada's balance of payments may be less important than the loss of creative energy. As will be seen, policymakers have tried sporadically to deal with both of these problems.

The cultural and political implications of the situation are somewhat more controversial. The view that the situation represents a serious problem rests on the assumption that television is "a uniquely powerful force in the socialization of individuals and in the formation of collective attitudes, values and aspirations," as Meisel puts it.[7] Although this assumption is not without its challengers, it is widely held and there is strong circumstantial evidence to support it.[8] In particular, broadcasting in Canada "provides the means through which Canadians communicate with each other across a vast, diversified country."[9] Although Canadians are exposed primarily to domestically-produced news and current affairs programming, there is reason to believe that significant incidental learning takes place as a result of viewing drama and entertainment programming. Despite many common cultural attributes, the two countries differ substantially in geography, demography, and role in the world, not to mention political institutions, making many U.S. models inappropriate for Canada. There is evidence that some Canadians who are

6. Paul Audley, *Canada's Cultural Industries,* Toronto (1983), p. 317.

7. John Meisel, "Escaping Extinction: Cultural Defence of an Undefended Border," *Canadian Journal of Political and Social Theory* 10, no. 1–2 (1986), pp. 248–265. In many respects, the present chapter is a gloss on this excellent article.

8. There are many useful discussions on this subject. See, for example, Doris A. Graber, *Processing the News: How People Tame the Information Tide,* New York (1984), pp. 1–9.

9. Government of Ontario, "Response of the Government of Ontario to the Report of the Federal Task Force on Broadcasting Policy," Ministry of Transportation and Communications, Toronto (1987), p. 22.

heavy viewers of U.S. television are confused about their own judicial, federal, and parliamentary systems, for example.[10]

More important, perhaps, American images crowd out Canadian ones. The pattern of dominance makes it difficult for Canadian programs to be made and distributed, with the result that many Canadians are not exposed to "the highly textured and varied character of their own land."[11] Such dominance makes it difficult not only to pursue one's own national interest but even to recognize it. Even if the cultural differences between the two countries are marginal, as some argue, the infiltration of foreign concerns and priorities makes the task of political mobilization in Canada more difficult. This pattern of communication, therefore, reduces the capacity of Canadians to come to grips with their own unique problems and to preserve their distinct values (civility, order, compassion, community responsibility). In addition, the legitimacy of Canadian governments may be undermined as Canadians absorb priorities established elsewhere on which they have no influence. The Canadian media themselves give the impression that what happens in Washington, New York, and Los Angeles (or Dallas) is significant, while not much happens in Ottawa, Toronto, or Vancouver.

The result is that we Canadians are "junior partners in our own cultural enterprise," and as such "net importers of informational and cultural products that each day influence our ideas, priorities, politics, personal ambitions and sense of the world."[12] R. Lorimer and J. McNulty state the problem as follows: "With so much cultural spill-over there is a very real problem that Canadian cultural creators cannot help but be tempted to address ... themes selected, by repetition if nothing else, as salient by ... American cultural producers."[13] However, the practical problem is not so much the presence of American materials as the absence of Canadian ones. The continuing problem then, as stated by Meisel, is: "what can be done to create conditions in which Canadians can make genuine choices between foreign and domestic offerings?"[14]

---

10. See, for example, E.D. Tate and R.L. Trach, "The Effects of U.S. Television Programs upon Canadian Beliefs about Legal Procedures," *Canadian Journal of Communication* 6, no. 4 (Spring, 1980), pp. 1–17.

11. Meisel, "Escaping Extinction," p. 252.

12. Lorimer and McNulty, *Mass Communication*, p. 37.

13. Ibidem, p. 38.

14. Meisel, "Escaping Extinction," p. 253.

The Historical Background

Virtually since its inception, Canadian broadcasting policy has been made in the context of developments in the United States. Canada's small market and proximity to the United States have combined to make government action necessary to preserve a place in the broadcasting system for Canadian content. Indeed, before the advent of radio, there was the problem of U.S. supremacy in the film industry. The U.S. domination of Canadian screens, which continues to this day, can be traced to a set of factors that continued to operate for radio and television. If this policy problem is as vital to Canadian society as we believe, "it is imperative that ... we [Canadians] understand fully why we are so dependent on the United States."[15]

First, from the beginning, physical proximity to the U.S. border has been a major factor. The easy delivery of films and other cultural goods was important, but the spillover of U.S. radio and television signals was of even greater significance. Because most Canadians live within 200 kilometers of the border, a majority were able to receive radio and television signals from the beginning of transmission in border cities. Subsequently, cable television and satellites made such signals available to almost all Canadians.

Second, the dynamism of the U.S. entertainment industry, which has made it popular throughout the world, has had a profound impact on Canada. Based on the highly successful American film industry, U.S. television programs and stars were almost instantly popular everywhere, but especially in Canada, with its similar culture and the already-established dominance of American cinema. From the beginning, cinema has been a "branch plant" operation in Canada. The commercial nature of U.S. television, with its high premium on mass appeal, has led to the creation of formats that have come to be regarded as the very definition of popular entertainment in Canada, as elsewhere.

A third factor, perhaps the most important, is the economic structure of television program production and distribution, especially drama. Because the cost of U.S. productions — up to US$ 1 million per episode — can be amortized in the rich domestic market, they can be offered abroad for as little as 3 to 6 percent of their original cost.[16] The Canadian market does not offer similar economies of scale. Whereas the typical U.S. import will return from ten to twenty times its cost, the typical successful Canadian-produced

---

15. Ibidem, p. 250.

16. Pierre Juneau, *Public Broadcasting in the New Technological Environment: A Canadian View*, Luxembourg, 16 July 1983, as cited in Meisel, "Escaping Extinction," p. 250.

drama will recoup only one-third to one-half of its production cost in the domestic market. The dominance of U.S. productions in theater and video distribution limits their capacity to help bear the costs of domestic production.[17] As a consequence, it makes no economic sense for private Canadian broadcasters to produce or purchase domestic drama productions.

The initial response of Canadian governments to the high costs of television program production and distribution in Canada was to turn to public ownership. The Canadian Broadcasting Corporation (CBC) was founded in 1936 though public radio had already begun in 1932. Television service commenced thirty years later. Even with public ownership, the high cost of television production and distribution outstripped government willingness to fund the CBC. As with radio, the CBC itself imported American shows and used commercial revenues to subsidize its domestic productions. Since 1968, however, the public networks have declined in significance relative to the commercial sector. There are now more commercial stations than public stations and they command a larger audience. As will be seen, the Canadian government accepted the increasing primacy of the private broadcasters and sought through Canadian content regulations to require them to adopt the cross-subsidy strategy developed by the CBC. However, neither public nor private sector dramas, of which there have been few, have been able to raise the proportion of domestic productions above 4 percent of the total, though 50 percent of all viewing time is devoted to drama.[18]

A factor of almost equal importance is the head start achieved by the United States in both radio and television. With respect to radio, the U.S. networks were well established by the time Canada was ready to move. They occupied most of the available frequencies and were serving substantial Canadian audiences when the government decided that private enterprise would not serve Canada's needs. The American networks were ready to move into Canada, regarding it as a natural extension of their market, as the film makers did (and do today). Even after the creation of the CBC, U.S. programming remained significant. Television was established in the United States in the 1940s and had emerged as a mass medium by 1948.[19] By the time the CBC was authorized to provide television service in 1952, many Canadians had purchased receivers and antennas and had become attached to American programming. The CBC and its private affiliates believed that

17. Lorimer and McNulty, *Mass Communication*, pp. 221 f.

18. Meisel, "Escaping Extinction," p. 251.

19. Frank W. Peers, "Canada and the United States: Comparative Origins and Approaches to Broadcasting Policy," in *Culture in Collision*, New York (1984), p. 20.

they could attract and hold viewers only if they themselves catered to the established appetite for the most popular American programs. The early dominance of American programs no doubt played an important role in shaping the tastes of Canadian audiences.

A final factor, stemming in large part from the others, is Canadian affinity for American popular culture. Whether or not this taste results from natural cultural affinity, early exposure, or American hype, it is absolutely essential that it be recognized if policies acceptable to the Canadian public are to be designed. As Meisel puts it:

> Canadians not only like American programs; they also believe that they are entitled to have full access to them. This strongly held view compelled the CRTC (Canadian Radio-Television and Telecommunications Commission, the regulator) to enable Canadian cable systems to carry the programs of American stations.[20]

In the main, concern for Canadian content emanates from intellectuals and from the cultural community. Nevertheless, Canadian programs often do attract large audiences and are watched approximately in proportion to their availability. The key problem, then, is not so much taste as availability.

For a variety of reasons, the Canadian state has been unwilling or unable to establish a Canadian public monopoly in broadcasting. Although the British heritage helped to promote the creation of the CBC on the model of the British Broadcasting Corporation, U.S. influences were too well-entrenched to permit a monopoly. The Canadian public supported public broadcasting but not a monopoly, and public funding was never quite sufficient to make the CBC the dominant force in broadcasting that its supporters envisioned. There was a long struggle between the commercial and public service lobbies as to which principle would predominate. Though public opinion provided some support for both groups, the business community, including advertisers as well as active and aspiring broadcasters, could mount a well-funded lobby. The influence of these competing pressures combined with the established public appetite for American commercial programs to promote the mixed system.

While some view this mixed system as a typical Canadian compromise, others see it as an expression of a deep-seated ambivalence in the political culture regarding the appropriate role of the state. In any case, the mixed system — including a public system partially funded by commercial advertising — emerged, along with the practice of cross-subsidy noted above. Since 1961, however, with the licensing of the CTV television network as the first private network, the commercial sector has grown steadily and has taken on

---

20. Meisel, "Escaping Extinction," p. 252.

a character of its own, reducing to a myth the notion that the arrangement would constitute a single system with the CBC at its core. The CBC continues to constitute the core of the system, at least in terms of the production and exhibition of quality Canadian programming, but the private sector no longer revolves around the core.

Policy Choices

Policy formulation may be said to involve the establishment of general objectives, the allocation of priorities to these objectives, and the selection of governing instruments (or policy tools). The history of Canadian broadcasting policy demonstrates that there have been difficulties in all three areas. As Frank Peers makes clear, the establishment of general objectives was hampered by a long struggle between those supporting public service aims and those concerned with commercial goals.[21] The objectives established in the Broadcasting Act of 1968 were the result of that struggle. By the 1980s, these goals had achieved general acceptance and were retained in the new Broadcasting Act passed in 1991, though they are flawed in some ways. Section 3 of the Act makes the following key points: That broadcast frequencies are public property (and, therefore, it implies, should be used in the public interest); that Canadian broadcasting outlets constitute a single system; that the system should be owned and controlled by Canadians "so as to safeguard, enrich and strengthen the cultural, political, social and economic fabric of Canada," using predominantly Canadian creative and other resources. Cultural and industrial goals are intertwined here. Nevertheless, both public and private sector supporters have come to support these goals, at least in public. The setting of priorities proved even more difficult as the cultural and industrial concerns struggled for ascendancy.

The choice of governing instruments has revolved around both the degree and type of government intervention. At one time or another, the state has used almost every conceivable policy tool, ranging from full or partial government ownership (as in the case of the CBC and the agencies that control Canadian satellites, Telesat Canada and Tele Globe Canada), to exhortation and negotiation. Between these extremes, it has employed a wide range of grants, subsidies, tax exemptions, and loans, as well as complex regulations dealing with both the content and the ownership of broadcasting entities. Over the years, the tools have had to be adjusted to the continual changes in

---

21. Peers, "Canada and the United States," pp. 12–24.

the economic and political environment and, especially, to the changes in the technologies of broadcasting.[22] The story of these choices is long and complex and we can touch on only a few central issues here.

Before 1957 (the date of the formation of the Canada Council to subsidize the arts in Canada), the CBC and the National Film Board (NFB), established in 1939 to produce Canadian films, were among the few outlets for Canadian cultural works. As noted above, cinemas were controlled by U.S. distributing companies and showed very few Canadian films; Canadian book publishing was primarily a branch plant operation; and Canadian radio stations played mostly American music.[23] Since that time, successive governments have brought in a number of policies designed to promote Canadian cultural production, though public expenditures still lag far behind those in most European countries (at about 2.2 percent of total federal expenditures, most of which goes to the CBC). The most important of these policies for television have been: the creation in 1959 of Canadian content quotas; the licensing of new networks, including CTV in 1961 and the Global Television Network more than a decade later in an effort to expand Canadian programming choices; the introduction of measures designed to encourage Canadian businesses to advertise on Canadian rather than on American stations, including restrictions on tax deductions and signal substitution on cable; and, most recently, direct support to television program production through investments by Telefilm Canada.

In general, regulation has been aimed mainly at encouraging Canadian content and expanding the size of the Canadian system by increasing the number of Canadian services available. The CBC always was intended to be at the center of the system, but the regulator leaned toward the development of the private sector after 1958. This was made manifest by the licensing of CTV and later by a permissive attitude toward the expansion of cable television, which increased substantially the availability of American signals without increasing real choice.[24] The Broadcasting Act of 1968 gave the first legislative recognition to the private sector and, with the permission of the CRTC, it has grown steadily. The CBC, however, continues to produce a majority of the Canadian content, at least in terms of dollars spent.[25] Nevertheless, the CBC has suffered from limited and unpredictable funding,

22. Eaman, *Media Society*, pp. 171 f.; see also Stephen Globerman, *Cultural Regulation in Canada*, Montreal (1983), pp. 7 f.

23. Eaman, *Media Society*, p. 174.

24. Stuart McFadyen, Colin Hoskins, and David Gillen, *Canadian Broadcasting: Market Structure and Economic Performance*, Montreal (1980), pp. 207–213.

25. Lorimer and McNulty, *Mass Communication*, p. 217.

especially in light of government pressure to concentrate its resources on expansion to underserved areas rather than on program production. Pressures from politicians in underserved areas and from those concerned with industrial development created a tradition of stressing hardware and distribution at the expense of programming.[26]

The Canadian content quota, first promulgated in 1959, was the primary policy tool chosen to gain some public service in return for licensing private broadcasters to use scarce frequencies for commercial purposes. Although they have been modified on numerous occasions to close loopholes or to adjust to changes in technology, the Canadian content requirements have remained the foundation of the regulatory system. Unwilling to enter into the difficult game of assessing quality, the regulators fell back on requiring a certain quantity of domestic programming.[27] In general, despite having some measurable success in fostering a Canadian recording industry and promoting news and current affairs programming, the regulations have been widely condemned as inadequate. They have been ineffective in encouraging high quality domestic drama and entertainment programming. Indeed, there is little Canadian programming of any kind in prime time (8:00 P.M. to 11:00 P.M.) on private stations. If the object was the cultural one of promoting the production and exhibition of truly distinctive, high quality, popular Canadian programming, the quotas have failed. The regulations, however, have provided jobs for Canadians, producing the resulting news, sports, and game shows (and occasional dramas) that have filled the quotas.

From a cultural perspective, the quotas were doomed to failure. The economic incentive structure of commercial broadcasting ensured that the private broadcasters would fill their quotas as cheaply and with as little disruption of their lucrative American prime time programming as possible. Indeed, careful analysis of the profit margins of individual Canadian stations shows that although they could do more, they simply do not have the financial base to compete with American spillover signals.[28] Recognizing this, the regulators have taken pains to protect the return on investment of their licensees in the hope that some of the profits would be diverted to Canadian production. Recent regulations, such as those requiring cable systems to

26. Ibidem, p. 203.

27. Canadian content must make up 60 percent of the time during the broadcast day. In prime time, between 6:00 P.M. and midnight, the percentage is 60 for the CBC and 50 for private broadcasters; Section 4 of the CRTC Regulations Respecting Television Broadcasting.

28. See, for example, Colin Hoskins and Stuart McFadyen, "Market Structure and Television Programming Performance in Canada and the U.K.: A Comparative Study," *Canadian Public Policy* 8, no. 3 (1982), pp. 347–357.

carry the Canadian signal whenever a Canadian station is carrying the same program as an imported border station (simulcasting), do protect domestic profit margins. However, they do little to promote cultural goals, unless one argues that Canadian commercials carry significant cultural content. Indeed, they merely reinforce the monopoly of American programming in Canadian prime time. In any case, poor Canadian programs in prime time would simply cause most Canadians to switch to imported channels. In fact, it could be argued that the cheap fillers used by many private stations to fill their quotas have contributed to the poor reputation of domestic Canadian productions.[29]

It must be noted that the Canadian state has operated under a very severe set of constraints in attempting to deal with the spillover problem. These include several noted above: the power of the commercial interests, the affinity of Canadian audiences for American programming, and the popular ambivalence regarding state intervention, particularly in matters of program content. To these must be added government fiscal restraint, which has limited the growth of the CBC, and pressures from U.S. interests. The impact of these constraints may be seen in two brief case studies.

In addition, it must be noted that the very basis of regulation has been undermined by technological change. The advent of cable television, which brought the offerings of the three major American networks within reach of more than 90 percent of Canadian homes, and direct-to-home satellite transmissions meant that Canadians could easily evade attempts at enforced Canadianization. Viewing of American channels in cabled homes is roughly double that of nonsubscribers.[30] Increasingly, it can be said that frequencies are not scarce and regulation must be justified in the public interest rather than in technical terms, though limited channel capacity is a common argument used by cable companies when resisting carriage of more Canadian services. Measures to promote Canadian content will succeed only if they are based on a recognition of the competitive situation that has emerged.

The Border Broadcasting Dispute

This dispute, which emerged after the passage in 1975 of an amendment to the Income Tax Act withdrawing the deduction for Canadian commercials on non-Canadian stations, set off a furor that is instructive. The measure was designed to stop the flow of Canadian advertising dollars to the U.S. border

---

29. Meisel, "Escaping Extinction," p. 257.

30. Minister of Supply and Service, "Report of the Task Force," p. 103.

stations, some of which existed primarily to sell Canadian audiences to advertisers (though not licensed to do so). The border stations lost about Cdn$ 15 million per year. The Canadian action, designed in theory to help fund Canadian content, elicited an angry response. The border stations successfully lobbied the Congress to pass retaliatory legislation, and the resulting restrictions on income tax deductions for Americans attending conferences in Canada apparently cost Canada much more than it gained from the initial action.

The vehemence of the dispute reflects deep-seated principles on both sides. On the Canadian side, the measure was seen as an attempt to redress in a relatively small way the massive imbalance in cultural balance of trade. As Meisel sums it up: "Although economic measures were being used to promote national goals, the purposes of the enterprise ... were cultural and were related to the very preservation of a distinct Canadian identity."[31]

The fact that Canadian broadcasters would benefit economically was viewed as incidental. From the American point of view, the action was seen not only as unfair to the border broadcasters but, more importantly, as interference with the free flow of information and the free market. The border stations argued that the prosperity of Canadian cable systems was based on the delivery of their signals without compensation and their only return came from selling Canadian advertising, an allegation not without justification. The advent of simulcasting was seen as adding insult to injury, even though the Canadian broadcasters were paying the license fee for access to their local audiences. The intensity of the U.S. reaction must be explained in large part by a commitment to free flow of information and by concern about the access to foreign markets of American cultural products in which they have a massive worldwide interest.

Canadian and U.S. communication policies differ substantially in emphasis. As Theodore Hagelin and Hudson Janisch put it,

> Canadian policy seeks cultural development; U.S. policy seeks consumer choice. Canadian policy relies on program content regulation and a strong public broadcasting system to achieve its objectives. U.S. policy relies on structural, or industrial regulation and a strong commercial broadcasting system to achieve its objectives.[32]

---

31. Meisel, "Escaping Extinction," p. 261. This section draws on Meisel's assessment of the case and the discussion in Theodore Hagelin and Hudson Janisch, "The Border Broadcasting Dispute in Context," in Frank W. Peers, *Culture in Collision,* pp. 40–99.

32. Hagelin and Janisch, "Broadcasting Dispute," p. 53.

The gap in understanding is great and, as Meisel suggests, resolution of such issues becomes difficult because the two systems of government are so different.

This case study is instructive in several respects. First, it illustrates the capacity of the United States to retaliate against measures aimed at restricting U.S. access to the Canadian media system. The recent strong reaction to attempts to open up the Canadian cinema to domestic films also illustrates the point. Second, it demonstrates clearly that most Americans have little understanding of or sympathy for Canadian cultural concerns. Finally, it shows the potential effectiveness of even relatively small lobby groups in the U.S. system. It is no wonder that the cultural community in Canada is concerned that the FTA will weaken the safeguards now in place.

More important than these observations, perhaps, is Meisel's conclusion that although the problem is an international one, in one sense, its solutions are inevitably domestic. Indeed, although the problem stems from the American cultural presence, its essence is domestic in the sense that Canadian entrepreneurs have welcomed these cultural imports and, indeed, built their prosperity on them. It appears that the best hope for a cultural contribution from the private sector is to accept this situation and to make the best use possible of the cross-subsidies that the U.S. imports permit.

Specialty Services: Old Issues, New Choices

In mid-1987, the CRTC reviewed applications for licences to offer a number of new, specialized, narrowcast services as part of the Canadian broadcasting system.[33] Motivated by the potential spillover of the proliferating U.S. specialty services delivered by satellite and cable, these hearings brought to the forefront the same policy issues that have faced the system from the beginning. The new technologies simply highlighted the old issues: the tension between the popular demand for access to the new services being offered in the United States and the need for a Canadian space in the system; the need to balance industrial and cultural goals; the relationship

---

33. This section draws on two documents issued by the Ontario Ministry of Transportation and Communications in response to the CRTC call for public comment on its policy regarding specialty television choices. They are: "Cable Carriage of Canadian Specialty Programming Services: Response of the Government of Ontario to CRTC Notice of Public Hearing 1987-48," Toronto (1987); and "Ontario Public Opinion on Specialty Television Services: Demand, Pricing and Packaging," Toronto (1987).

between these services and their American counterparts as well as their relationship to other parts of the Canadian broadcasting system such as the traditional broadcasters and the cable systems; and the public response to and ambivalence toward state intervention in a matter that some see as properly a matter of unfettered consumer choice.

For the CRTC, the industrial and cultural goals were clear. Commission Chairman André Bureau since the beginning of his term had made it clear that the commission placed high priority on the financial viability of all prospective licensees. Applicants would have to present a sound business plan in their applications and would be protected from domestic competition within the same format as well as from competition from their American counterparts. (It was the domestic competition that had proved disastrous for the early pay services offering movies.) In exchange, applicants would be expected to contribute to the cultural goals of the system by providing Canadian content as mandated in Section 3 of the Broadcasting Act.

For their fellow players in the broadcasting system, the new services offered threat and opportunity. More services inherently offer more choices on television and with them the threat of fragmentation of the audience, threatening the audience share of the conventional broadcasters and, therefore, their rate cards. This threat is magnified when the new services compete for advertisers as well as audiences. For cable systems, new services, which are available only to cable subscribers, offer the means to attract new subscribers and to sell more services to old ones. But the importance of this opportunity to cable systems is affected by the popular appeal of the successful applicants, the extent to which they may preclude carriage of more economically advantageous American services, and the freedom the cable operator has to offer them in combinations that bring the greatest return.

Though there is clearly a vocal segment of the public that can be mobilized behind ideas such as the free flow of information (a code for free flow of U.S. programming into Canada) and consumer choice as the sole determinant of which services should be made available, it also appears that there is clear support for the provision of services that are important social and cultural "goods." In the survey commissioned by the Ontario government to assist in the development of its intervention in the specialty services hearing, respondents were asked to rate the major service types — news, children's, religious, multicultural, national general interest, distant conventional broadcasters — on the two dimensions of attractiveness to the respondent's particular household and of the degree to which its provision would be good for Canada as a country. Respondents accepted this distinction readily, rejecting the notion that the consumer interest and the public interest are one and the same thing. Support for a children's channel, for example, was high, though respondents without children freely conceded that it would not be of interest to them as consumers.

The Ontario survey data make it clear that Ontario citizens take a more sophisticated view of the distinction between public interest and consumer interest than do many commentators. It appears that they are willing to make the distinction between self-regarding and other-regarding policy preferences that voters make in selecting among policy proposals during election campaigns. The extent to which they are willing to pay for cultural public goods that they would not use themselves, as citizens do for schools and other public goods, remains unclear, but the concept deserves further examination. Certainly, public support for the CBC, which often exceeds its audience share, indicates some willingness to consider such expenditures. Many citizens who do not regularly watch such services as the parliamentary channel or the CBC's "The Journal" apparently wish them to be available when they want them.

Some Concluding Comments

The foregoing discussion has made clear some of the parameters within which the solution to the Canadian policy problem must be found. It has also suggested that failure to distinguish clearly among policy objectives and priorities has hampered the search for a solution. Let us examine some of the distinctions that we have come to regard as crucial.

First, we must define clearly what it is that Canada wishes to encourage and protect. Opponents of measures to promote Canada's distinct identity can be found arguing that there is little to protect or promote, that Canada's differences from the United States are marginal, therefore, unimportant, or conversely that Canada's culture is strongly rooted and not at risk, that Canadians can be continually exposed to American images and yet retain a clear sense of themselves. The argument that Canadians will filter American images through their own experiences is, of course, correct[34], but increasingly the psychic experiences of Canadians, derived in large part from television, is American. The values expressed in many U.S. programs, for example, with respect to violence and the use of firearms, differ sharply from those held by most Canadians.[35] If Eaman is correct in suggesting that culture can best be defined as "the representations of reality that a society has selected

34. Eaman, *Media Society*, p. 181.

35. Globerman, *Cultural Regulation*, pp. 44 f.

as having meaning for itself," then Canada's problem is that Canadians have little or no impact on much of the (American) material available to them. Viewed from this perspective, as Eaman puts it,

> cultural policy does not have to be defended on the grounds that it somehow stimulates common national characteristics which distinguish Canadians from Americans. It is enough to show that government support is essential for there to be adequate opportunities for Canadians to create and relate to meaningful indigenous interpretations of their own experience ... We can provide a perfectly good defence [for government support mechanisms] in terms of their being essential for a reasonable degree of communication among Canadians.[36]

What Canada needs, in short, is a communication policy, rather than a cultural policy as such.

Second, in this connection, the supply- and demand-side elements of the problem have to be distinguished. As Paul Audley has pointed out, the problem "is not that properly financed Canadian cultural materials are being offered to the Canadian public and being rejected, but that, as a general rule, they are in limited supply, have limited financing available, and receive inadequate distribution or exhibition."[37] In this interpretation, the problem exists primarily on the supply side. Because U.S. materials are available cheaply, having amortized their costs in their domestic market, Canadian producers are not competing on a level playing field. The economic incentive structure almost impels private broadcasters (and the underfunded CBC) to meet the consumer demand for popular drama with imported programs. Canadians appear to select Canadian programs roughly in proportion to their availability.[38] The propaganda from private broadcasters that Canadians do not like Canadian programs per se appears to have little foundation. As Lorimer and McNulty put it, "Once room is created in the distribution system for Canadian cultural products, then Canadian audiences apparently will jump at the chance to consume them."[39] Many examples could be given. The lesson is that government intervention should be focused on the supply side, though better promotion of Canadian programming would not hurt. Effective government policy must create incentives for production, distribution, and promotion.

---

36. See, for example, Benjamin D. Singer, "Violence, Protest and War in Television News: The United States and Canada Compared," in B.D. Singer (ed.), *Communications in Canadian Society,* Don Mills, Ontario (1983), pp. 192–196.

37. Audley, *Cultural Industries,* p. 320.

38. A.W. Johnson, "Canadian Programming on Television: Do Canadians Want It?" A talk to the Broadcast Executives Society, Toronto, 19 February 1981.

39. Lorimer and McNulty, *Mass Communication,* p. 273.

Third, one must distinguish clearly between industrial and cultural objectives. Though not always incompatible, policies designed to boost the revenues of private broadcasters have not generally produced the cultural benefits promised. Recent policies with the objective of harnessing Canadian market power and creativity in order to become competitive domestically and internationally tend to confuse the two goals. The measure of success tends to become the size of the audience or the amount of international sales, not the cultural significance of the product. "The cultural industries face a tough choice of trying to sell Canadian materials to a very small domestic market or aiming to produce 'international' products that appeal to a worldwide audience accustomed to American mass cultural products," as Lorimer and McNulty put it.[40] International coproductions have many benefits but, with some exceptions, they are unlikely to contribute to Canadians' understanding of themselves. Though private broadcasters, motivated by a combination of market forces and quota requirements, have contributed significant Canadian content to news, current affairs, and sports, they are unlikely to make a major contribution to drama without direct incentives. By abandoning the myth of the single system and clearly specifying the contributions of the public and private sectors, it should be possible through a combination of subsidies, tax incentives, and more realistic quotas based on investment and audience achieved to create a small but important space in the private sector for Canadian cultural materials. Cross-subsidy could be maintained through tax measures.

The CBC will inevitably remain the major vehicle for the realization of Canadian cultural goals. The temptation to turn the corporation into a "high culture" operation, however, should be resisted. An effective *communication policy* requires that the CBC continue to program high quality Canadian programs with mass audience appeal. Finances permitting, it would be desirable for CBC television to withdraw from the commercial field and to become a predominantly Canadian service as CBC radio has done. To fulfill the objectives envisioned here, however, it would have to remain competitive in audience appeal as the radio networks have done. As we have suggested, Canadians appear prepared to pay for a public network that offers the whole range of programming — from ballet to baseball — but want to reserve the right to watch whatever appeals to them.

Above all, Canadian broadcasting policy must be realistic. This means admitting that the options open to the state are limited by both international and domestic considerations. It must be recognized, for example, that no amount of lobbying in Washington will alter U.S. views on the free flow of information and trade in cultural products. Nor can American producers be

40. Ibidem, p. 226.

induced to market their wares less aggressively. American off-air and satellite transmissions will continue to flow across the border, and Canadian entrepreneurs will continue to import them and to sell the equipment necessary to receive them, complete with descramblers if necessary. Canada's dependence on the United States and on worldwide trends away from national distinctiveness and from public broadcasting are realities that cannot be escaped. The available options, then, are entirely domestic.

It is also important to recognize that wholesale repatriation of Canadian audiences is impossible and, perhaps, neither necessary nor desirable. Given Canada's small market, ambivalence about state intervention, shared language and culture, and desire for maximizing program choice, the only realistic objective is to maintain and to gradually expand the space available in the system for Canadian messages. At the national level, this involves

1. financial incentives for domestic production, along with realistic content quotas and provision for exhibition
2. encouragement of domestic production
3. better funding and a clearer mandate for the CBC, including consideration of additional outlets when program production warrants it

At the provincial and local level, there is considerable potential for the expansion of educational and community broadcasting, but that would be another chapter.

The fact remains, however, that Canada's dependence on the United States seriously limits its options. For example, Canada's ties with the large market to the south means that it will have to wait for decisions to be made there before it can move in a serious way into high definition television. It would be infeasible for the Canadian broadcasting signals to be incompatible with American ones. In addition, the FTA, made necessary by Canada's economic dependence, may make certain policies impermissible. Many Americans view Canadian attempts to protect Canada's broadcasting space as simply disguised barriers to trade. The agreement might well restrict the use of quotas or limit subsidies to programs for domestic exhibition only. Nevertheless, there appears to be a sufficient appetite for Canadian programming to justify a serious effort to promote it.

Abbreviations and Acronyms

AdÖG	Arbeitsgemeinschaft der Österreichischen Gemeinwirtschaft
AECQ	Association des entrepreneurs en construction du Québec
AEG	Allgemeine Elektrische Geräte
AG	Aktiengesellschaft
AIDS	Acquired Immune Deficiency Syndrome
APA	Austria Presse Agentur
ARD	Arbeitsgemeinschaft der öffentlich-rechtlichen Rundfunkanstalten der Bundesrepublik Deutschland
ARGE Alp	Arbeitsgemeinschaft Alpenländer
BMW	Bayrische Motorenwerke
CBC	Canadian Broadcasting Corporation
CCF/NDP	Cooperative Commonwealth Federation/New Democratic Party
CCP	Central Canada Potash
CDU	Christlich Demokratische Union
CEN	Comité Européen de Normalisation
CENELEC	Comité Européen de Normalisation Electrotechnique
CPQ	Conseil du patronat du Québec
CRA	Canadian Reconstruction Association
CRTC	Canadian Radio-Television and Telecommunications Commission
CSCE	Conference on Security and Cooperation in Europe
CSU	Christlich Soziale Union
CTV	Canadian Television
EC	European Community
ECSC	European Coal and Steel Community
EDU	European Democratic Union
EEA	European Economic Area
EEC	European Economic Community

EFTA	European Free Trade Association
EPC	European Political Cooperation
Euratom	European Atomic Community
EWG	Europäische Wirtschaftsgemeinschaft
f.o.b.	free on board
FORD	Foreign Office Research Department
FRG	Federal Republic of Germany
FTA	free trade agreement
GATT	General Agreement on Tariffs and Trade
GDP	gross domestic product
GDR	German Democratic Republic
GNP	Gross National Product
GOP	Grand Old Party
IBM	Internationale Büromaschinen
IDU	International Democratic Union
ITT	Internationale Telefon & Telegraph
KPÖ	Kommunistische Partei Österreichs
MRP	Mouvement Républicain Populaire
NDP	New Democratic Party
N+N	neutral and nonaligned
NATO	North Atlantic Treaty Organization
NFB	National Film Board
NORAD	North American Aerospace Defense Command
NSDAP	Nationalsozialistische Deutsche Arbeiterpartei
NTB	nontariff trade barriers
OEEC	Organization for European Economic Cooperation
ORF	Österreichischer Rundfunk Fernsehen
ÖAKT	Österreichischer Arbeiterkammertag
ÖStZ	Österreichisches Statistisches Zentralamt
ÖVP	Österreichische Volkspartei
ÖZAP	Österreichische Zeitschrift für Außenpolitik
PC	Progressive Conservative party of Canada
PCS	Potash Corporation of Saskatchewan
PJBD	Permanent Joint Board on Defense
RAVAG	Radio Verkehrs AG
RTL	Radio Tele Luxemburg
R&D	research and development

SEA	Single European Act
SITC	Standard International Trade Classification
SRG	Schweizer Radio- und Fernseh-Gesellschaft
SPD	Sozialdemokratische Partei Deutschlands
SPÖ	Sozialistische Partei Österreichs (since 1991 – Sozialdemokratische Partei Österreichs)
U.K.	United Kingdom
UN	United Nations
USITA	U.S. International Trade Administration
USITC	U.S. International Trade Commission
USSR	Union of Soviet Socialist Republics
VÖI	Vereinigung Österreichischer Industrieller
WAZ	Westdeutsche Allgemeine Zeitung
WTO	Warsaw Treaty Organization
ZDF	Zweites Deutsches Fernsehen

About the Contributors

Günter BISCHOF

Assistant Professor of History and Associate Director, University of New Orleans, Louisiana.

Frederick C. ENGELMANN

Professor Emeritus of Political Science, University of Alberta, Edmonton, Alberta.

Hans Heinz FABRIS

Professor of Communications, University of Salzburg.

Frederick J. FLETCHER

Professor of Political Science, York University, Toronto; Research Coordinator (Broadcasting/Media), Royal Commission on Electoral Reform and Party Financing.

Martha FLETCHER

Manager, Broadcasting Office, Ontario Ministry of Culture and Communications, Toronto.

Stanley FOGEL

Professor of English Literature, St. Jerome's College, University of Waterloo.

Adolf HASLINGER

Professor of German Language and Literature, University of Salzburg.

285

Henry J. JACEK

Professor of Political Science, McMaster University, Hamilton, Ontario.

Joseph LEVITT

Professor Emeritus of History, University of Ottawa.

David LEYTON-BROWN

Professor of Political Science and Dean of Graduate Studies, York University, Toronto.

Hanspeter NEUHOLD

Professor of International Relations and International Law, University of Vienna; Director, Austrian Institute for International Affairs, Laxenburg.

Harald von RIEKHOFF

Professor of Political Science, Carleton University, Ottawa.

D. Mark SCHULTZ

Dr. Phil., Analyst, Country Strategies Group, Royal Bank of Canada, Toronto, Ontario.

Bruce W. WILKINSON

Professor of Economics, University of Alberta, Edmonton, Alberta.

Georg WINCKLER

Professor of Economics, University of Vienna.